Year-Round Programs
for
Young Players

Year-Round Programs

for

Young Players

*One hundred plays, skits, poems,
choral readings, spelldowns,
recitations, and pantomimes
for celebrating holidays
and special occasions*

By

AILEEN FISHER

Publishers   PLAYS, INC.   *Boston*

Library of Congress Cataloging in Publication Data

Fisher, Aileen Lucia, 1906–
  Year-round programs for young players.

  Summary: A collection of plays, recitations, poems, and other material which can be performed at holidays and special occasions throughout the year.
  1. Children's poetry, American. 2. Children's plays, American. 3. Recitations. 4. Holidays— Exercises, recitations, etc. 5. Schools—Exercises and recreations. [1. Holidays. 2. Plays.
3. American poetry. 4. Recitations] I. Title.
PS3511.I29Y   818'.5209   85–8153
ISBN 0-8238-0266-3

Manufactured in the United States of America

CONTENTS

JANUARY

FEBRUARY

MARCH

JUNE

JULY–AUGUST

SEPTEMBER

OCTOBER

Year-Round Programs
for
Young Players

JANUARY

Roll Call for a New Year

Twelve boys and girls represent the months of the year. Each enters and acts out lines—January comes "skating" in, blowing horn. February is cutting red hearts. March runs in with a kite, etc.

JANUARY: January skis and skates,
and makes resolves, and celebrates.
FEBRUARY: February cuts designs
for scores of showy Valentines.
MARCH: March comes puffing, on the run,
blowing kites across the sun.
ALL: There go sleds and coasting fun!
APRIL: April plays at "April Fool,"
changing sunny days to cool.
MAY: May strews flowers along the way
for baskets and for Mother's Day.
JUNE: June is apt to start too late,
then come rushing through the gate.
ALL: There goes Spring! It will not wait.
JULY: Noisy fireworks mark July
as parades and flags go by.

AUGUST: August suntans on the lawn,
  feeling lazy as a yawn!
SEPTEMBER: Bright September paints the
   trees,
  and school begins, and gardens freeze.
ALL: There goes Summer . . . like a breeze.
OCTOBER: Now October decks the scene
  with pumpkins—made for Halloween!
NOVEMBER: Brisk November scatters
   cheer
  with *Thanksgiving* almost here.
DECEMBER: Then December with a bell
  and wreath comes dancing in to tell
  that Christmas is alive and well . . .
ALL: And then the year is through and
   done
  and we will get another one!

January

Once a god of Roman days
had a face that looked two ways:
Janus looked ahead, and back,
at a past and coming track.

And his name you still can hear
in the month that starts the year:
January sees what's through
and looks ahead to something new.

Martin Luther King's Birthday
(January 15)

I Have a Dream

Characters

JEFF
SUSAN
GRANDFATHER
SAMUEL
OTHER AUDIENCE MEMBERS
M.C.
BUS DRIVER
MRS. ROSA PARKS
BUS PASSENGERS
POLICE OFFICER
MARTIN LUTHER KING
BLACK MEN AND WOMEN
DALTON
COREY
CHORUS, *6 or more male and female*
STAGEHANDS
MARCHERS
LOUDSPEAKER VOICE

BEFORE RISE: *Music of "We Shall Overcome" is played in background as several audience members enter from back of auditorium and go to front rows to take seats. JEFF and SUSAN enter, carrying on conversation.*

JEFF: Until we studied about Martin Luther King in school, I never realized what a difference he made to this country.

SUSAN (*Nodding*): He was a great man. I'm glad the school is honoring his birthday with this program. (*Looks around for seats*) Jeff, here are two good seats together. (*They sit. GRANDFATHER and SAMUEL enter at back of auditorium, start walking toward front.*)

SAMUEL: Where do you want to sit, Grandpa?

GRANDFATHER: Thanks to Martin Luther King, Samuel, we can sit any place we please. We black folks couldn't always do that.

SAMUEL: I know. We were considered second-class citizens, weren't we? When I hear you and Grandma talk about it, I wonder why it was like that.

GRANDFATHER: That's what Martin Luther King was always wondering—and asking. And he did something about it—something that changed the whole country. He reminded everyone that people in the United States should all have the same chance. That's what the Constitution says—"with liberty and justice for all."

SAMUEL (*Pointing to two seats*): Let's sit right here, Grandpa. (*Lights dim.*) The program's about to begin.

* * *

SETTING: *Stage is bare. M.C.'s stand is at one side of stage. At the other side are two rows of chairs, angled so that they face the audience. A large sign reading* RESERVED FOR WHITES *is placed near the chairs in front. Chairs at the back have sign reading* COLORED SECTION. *A single chair for Bus Driver is placed in front of the two rows. On the backdrop is a large picture of Martin Luther King. If available, slides of Martin Luther King and activities in which he was engaged may be flashed on the backdrop from a projector throughout the play.*

AT RISE: *Spotlight goes up on* M.C.'s *stand.* M.C. *enters and addresses audience.*

M.C.: We are gathered here today to celebrate the birthday of a great American—Martin Luther King—who made a lasting impression on our history in his short life of 39 years. Actually, his career as a leader in the freedom movement didn't begin until he was 26 years old. Before that his life ran smoothly enough. He went to college, received a doctorate in theology, married, and became pastor of a Baptist church in Montgomery, Alabama. But on a December night in 1955, something happened that changed the direction of his life. Picture a crowded bus in the city of Montgomery, carrying passengers home after a busy day. (BUS DRIVER *enters, sits in single chair.* BUS PASSENGERS *enter and sit in chairs—white passengers in front section, blacks in back section. Spotlight goes up on chairs.* BUS DRIVER *pantomimes driving for a few moments, then stops. More* PASSENGERS *enter, pay fare to* DRIVER, *and take seats.* MRS. ROSA PARKS, *a black woman carrying heavy bags, enters, pays fare to* DRIVER, *then looks wearily at the chairs—mostly filled except for one in front section. She sits there.*)

PASSENGER (*Angrily; to* ROSA): You'll have to move to

the back of the bus, lady. (ROSA *doesn't move.*) Can't you read? (*Points to* RESERVED FOR WHITES *sign*) These seats are for whites only. (DRIVER *looks around, gets up, and goes over to* ROSA.)

DRIVER: Lady, these seats are reserved. Go to the back of the bus where you belong. (ROSA *doesn't move or speak.*)

OTHER WHITE PASSENGERS (*Ad lib*): She won't move! Doesn't she know she can't sit in the front of the bus? (*Etc.*)

DRIVER (*Angrily*): All right, lady. You asked for it. (*Steps to center stage, calls off*) Officer! Officer, would you come here, please? (OFFICER *enters.*)

OFFICER: What seems to be the problem?

DRIVER (*Pointing to* ROSA): This lady is the problem. She won't move to the back of the bus.

OFFICER (*To* ROSA): You won't move, eh? (*Grabs her arm, pulls her out of chair*) Then you're under arrest. (*He drags* ROSA *off. Light goes out on chairs.* DRIVER *and* PASSENGERS *exit;* STAGEHANDS *remove chairs and signs. Spotlight goes up on* M.C.)

M.C.: For years black people in Alabama and other southern states had been treated as if they had no rights. If they complained, they were put in jail. White people made the rules, and black people were expected to follow them. But the arrest of Mrs. Parks aroused the black community in Montgomery to do something about the injustice of the episode. They turned to their pastor, Martin Luther King, for help. (MARTIN LUTHER KING, COREY, DALTON, *and several* BLACK MEN *and* WOMEN *enter, stand center stage.*)

1ST MAN: Reverend King, we have to fight against this injustice.

1ST WOMAN: What happened to Rosa Parks is a disgrace.

8

We've all suffered enough from white people's laws.

COREY: Let's take action—now! Not next week or next year!

OTHERS (*Ad lib; angrily*): Yes, that's right! Let's fight! (*Etc.*)

KING (*Holding up hand for silence*): I agree the time has come to act. But we must do it peacefully, not with meanness and violence. Excited talk blocks common sense, and the only way for us to fight unjust laws is to unite against them. We have to fight injustice with words and nonviolent action instead of clubs or guns.

DALTON: Reverend King, I have an idea. What if we all boycott the buses—walk to our jobs and have our children walk to school, instead of riding in the back of the bus.

2ND WOMAN: But my job is five miles away! I can't walk that far twice a day!

KING: Dalton has a good idea. (*To* 2ND WOMAN) You could find a ride with someone who has a car. Anything but ride the bus. If we all unite to boycott the buses, then maybe the white men who make the laws will change those laws!

OTHERS (*Ad lib*): Maybe a boycott could work! Yes, let's try it. (*Etc.*)

KING: But always remember the boycott must be orderly, and peaceful. No threats, no fighting, no violence. We're not doing this out of hatred of the white men, but to make them see that our cause is just.

COREY: That's right, Reverend King. We're tired of being mistreated, tired of being kicked about. It's time to act, but in a peaceful way! When will the boycott start?

KING: Tomorrow morning! Let's spread the news to our brothers and sisters, and remember to impress upon them the importance of nonviolence. "He who lives by the sword shall perish by the sword." (KING *and others exit. Spotlight goes up on* M.C.)

M.C.: The very next day, December 5, 1955, the boycott began. Bus after bus clattered down the street with no black passengers. Bus after bus, day after day, month after month—until finally, the law was changed and blacks could sit anywhere on a bus, not only in Montgomery, Alabama, but in other cities and states as well. (MARTIN LUTHER KING *enters and crosses to center stage. Spotlight comes up on him.*)

KING: At last the words of our Declaration of Independence are beginning to have some meaning! "We hold these truths to be self-evident—that all men are created equal; that they are endowed by their Creator with certain inalienable rights; that among these are life, liberty, and the pursuit of happiness."

M.C.: Other words, bold words, mighty words, were written into the preamble to the Constitution of the United States:

KING: "We the people of the United States, in order to form a more perfect Union, establish justice, insure domestic tranquillity, provide for the common defense, promote the general welfare, and secure the blessings of liberty to ourselves and our posterity . . ." (KING *exits. Spot up on* M.C.)

M.C.: Martin Luther King's work for liberty had just begun. In many states, particularly in the South, white children and black children were not permitted to go to the same school; black children could not play in public parks. Many restaurants had signs in their windows: COLORED NOT WELCOME. One by one, Martin Luther King tackled the issues, driven on by his dreams of justice, and more and more black people looked to him for leadership. Meanwhile, Reverend King was put in jail again and again for his uncompromising stand on equality. His house was bombed. Still, his faith never wavered. (CHORUS *crosses backstage, singing first stanza of "We Shall Overcome."*)

CHORUS: We shall overcome
We shall overcome
We shall overcome some day.
Oh, deep in my heart
I do believe
We shall overcome some day.

M.C.: Then came August, 1963, one hundred years after Abraham Lincoln issued his Emancipation Proclamation freeing the slaves. With the blessing of Martin Luther King, more than 200,000 people, black and white, took part in a "march for jobs and freedom" and gathered at the Lincoln Memorial in Washington, D.C., where Dr. King gave his famous "I Have a Dream" speech. It was carried in newspapers all over the country. (KING *enters, crosses center. Spotlight goes up on him.*)

KING: I have a dream that my four little children will one day live in a nation where they will not be judged by the color of their skin but by the content of their character.

I have a dream today.

I have a dream that one day the state of Alabama will be transformed into a situation where little black boys and black girls will be able to join hands with little white boys and white girls and walk together as sisters and brothers.

I have a dream today. . . .

And if America is to be a great nation this must become true. So let freedom ring from the prodigious hilltops of New Hampshire! . . .

Let freedom ring from every hill and mole hill of Mississippi. From every mountainside, let freedom ring.

11

When we let freedom ring, when we let it ring from every village and every hamlet, from every state and every city, we will be able to speed up that day when all of God's children, black men and white men, Jews and Gentiles, Protestants and Catholics, will be able to join hands and sing that old Negro spiritual, "Free at last! Free at last! Thank God almighty, we are free at last!" *(Exits)**

M.C.: Martin Luther King's success in promoting non-violence as a solution to racial problems was recognized by the world in 1964, when he received the Nobel Peace Prize. He was only 35 years old, the youngest person ever to receive the prize. All over the world people watched on television as he accepted the award of $54,000. He donated it all to the civil rights movement. (KING *enters; spotlight goes up on him.*)

KING: On behalf of all men who love peace and brotherhood, I accept this award . . . with an abiding faith in America and an audacious faith in the future of mankind . . . and a profound recognition that nonviolence is the answer to the crucial political and moral question of our time. Though 22 million of our black brothers and sisters in the United States are still fighting for full freedom and justice in nonviolent ways, I have faith that eventually they will achieve their goal, and that the long night of racial injustice will be over. I still believe that we shall overcome. (*Exits;* CHORUS *sings offstage.*)

CHORUS: We'll walk hand in hand
We'll walk hand in hand
We'll walk hand in hand some day.
Oh, deep in my heart
I do believe
We'll walk hand in hand some day.

*The complete text of this speech may be found in libraries.

M.C.: The climax of Martin Luther King's career came in the spring of 1965, with the 54-mile march from Selma, Alabama, to Montgomery. It was a march to dramatize the "right to vote" problem. Although the 15th Amendment, ratified almost 100 years before the Selma march, gave blacks the right to vote, they were still unable to vote in some states because they were not allowed to register. Martin Luther King decided to fight this injustice. He faced bitter opposition in Alabama.

Hundreds of marchers, of every faith and race, started on the walk from Selma under a sweltering spring sun. But they had gone only a few blocks when they were met at a bridge by a living blockade of state troopers wearing helmets and swinging billy clubs. They carried canisters of tear gas. The marchers knelt down before the troopers, who pressed ahead swinging their clubs with abandon and spraying the air with gas. Dr. King saw that there was nothing to do but to retreat.

Two weeks later he tried again, this time leading 8,000 black and white supporters on the long march to the state capital. Meanwhile, a federal court order was issued to protect the marchers, and National Guard troops were on hand in case of trouble. Five days later the long march ended at the capitol building in Montgomery, where 25,000 people had gathered to welcome Reverend King and his fellow marchers. (MARTIN LUTHER KING *and* MARCHERS *enter, gather at center.*)

KING: We are on the move! And we are not about to go back. We will go on, with faith in nonviolent action, for our cause is humane and just. It will not take long, because the arm of the universe bends toward justice. . . .

MARCHERS (*Ad lib*): We will go on! (*Etc.*)

M.C.: As a champion of peace, Martin Luther King opposed the war in Vietnam. He spoke out against it with anxiety and sorrow.

KING: We must work for peace by peaceful means. War is madness, and this madness must cease. Those who love peace must organize as effectively as those who love war. (*Exits with* MARCHERS)

M.C.: For his outspoken views on this and many other national problems, Martin Luther King was continually in danger for his life. His family, too, suffered from threats, and several times the King home was bombed. In April, 1968, he went to Memphis to address some striking workers. As usual his message was for peace, justice, and equality. No one was prepared for the violence that erupted. While Dr. King was speaking to a friend from the balcony of his motel, a shot rang out. Dr. King slumped to the floor. . . .

LOUDSPEAKER: Special news bulletin from Memphis, Tennessee! Martin Luther King has just been assassinated! Who the assassin is, no one knows at this point. We will supply more details as they come in. . . .

M.C.: Martin Luther King died just an hour after the shooting, a martyr to the cause of equality and peace. He was not yet forty years old. (*Music of "We Shall Overcome" is heard softly offstage.*) Yes, Martin Luther King had a dream, a dream for the future that will bring hope to the oppressed wherever they are, a dream to overcome injustice with fairness and equality. For as Reverend King said, the arm of the universe bends toward justice. (*Music of "We Shall Overcome" swells as curtain falls.*)

THE END

PRODUCTION NOTES
I HAVE A DREAM

Characters: 8 male; 2 female; 1 male or female for M.C.; as many male and
female extras as desired for all other characters.

Playing Time: 20 minutes.

Costumes: Jeff, Susan, Grandfather, Samuel, Other Audience Members and
M.C. wear modern, everyday dress. All other characters wear clothes
appropriate for the 1950's and early 1960's.

Properties: Shopping bags for Rosa Parks.

Setting: Stage is bare. M.C.'s stand is at one side of stage. At other side are
two rows of chairs, angled so that they face the audience. Large sign
reading RESERVED FOR WHITES is near chairs in front. Chairs at the back
have sign reading COLORED SECTION. Single chair for Bus Driver is in
front of the two rows. On the backdrop is a large picture of Martin Luther
King. If available, slides of Martin Luther King and activities in which he
was engaged may be flashed on backdrop from a projector throughout the
play.

Lighting: Spotlights, as indicated.

Music: "We Shall Overcome."

Martin Luther King

Because he took a stand for peace
and dreamed that he would find
a way to spread equality
to all of humankind,

Because he hated violence
and fought with words, not guns,
and won a timely victory
as one of freedom's sons,

Because he died for liberty . . .
the bells of history ring
to honor the accomplishments
of Martin Luther King.

Benjamin Franklin's Birthday
(January 17)

Who Is It?

Characters

BETTY
BRUCE
TWELVE BOYS AND GIRLS

SETTING: *There is a big "History Book" toward back of stage. Only the covers show, and they can be made of screens that will open. It can be very simple.* TWELVE BOYS *and* GIRLS *are behind the "Book."* BETTY, *dressed in colonial costume, is at one side of the stage;* BRUCE, *in modern clothes, at the other side.*

BETTY: There was a man in our town
And he was wondrous wise:
He did so many helpful things
His neighbors rubbed their eyes.
BRUCE: Who was the man in your town
Who was so wondrous wise?
I wouldn't think that *one* man
Could make you rub your eyes!

16

BETTY: He didn't act like one man,
He acted more like ten,
And everybody called him
"Our Leading Citizen."

BRUCE: What was his name and station?
How long ago and when?
What did he do that made him
Your Leading Citizen?

BETTY: Oh, everybody knows him!
Why don't you guess his name?

BRUCE: All right . . . if you will give me
Some hints about his fame.

(BETTY *runs to "History Book" and opens covers.*
BOYS *and* GIRLS *enter one by one, as they speak their
lines.*)

1ST: He was the first man to propose a union of the
thirteen colonies, way back in 1754.

2ND: He started the first public library in America.

3RD: He helped found the first hospital in Philadelphia, and persuaded the people to light the
streets, and have them swept.

4TH: He organized the first fire insurance company
and a volunteer fire department.

5TH: As Postmaster-General of the colonies, he im-
proved the service so mail was delivered more
quickly.

6TH: He wrote and published a famous Almanac, in
which he said: "Little strokes fell great oaks."

1ST: "He that goes a borrowing goes a sorrowing."

2ND: "Plough deep while sluggards sleep;
And you shall have corn to sell and to reap."

3RD: "Early to bed and early to rise,
Makes a man healthy, wealthy, and wise."

4TH: "Never leave that till to-morrow which you can
do today."

5TH:	"Vessels large may venture more, But little boats should keep near shore."
7TH:	He invented a new kind of stove which became very famous because it didn't waste heat like a fireplace.
8TH:	He held many public offices, and went to England to try to get Parliament to give the colonies their rights.
9TH:	He helped to frame the Declaration of Independence and the Constitution of the United States, and signed them both.
10TH:	He persuaded France to send us ships and soldiers and supplies in our fight for freedom.
11TH:	He arranged the Treaty of Peace with England after the Revolutionary War.
12TH:	By using a kite with a key on the end of the string, he discovered that there was electricity in lightning . . .
BRUCE:	Benjamin Franklin!
ALL:	Benjamin Franklin! He didn't act like one man, He acted more like ten, No wonder people called him Our Leading Citizen!

FEBRUARY

Groundhog Day
(February 2)

To a Groundhog on February 2

ALL: Wake up, sleepyhead!
       Put your dreams away.
       Everyone is waiting
       for what you have to say:
GIRL: Will your shadow make a blot
       on the snow today or not?
BOY: Will the sun start turning hot?
       Will the month be cold, or what?
       Hurry, sir, and tell us on this Groundhog Day.

ALL: Wake up, sleepyhead!
       What's a little snow?
       If your shadow follows you,
       back inside you'll go.
BOY: Will the coming six weeks be
       wintry, cold, and shivery?
GIRL: Balmy, warm, and summery?
ALL: Groundhog, what's your prophecy?
       Better put your *glasses* on, so you'll really know!

Groundhog Day

Halfway into winter,
halfway on to spring . . .
February second
has some news to bring:

Are the worst days over?
Are there more to come?
Who's better than a groundhog
to get an answer from?

He has no vested interests,
no causes to promote,
no positive opinions
of how he ought to vote.

And so it's safe to watch him
emerging from his door . . .
if he should see his shadow
he'll sleep for six weeks more.

It's really very simple,
and some folks swear it's true:
he knows more lore of weather
than either I or you.

P.S. But Groundhog Day is different
in Canada . . . beware!
Folks don't consult a groundhog,
they much prefer a *bear*.

Lincoln's Birthday
(February 12)

Sing the Songs of Lincoln

Characters

READER
NANCY HANKS LINCOLN
SARAH LINCOLN (SAIRY)
ABRAHAM LINCOLN (ABE)
THOMAS LINCOLN (TOM)
DENNIS HANKS
ELIZABETH JOHNSTON
JOHNNY JOHNSTON
SARAH BUSH JOHNSTON LINCOLN
ANN RUTLEDGE
TWO MEN
BAND AND CAMPAIGNERS
SALLY
WOMAN FROM VIRGINIA
GIRL
JOHN HAY
ACTORS
OFFSTAGE CHORUS

BEFORE RISE: READER *enters, takes place at reading stand at one side, and opens book.*

READER: She had something of a singing voice, Nancy Hanks Lincoln had. But she didn't have much to sing about . . . leastwise most women nowadays wouldn't be in a singing mood with a life like hers. Maybe that's why Nancy Lincoln sang—to forget the drudgery and the hardships and the poverty . . . the washing and cooking and scrubbing, the spinning and weaving and soapmaking, the sewing and patching and fixing . . . (*Curtain rises.*)

SETTING: *A one-room cabin, furnished in frontier fashion.*

AT RISE: NANCY HANKS LINCOLN *enters, carrying old clothes and sewing basket over her arm. She sits on a stool and begins to sew, humming tune of "William Riley."**

READER: No, Nancy Hanks didn't have much to sing about after she'd been married to Tom Lincoln for ten years. Not that he was a mean man, or a worse provider than other farmers in the Cabin country of Kentucky. Still, he wasn't what you'd call enterprising, and as a rolling stone he had an uncanny way of choosing the wrong direction to roll. (NANCY *picks up sewing, goes to cabin door, and looks out.*)

NANCY (*Calling*): Sairy! Abe! (*There is no answer. She goes back to her sewing.*)

READER: The first two years in Elizabethtown, Kentucky, when Tom Lincoln was carpentering, weren't so bad. That's where Sarah, their first baby, was born.

*Most of the songs in this play can be found in *Songs that Lincoln Loved* by John Lair, Duell, Sloan and Pearce, N.Y., and Little, Brown and Company, Boston, 1954. Or early American songs written prior to 1800 can be used.

The next three years, on the South Fork of Nolin's Creek where Tom was trying to farm, were harder. That's where Abe was born, in a small log cabin with a dirt floor and only one window, and a stick-and-clay fireplace. (NANCY *goes to door again.*)

NANCY: Abe! Sairy! (*After a moment, she turns, puts wood on fire.*)

READER: When Abe was two years old, Tom Lincoln moved his family again, to a farm on Knob Creek, close to the old Cumberland Trail. That's where another son was born—named after his father. But little Thomas died when he was three days old, and Nancy Lincoln didn't sing again for a while. (NANCY *pulls her old shawl around her, looks off dreamily, then resumes her sewing.*) Things didn't improve any at Knob Creek. But when Nancy's voice came back, she sang in spite of everything, because Abe and Sarah liked to sit and listen, learning the tunes and words. (NANCY *sings a stanza or two of "William Riley."* NOTE: *An offstage chorus, or offstage record, may be substituted for onstage singing throughout.*) When Sarah was nine and Abe seven, Tom Lincoln's title to the Knob Creek farm came under question. Silent and discouraged, he headed north, across the Ohio River to Indiana where government land was up for sale at two dollars an acre. Surely nobody could question a government title. (NANCY *gets up to put something in the iron kettle at fireplace. She looks out expectantly when she passes the door, then goes back to her patching.*) At the Knob Creek farm, Nancy Lincoln waited restlessly for Tom to return. She worked hard so the children could go to school. And she felt singing glad to do it! (NANCY *sings first two stanzas of "Barbara Allen."* SAIRY *enters, carrying heavy buckskin bag, which she sets on floor.*)

SAIRY: Here's the meal, Mammy. Abe's got the rest of it. (*Goes to fire to warm hands*) Seems like the sun doesn't make any heat today.

NANCY: That's the way with a December sun, Sairy. (*Apologetically*) It grieved me to have you and Abe lose part of a day at school to tote that corn to the mill, Sairy. Goodness knows you don't get to school half enough as it is. But we were clean out of meal. (*Sighs*) I wish your Pappy'd come back. . . .

SAIRY: Is the land really better there?

NANCY: That's what your Pappy heard. Couldn't be much worse'n this creek bottom where the crops wash out, with every bad rain. There's nothing to do if your Pappy gets it in his head to move.

SAIRY: I hope we don't have to move to Indianny, though. Here it's only two miles to school, and maybe there won't be any school at all in Indianny. (*Pause*) The teacher says Abe's got a learning mind.

ABE (*Bursting in carrying bag of meal*): Mammy, the miller's wife calls the song "Barbara *Ellen*" 'stead of *Allen*, and her words are all different.

NANCY: Barbara Ellen, Barbara Allen—reckon there's a dozen ways to sing it. It's not written down anywhere, that I know, and we couldn't read it if it were. That's why I want you to get all the learning you can, Abe, so you can read for yourself. Come, now, let's sing "Barbara Allen." (*They begin to sing. Suddenly, TOM LINCOLN, a pack on his back, enters, and they abruptly stop singing.*)

TOM (*Walking towards fire; grumpily*): Gets so a man can't hear himself think in his own house.

NANCY (*With surprise; hurrying to greet him*): Tom! You're back!

SAIRY *and* ABE: Pappy!

TOM: Rustle up some wood, Abe. Get a kettle on to boil,

Sairy. I shot us a wild turkey, coming through the woods. Hoecakes taste mighty good with fresh game, Nancy. (*They scatter to their tasks.* TOM *throws down pack and coat.*) D'ya reckon we can be ready to start in a few days?

NANCY: Where to, Tom?

TOM: Indianny. No use waiting for the weather to get colder. I'd like to be over there and settled before year-end, and it's a good piece away. (*Glances at* ABE, *who slips out for the wood*)

NANCY (*Hopefully*): Settled? There's a cabin, then, or somewhere to stay?

TOM (*Gruffly*): Cabin! We'll be lucky if we get ourselves a pole-shed before the snow piles up. It's wild, unbroken country, Nancy, but there'll be deep rich soil once we get a clearing. I've never seen such big oaks and elms, and sycamores and maples and birches, looped up and around with wild grapevines. Never seen such cover for game. We won't be going hungry for meat this winter, I can tell you that.

SAIRY (*Tentatively*): And Indians . . . ?

TOM: Nary an Indian all the time I was in Indianny.

NANCY: Any folks to neighbor with, Tom?

TOM: Not enough to cause any bother. One family every square mile, I reckon.

ABE (*Entering with wood in time to hear*): Any school?

TOM: Not closer'n eight–nine miles. But you young 'uns won't have time for schooling anyhow, what with all the work to be done. Have to carry spring water almost a mile for one thing. That's a job for you and Sairy, Abe. (*Turns toward door*) Well, I'll be walking over to Redman's to see about selling the cows and chickens and extry corn. Best start packing, Nancy.

SAIRY: How far is it, Pappy?

TOM: Reckon a hundred miles, the way we'll have to go. Only about fifty, as crows fly.

NANCY (*Looking after him*): Sometimes when you don't feel much like it, it's the best time for singing.

ABE: "All Through the Night," Mammy?

NANCY: Fine, Abe. (*They sing, as curtain falls.*)

READER: As it turned out, Indiana wasn't a land of promise for the Lincolns. They reached Tom's wilderness claim near Pigeon Creek with not much more than the clothes on their backs. Wind whistled through the bare treetops, and frost shone white on the leaf mold.

Tom Lincoln set about building what settlers called a half-faced camp—three sides of logs and boughs and the fourth side open—and that's where the Lincolns spent the winter, hovering around the fire they always kept burning at the open side. In the spring, when Abe was eight, he helped his father clear a small piece of ground to plant corn and wheat. With the help of neighbors, they built a log cabin with a dirt floor and no windows, chinking and daubing the cracks with mud. They turned the half-faced camp over to Nancy's aunt and uncle, who'd come to find the promised land, too. They brought along their adopted son, Dennis Hanks, almost ten years older than Abe. (DENNIS, *18 and* ABE, *8, enter before curtain.*)

DENNIS: You catch onto the words quick enough, Abe, but what you do to the tune I can't figure.

ABE: The tune sounds all right inside my head. It just comes out different somehow, Dennis.

DENNIS: Try it again now. Listen hard how the tune goes. (DENNIS *sings first stanza of "A Frog Went A-Courtin'."*)

ABE (*Trying to sing*): "A frog went a-courtin' and he did ride . . ."

27

DENNIS: What did you sing a different song for, Abe?

ABE: I wasn't singing a different song. (*Begins to laugh*) I was singing "A Frog Went A-Courtin'," same as you.

DENNIS: Guess what we need is a harmonica. You could carry a tune on that without having to sing it.

ABE: Pappy'd never buy me one, and I've got nothing to trade.

DENNIS: Maybe you can trade work some time, chopping wood or something. I've never seen a young'un handle an axe the way you can, Abe. (*They exit.*)

READER: Nancy Lincoln had lived in the new cabin less than a year, when come the fall of 1818, an epidemic swept through southern Indiana. Nancy's aunt and uncle caught the fever and died. Then on October 5, when leaves were fluttering bright in the treetops, and a purple haze showed beyond the knoll, Nancy took sick. Tom Lincoln did what he could to make her comfortable, but the fever took her, too. Abe and Sarah were frightened and silent.

Their mother never sang again . . . and for a long time Abe could find no music inside of him. (OFFSTAGE CHORUS *sings* "All Through the Night.") The year after Nancy Lincoln's death was a year young Abe would never forget. Twelve-year-old Sarah did her best to keep the cabin orderly, the stew kettle boiling, the clothes patched. Ten-year-old Abe chopped wood and helped tend the crops, but his mind whirled with questions. Why did his mother, his good, kind mother, have to die? Why was his father so sullen? What was going to happen to them off in the wilderness?

Then in November, Tom Lincoln went back to Elizabethtown, Kentucky, to find himself another wife. (*Curtain opens on yard in front of Lincoln cabin. There is a chopping block and wood. ABE sits on a log, deep in thought. DENNIS, now 20, enters, singing "Hey, Betty Martin."*)

DENNIS: What're you doing, Abe?

ABE: Thinking.

DENNIS: What about?

ABE: About Pappy bringing someone to take Mammy's place. Can't be anyone to do that.

DENNIS: Maybe it won't be so bad. (*Sits on log next to* ABE)

ABE: Or so good. *You* know how kind Mammy was, Dennis. Couldn't be anyone better. (SAIRY *comes out of cabin, a shawl around her shoulders.*)

SAIRY: You'd best bring in a pile o' wood, Abe. If they come today, they'll be wanting to thaw out.

DENNIS: On a nice bright December day like this?

SAIRY: I'm cold. (*She shivers.*) Or maybe I'm just plain skeered . . . (ABE *looks at her, surprised.*)

ABE: What you skeered of, Sairy?

SAIRY: What if Pappy's new wife can't take a liking to me, or me to her? (*She sighs.*)

DENNIS: It appears we're all skeered. (*Rises*) Reckon Sairy's right about the wood, Abe.

ABE: We've been getting ready for them every afternoon for a week.

DENNIS: They're bound to get here *some* time. (*He carries armload of wood into cabin, returning with his gun.* ABE *and* SAIRY *sit side by side on log.*) You finish the wood, Abe. After that long drive from Kentucky they might fancy a little fresh game for supper. (*Exits*)

ABE (*Glumly*): Can't anyone take Mammy's place.

SAIRY (*Trying to be comforting*): But Mammy wouldn't want us to be sad, Abe. She never had things easy, but she wasn't sad.

ABE: Not that she let us see.

SAIRY: I still remember all the songs she sang to us. When you and Dennis are away, I sing them to keep myself company. Do you remember them, Abe?

ABE (*Nodding*): Yes, but Dennis thinks I sing like a donkey.

SAIRY: When I'm a-working around and singing, I don't have so much time to be skeered.

ABE: Doing things helps. (*Gets up, picks up armload of wood, and takes it into cabin. He returns, pauses at the door, listening.*) Hear anything, Sairy? Way off?

SAIRY (*Listening intently*): Seems like I *do* hear something, too. Can't be wagon wheels, can it, Abe?

ABE: Maybe. But something else, too, above the sound of wheels grinding and creaking. (*Listens again*) Listen! There's someone a-coming, singing "All Through the Night."

SAIRY: Do you think it's *her*—Pappy's new wife?

ABE: It's more than just her . . . (*Sound of singing comes faintly from offstage, getting louder gradually.*) Look! There's Pappy with a big old wagon and horses. (*Points off*)

SAIRY: *She's* a-sitting on the seat next to him. And look, Abe! A real true bureau, a table and chairs, and feather beds! And three children . . . perched on the load. Two girls and a boy.

ABE: 'Pears to me two of them are singing. The biggest girl's playing a harmonica, Sairy. A harmonica!

SAIRY: I'm not so skeered now. When they come a-singing, it's a good sign, don't you think? Mammy'd run out to meet them with her arms open, I know she would. (SAIRY *runs off excitedly, arms outstretched.* ABE *stands watching doubtfully, as curtain falls.*)

READER: They came a-singing . . . Sarah Bush Lincoln and her three young 'uns. And before the month was out Abe was beginning to sing, too, not so Dennis Hanks could hear, but down inside where it mattered most. First off the new stepmother stretched out her arms to Abe, and laughed good-naturedly when he drew back. She could wait.

Solemnly Abe watched the unloading. His new mammy had brought something besides furniture and feather beds and shiny pots and pans. She'd brought books, a few wonderful books! And then there was the harmonica her oldest daughter Elizabeth could play. (ABE *and* ELIZABETH *come before curtain.*)

ABE: Where'd you get the harmonica, Betsy?

ELIZABETH: It belonged to my Pappy, Mr. Johnston. (*Sadly*) He died. He could play really well.

ABE: So can you. I heard you a long way off.

ELIZABETH: Only "All Through the Night" and "Yankee Doodle." That's all I've practiced. It's harder'n singing.

ABE: Not for *me* it wouldn't be. I'm no shakes when it comes to singing. Ask my cousin Dennis.

ELIZABETH: Well, I'm no shakes playing the harmonica.

ABE: You know "Barbara Allen"? That was my mother's favorite song.

ELIZABETH: I know it to sing, sort of. (*Tries to play it*) It doesn't go right on the harmonica, though. (*Tries again*) *You* try, Abe.

ABE: Me? What do I do?

ELIZABETH: Just pull your breath back and forth. (*She wipes harmonica on her apron and hands it to* ABE. *He tries tentatively.*) That's right, in and out. (ABE *gets the first few notes of "Barbara Allen."*) That's good. (*He gets a few more notes.*) Real good. I can almost tell what you're playin'. You can practice the rest of the day if you want.

ABE: Honest? I'll do something for you, Betsy . . . whittle you something, or make you a buckskin pouch.

ELIZABETH: Maybe you can tell me a story . . . all for myself.

ABE: I'll do that. Wait till Dennis hears me keep in tune tonight! (*They hurry out.*)

31

READER: He had music in his bones, Abe did, if not in his voice. When he was twelve years old, he began making up poems and songs. Folks thought of him as a mimic and a storyteller, not a poet. But he had one good audience—his stepmother. She fancied Abe was one of the best rhymsters she ever listened to. Fact is, most everything Abe did struck his stepmother as right smart. She urged Abe to go to school every chance he got, and stood up for him whenever his father talked against too much "eddication."

Life was good for Abe and Sairy and Dennis Hanks after Sarah Bush Lincoln came to live in the log cabin. Her son, Johnny, a year or two younger than Abe, followed him around like a pet dog.

Abe grew lanky and rawboned and muscular. When Abe was 17, he stood six feet four inches tall. That was the year his sister Sarah and Aaron Grigsby were married. (ABE *and* DENNIS *enter before curtain.*)

DENNIS: Girls can't stay home forever, Abe. Sairy'll be happy with Aaron.

ABE (*Sadly*): I'm sure going to miss Sairy. 'Taint everyone has a sister like her. (*Looks off dreamily*) Sometimes I get a feeling about it, Dennis. . . . I know she loves Aaron, and he'll be good to her . . . but I wish she weren't getting married and all. I have a foreboding. If anything happened to Sairy, I'd feel mighty bad. (*They exit.*)

READER: Poor Abe. The next year Sairy died, and the sorrow of it bit to the marrow of Abe's bones. He felt melancholy again, the way he did when his mother died. His heart lost its singing. He jumped at a chance to help Allen Gentry build a flatboat and load it with farm produce to take down to New Orleans, thinking it would help him forget.

He was gone three months, seeing things, hearing

things, smelling things he never knew existed. And thinking things, too. He saw slavery in practice . . . men and women sold at auction in New Orleans. . . . He saw slaves working and singing in the fields, singing around campfires at night, even singing when their backs were bent over their hard labors.

Back home again, Abe was caught up in the excitement of the election of 1828. Now that he was 19 and had seen a big piece of his country from a flatboat, now that he had watched the waterfront, walked the streets of New Orleans, visited the slave market, and listened to all kinds of talk, he felt equal to entering into election talk. John Quincy Adams was running for a second term against Andrew Jackson, a man of the frontier. Adams stood for the rich, Jackson for men who knew hardship and work. (*Curtain opens on Lincoln cabin.* SARAH BUSH LINCOLN *is knitting,* ABE *is sitting on a stool, writting on a slate.*)

ABE: Reckon Jackson's going to get elected come November, Mammy?

SARAH: Why, I've not bothered my head about it, Abe. Always did say politics is for the menfolks.

ABE: Jackson's a man of the people, people like us. Nothing fancy and high-stepping about him.

SARAH: If he's a man of the people, I reckon they'll elect him. I notice most people have common sense even if they haven't much education. You writing a campaign speech, Abe?

ABE: Only four lines so far, as they came to my mind. You recollect the tune of "Auld Lang Syne," Mammy?

SARAH: 'Course I do. (*Stops her work to hum tune and beat time*)

ABE: Let's see how this goes, then, with you taking the tune and me saying the words. All right, from the beginning . . .

"Let auld acquaintance be forgot
And never brought to mind;
May Jackson be our President,
And Adams left behind."

SARAH: Why, Abe! That's good enough to be put in a book. Reckon you won't ever get a chance to be President, but I'm countin' on you turning into a powerful big poet or something. (*Curtain*)

READER: Abe had just turned 21, when Tom Lincoln sold the Pigeon Creek farm. A week later the Lincolns, with Dennis Hanks and his family, packed their belongings and turned their ox teams toward central Illinois. To Tom Lincoln, always hankering after a land of milk and honey, Illinois sounded like the promised land. Abe had come of age . . . but it took him a few years to find himself. He tried splitting rails for wages and keep; he took another cargo down to New Orleans; he read books and studied grammar, and clerked in a store; he enlisted in the militia in the Black Hawk War; he went into the store business with a partner and lost money; he became postmaster of the frontier town of New Salem, Illinois; he ran survey lines; he studied law, and tried his luck at politics. When he was 25 years old, he ran for the State Legislature and was elected. And then he fell in love with Ann Rutledge. (*Curtain up on dimly-lit stage, an outdoor scene in spring. ABE and ANN enter.*)

ABE (*Looking around*): It was here I first heard you sing, Miss Ann. I was walking by myself in the evening when I heard your voice. I stood still to listen . . .

ANN: How did you know who was singing, Mr. Lincoln?

ABE: Hadn't I been boarding at your father's tavern for a good long time? I knew from talk around that the tavern-keeper's daughter had a singing voice. It didn't take a lawyer to put two and two together.

ANN: But you *are* a lawyer, Mr. Lincoln.

ABE: Not yet, though I'm determined to become one. Next year perhaps I can get my license.

ANN: Well then, you're *almost* a lawyer, and a Congressman in the Legislature, too. And you're still so young.

ABE: Makes me feel old as the hills sometimes to recollect I was 26 on the twelfth of February last.

ANN (*With a sigh*): Sometimes I feel as old as the hills, too. (*Sings softly from "Pilgrim Stranger"*)
"Here in this country, so dark and dreary,
I long have wander'd, forlorn and weary . . ."

ABE: That's the song you were singing the first time I heard you! It would pleasure me more than I can say to you to hear you sing it again.

ANN: And it would pleasure me to sing it. (ANN *sings first, second, and fourth stanzas of "Pilgrim Stranger." ABE listens.*)

ABE: Thank you, Miss Ann. The song moves me deeply. But I rebel against some of the words.

ANN: Why, Mr. Lincoln!

ABE: "Do not detain me, for I am going," it says. But I *want* to detain you. I don't want you to go.

ANN (*Laughing*): I'm in no hurry right now, Mr. Lincoln. And it's only a song. You mustn't take it so seriously. Folks say you are a great one for telling funny stories, Mr. Lincoln, and I've seen you set the whole table a-laughing at the tavern. But tonight you seem so serious . . . about a little song. Come, tell me what it's like in the capital city of Vandalia where the Legislature meets. (*They exit, holding hands.*)

READER: In August of that year Ann Rutledge died of the fever. Abe was shattered by overwhelming grief, for the third time in his life . . . first for his mother, then for his sister Sarah, and now for Ann. Finally, he went back to reading law, and got his license to practice. (OFFSTAGE CHORUS *sings "Pilgrim Stranger." Voices gradually fade out.*)

At 28, Abraham Lincoln, prairie lawyer, hung up his shingle in Springfield, Illinois, which soon became the capital city. Practicing law in those days meant traveling the circuit. For years Lincoln spent almost half his time on the road, often traveling in the company of the Judge and other lawyers. Lincoln enjoyed the trips, meeting people and making new friends, spinning yarns, exchanging stories, and adding his voice to a lusty chorus. (OFFSTAGE CHORUS *sings "Kathleen Mavourneen."*)

Lincoln did not marry until he was 33 years old, and then, some folks think, he made a mighty strange choice. Mary Todd, a Kentucky belle with all the social graces, seemed an unlikely mate for a man like Abraham Lincoln who'd been brought up in a log cabin. But he married her. And folks who knew the Lincolns when they lived in Springfield said that Abe didn't always have occasion to go around with a singing heart. But he delighted in his sons—playing with them, telling them stories, indulging them, yes, and spoiling them. He would always give in to the boys when they sang "Jimmy Crack Corn," one of his favorite songs. (OFFSTAGE CHORUS *sings song.*)

Lincoln went to Washington, D.C., in 1847 to serve a term in Congress. A few years later he ran for the Senate and was defeated. Then came the famous campaign of 1858 when Abraham Lincoln, the big giant, and Stephen A. Douglas, "The Little Giant," ran against each other for Senator from Illinois. Douglas was favored to win: He was already serving a term in the Senate and was running for re-election.

The two men were as different as sunflowers and roses—Lincoln tall and ungainly, Douglas short and well-groomed; Lincoln simple and unpretentious, Douglas traveling around the state in a private railroad car, with a brass band to meet him at the station. (ABE *enters before curtain, with* TWO MEN.)

The great issue of the campaign was the extension of slavery. Lincoln took a firm stand that the territories be free from slavery. Douglas insisted that the people of each territory should decide. Although not an abolitionist, Lincoln did not believe in slavery, and he denounced Douglas's indifference to the right or wrong of it. The great debates went on. . . .

ABE: How do you think the debates are going, boys?

1ST MAN: You have Douglas on the run, Abe. Your "house divided" speech is being quoted all over the country.

2ND MAN (*Orating*): "A house divided against itself cannot stand. I believe this government cannot endure permanently half slave and half free."

1ST MAN: And folks are still chuckling over the speech you made in Springfield in July. "In my poor, lean, lank face," you said, "nobody has ever seen that any cabbages were sprouting." (*Laughs*)

2ND MAN: Somehow—don't ask me how—Douglas is able to afford a private railroad car.

ABE (*Shrugging*): As for me, coach or freight caboose is good enough, and a haywagon to ride to my lodgings.

2ND MAN: What about the brass bands, though, Abe? Every place we go there's three times as much trumped-up noise for Douglas as for you.

ABE: Just as a matter of taste and principle, I prefer a harmonica. (*Takes out harmonica and plays a snatch of "America"*)

2ND MAN: Why, I didn't know you played one of those things, Abe!

ABE: Fooled around with one from the time I was a kid

in Indiana. Always liked the sound of a harmonica. Let Douglas have his brass bands . . . this will do for me. (*He plays "Home, Sweet Home."*)

2ND MAN: Abe! Now don't tell me not to spread the news! The harmonica is the musical instrument of the common people. You're one of them. You're for them. You speak their language. I'm going to make a point of that harmonica for the newspapers! (*They exit.*)

READER: Lincoln received the greater number of popular votes in that senatorial contest, but the State Legislature had the last word in those days, and there Douglas received the majority. Although Lincoln lost, the debates made him a figure of national importance, and the newly formed Republican party nominated him for President in 1860.

The campaign was a long one and a hard one, with Abe opposed by men who had long been in the public eye—governors, senators, judges. When he went East to speak, large crowds turned out to see the rail-splitter, the lanky prairie lawyer who had debated so forcefully with Douglas. There were torchlight processions and noisy demonstrations . . . and brass bands. (*Band music, live or recorded, is heard playing "Hail, Columbia." Curtain rises on* BAND *crossing stage, if practical, with noisy* CAMPAIGNERS *shouting and carrying placards: "Abe Lincoln for President," "A Vote for Abe is a Vote for the People," "Elect the Rail-Splitter from Illinois," "Honest Abe," etc. Curtain closes.*)

Abraham Lincoln was elected President, the sixteenth President of the United States. A backwoods boy, President of the United States!

Before he left for Washington, Lincoln made a pilgrimage through the slush and cold of a late January day to a little farm near Charleston, Illinois. His father had died some years before, but his stepmother was still living. (*Curtain rises on front room of a farmhouse.* SARAH BUSH LINCOLN *is sitting in rocking chair, knitting.* SALLY, *her granddaughter, rushes in.*)

SALLY: Granny! Granny! Uncle Abe is here!

SARAH (*Suddenly roused*): Abe?

SALLY: Uncle Abe's come to see you, Granny.

SARAH: Busy man like Abe coming to see his old Mammy? (*Alert, excited*) Do I look all right, Sally?

SALLY: Hasn't anybody ever seen you frowsed-up yet? Here, let me pretty your collar a bit.

ABE (*In doorway*): Don't go fixing up my best girl too pretty, Sally, or I won't be able to tear myself away.

SARAH (*Starting to rise*): Abe! (SALLY *exits.*)

ABE (*Striding to her*): Don't you get up, Mammy. I've just come to tell you goodbye.

SARAH: What kind of way is that, Abe? Minute you get in the door you tell me you've come to say goodbye!

ABE (*Laughing*): Oh, I'm intending to sit a while first. (*Sits near her*) How've you all been? All the grandchildren? And Dennis? And Johnny's young uns?

SARAH: We're all fine, Abe . . . getting a mite older, though.

ABE: It's a way we have.

SARAH: Stand close and let me have a good look at you, son. (ABE *stands for inspection.*) You're a bit stooped. A bit tired-looking, seems like. Been working too hard, Abe? And now you're going off to Washington. Oh, I'm *that* proud of you . . . but it's a big burden they've put on your shoulders.

ABE (*With a sigh as he sits again*): Too big, I sometimes think.

SARAH: You can handle it, though. I never will forget those big trees you used to chop down when you were

39

just a stripling. (*Chuckles*) And to think I reckoned you'd turn out to be a writin' man. Never entered my head you'd be President.

ABE: Nobody else thought I'd be either, Mammy. Least of all me.

SARAH: You still versify, Abe?

ABE: Haven't had much time for that lately.

SARAH: Remember the lines you wrote for Jackson? You'd just come back from that flatboat trip to New Orleans. (*Begins to beat out tune of "Auld Lang Syne"*)

ABE: Haven't thought of that for a good long time. Let me see if I can remember the words. (*Hesitates*)
"Let auld acquaintance be forgot
And never brought to mind;
May Jackson be our President,
And Adams left behind."

SARAH: Reckon you'll have to change the words now, Abe. I been spending considerable thought on it. Finally worked it out.
"Now Lincoln is our President,
The others left behind."

ABE (*Laughing*): So it's *you* who's turned out to be the poet, Mammy. (*Sobering*) But I reckon now we've come to parting it's the good old words that are best of all (*Singing*)
"For Auld Lang Syne, my dear,
For Auld Lang Syne;
We'll take a cup of kindness yet,
For Auld Lang Syne."
(*Curtain closes.*)

READER: It was a rainy, cold morning in February, 1861, when Lincoln left Springfield for Washington. Old friends had gathered at the station to say goodbye. There was even a feeble band playing "The Star-

Spangled Banner." (*Offstage band music, then cheers and shouts are heard.*) Lincoln stood on the observation platform to say goodbye. (*Curtain opens on empty stage.* LINCOLN *comes in, waves.*)

ABE: My friends: No one, not in my situation, can appreciate my feeling of sadness at this parting. To this place, and the kindness of these people, I owe everything. Here I have lived a quarter of a century, and have passed from a young to an old man. Here my children have been born, and one is buried. I now leave, not knowing when or whether ever I may return . . . (*Curtain closes. Sound of a train whistle is heard offstage.*)

READER: Less than two months after Lincoln reached Washington, Fort Sumter was fired upon, and the War between the States began. Feeling sorrow rather than anger against the South for bombarding the Fort, Lincoln's one thought was to preserve the Union . . . even if a war had to be fought to do it. Lincoln's days and nights were full of anguish. He was condemned by abolitionists for being too mild, and by anti-abolitionists for being too harsh. A continual stream of people tried to see him. (*Curtain opens on room in White House.* LINCOLN *is at a desk writing, piles of papers and maps in front of him. Piano is at right.* JOHN HAY, *assistant to Lincoln's secretary, enters.*)

HAY: A Virginia lady to see you next, sir. About her son in prison.

ABE (*Wearily*): Another?

HAY: She has her young daughter with her. About the age of your boy Willie, I should say. They've been waiting a long time.

ABE: There are so many of them, Hay . . . waiting, waiting. . . . Warn her that I can do little, much as I might like to. (*Sighs*) Show her in. (HAY *returns with* WOMAN *and* GIRL.)

41

WOMAN (*Going toward desk*): Oh, Mr. President, now that I am face to face with you . . . (*Hesitates*) My son . . . (*Breaks down*)

ABE (*Kindly*): He is a prisoner?

WOMAN (*Nodding, handing* LINCOLN *a slip of paper*): His name . . . and the prison. He is badly wounded. (GIRL *meanwhile sees piano and moves toward it.*)

ABE (*Looking at paper*): He's only eighteen years old. Wounded at the Battle of Bull Run.

WOMAN: He will die if he is kept in prison. (GIRL *sits down at piano, runs fingers over keys. Begins to play "Annie Laurie" very softly.*) Why, Lucy Belle! (GIRL *stops, embarrassed.*)

ABE: Let her be, Madam. There's little enough these days that isn't war, war, war. (*To* GIRL) Play it. Do you know the words? It's a song I specially like. (GIRL *sings "Annie Laurie."* LINCOLN *gets up and stands at the window as he listens. At the end of the song he turns to* GIRL.) And do you know the little song called "Down in the Valley"? I have always loved it.

GIRL: I know it! My brother taught me. (*She plays and sings several stanzas of "Down in the Valley."*)

ABE (*Turning to* WOMAN): I shall see that your boy is released to you, Madam. Nurse him well. Have your little girl play for him. I thank her for the welcome respite she has given me from this terrible war.

WOMAN: Thank you, Mr. President. (WOMAN *and* GIRL *exit as curtain falls.*)

READER: The terrible war went on . . . and on. 1861. 1862. 1863. 1864. In that year Lincoln was re-elected President by a large majority, who agreed with him that it was best "not to swap horses when crossing a stream." Union troops were marching to "The Battle Hymn of the Republic." (*Sound of music and marching feet offstage, right wing.*) Confederate troops had appropriated "Dixie" as their marching song. (*Sound of music and marching feet to left offstage.*)

1865. On Sunday April 9th, Lee surrendered to Grant at Appomattox Court House. The Union was saved! Word reached Washington that night, and the next morning wild celebrating began. Bells rang, whistles blew, shouting crowds surged toward the White House to serenade the President. (*Offstage noise—shouting, singing, music*) Lincoln finally appeared at an upstairs window of the White House. (LINCOLN *enters, holding up hand for silence.*)

ABE: I see you have a band there.

OFFSTAGE VOICES: Three of them!

ABE: I propose now that you play a certain well-known piece of music. "Dixie" was always one of the best tunes I ever heard. (*Shouting*) I know our adversaries attempted to appropriate it. Yesterday we fairly captured it. (*Mores cheers and shouts*) It's everyone's tune now—North and South. I ask the band to give us a good turn upon it. (BAND, *offstage, or marching on, plays "Dixie."* LINCOLN *waves and retires.*)

READER: Four days later, on the night of April 14th, the President and his wife went to Ford's Theater in Washington to see a play. When the Presidential party took their seats in the box a few minutes after the curtain had gone up, the orchestra interrupted the play with the stirring music of "Hail to the Chief." Actors joined in, singing. (*A group of* ACTORS, *a few men and women, stand at wings and sing several stanzas of "Hail to the Chief."*) It was the last song Abraham Lincoln ever heard. Two hours later, near the end of the play, he was shot in the head by actor

43

John Wilkes Booth, a fanatical advocate of slavery. The next morning the President lay dead. (OFFSTAGE CHORUS *sings "Gentle Annie" as background.*)

Abraham Lincoln's life and work were over. A wave of grief swept the country. Thousands of mourners thronged the White House and lined the route of the funeral train. Bells tolled, tears were shed. In Washington, Walt Whitman, then a little-known poet, poured into words his own grief and the grief that was in millions of hearts:

"My Captain does not answer, his lips are pale and
　　still,
My father does not feel my arm, he has no pulse nor
　　will,
The ship is anchor'd safe and sound, its voyage closed
　　and done,
From fearful trip the victor ship comes in with object
　　won:
Exult O shores, and ring O bells!
But I with mournful tread,
Walk the deck my Captain lies,
Fallen cold and dead."

Abraham Lincoln was dead. Yet not dead, either. For what he stood for, what he lived by, never dies—courage, justice, freedom, compassion, faith. One mourner put it all in six words when he said of the martyred President:

"Now he belongs to the ages."

THE END

PRODUCTION NOTES
SING THE SONGS OF LINCOLN

Characters: 7 male; 8 female; 1 male or female for Reader; male and female extras for Band Members, Campaigners, Actors, and Offstage Chorus. (It is advisable to have two actors for the role of Lincoln, one to play young Abe, the other Lincoln, the man.)

Playing Time: 45 minutes. (If a shorter production is desired, the play could be cut so that only the scenes dealing with Lincoln's youth are presented.)

Costumes: All characters wear plain clothes of the period: overalls and work shirts for men, long skirts, aprons and shawls for women. As a candidate and as President, Lincoln wears familiar costume with battered stovepipe hat, black coat and trousers, etc. (As President, Lincoln wears a beard.) Hay wears a suit. The actors may wear elaborate costumes. The band should wear uniforms if it appears onstage.

Properties: Mending for Nancy; buckskin bag for Sairy; pack for Tom; gun, paper, for Dennis; harmonica for Elizabeth; knitting for Sarah; placards, as indicated in the text, for campaigners; buckskin bag, harmonica, paper for Abe, wood.

Setting: The various scenes may take place on different parts of the stage, with a spotlight on the action while the rest of the stage is dark. They may also be presented as regular scenes with as many furnishings as desired. The scene in the Lincoln cabin may have a table, a bed built in one corner, some rough stools, a fireplace with wood piled near it, and a door at center. The scene in front of the cabin has a chopping block, logs, and a backdrop showing the cabin. The scene with Ann Rutledge may have a backdrop of trees. The farmhouse scene has a rocking chair for Sarah Bush Lincoln, the White House scene has a desk piled with papers and maps (the piano may be at the front of the auditorium).

Lighting: No special effects (unless a spotlight technique is used for scenes).

Lincoln Memorial

MC., GIRL, WOMAN *and* MAN *enter and stand center. If possible, a large poster of the Lincoln Memorial hangs behind them, on backdrop.*

M.C.: Why do they come . . .
more than two and a half million people
every year, year after year?
Why do they climb
the long, imposing flight of steps?
To admire the 36 Doric columns
that stand for the 36 states in the Union
at the time of Lincoln's death?
To regard the beauty of the sculpture
by Daniel Chester French?
Why do they come . . .
To marvel at the finely-fitted blocks
of white marble?
The massive armchair
with the colossal figure of a brooding man
nineteen feet high from head to foot?
Do they come to refresh their recollection
of the Gettysburg Address
engraved on the south wall,
or the excerpts from the Second Inaugural
on the north?

GIRL: No. They come with reverence
     more than curiosity.
     They come with awe, wondering.
     They come with a sense of history,
     asking where our twentieth-century Lincoln
     hides himself.
     They come with a welling up of gratitude,
     a yearning for communion with something great.
WOMAN: I'm just an ordinary citizen from Oklahoma,
     visiting the capital for the first time.
     They told me not to miss the Lincoln Memorial,
     and I wondered why.
     Now I know.
     Because something of Lincoln is here!
     I suppose everyone has a different name for it,
     but to me it's . . . serenity.
     Serenity and strength.
     I'm glad I came.
MAN: I've been here many times,
     and I keep coming back.
     There's faith and bigness here . . .
     you notice how the men take off their hats?
     Some women wipe their eyes.
     It's hard to put in words,
     but I find something here that gives me hope.
     Yes, that's it:
     hope for brotherhood, and peace,
     and understanding in a frightened world.
GIRL: In South America
     we learn about Lincoln in our schools,
     and because of the way he felt about freedom,
     we love him deeply.
     His name is as familiar to us
     as that of Bolivar and San Martin.
     One of the first things I wished to do
     in the United States

was to bow my head before the statue
of this Man of Freedom.
He belongs to all the world, to every age,
to generations still to come.
MAN: I'm not a man of fancy words or phrases.
A board, a saw, a hammer, and nails . . .
that's the language I know best.
My tongue is thick.
But here it doesn't matter—
Lincoln would understand.
He'd know what was welling up inside of me
without my saying it.
He'd just say, "Carry on."
And I would understand him, too.
M.C.: They come . . .
more than a million and a half people
year after year
because Abraham Lincoln
still has a hold on the heart of everyone
who believes in justice,
honor, integrity, freedom, and compassion.
For here was a man *of* the people
and *for* the people,
whose vision of the future
was not engulfed by the present.
A man of yesterday and tomorrow
whose voice still rings out loud and clear:
ALL: "With malice toward none;
with charity for all;
with firmness in the right,
as God gives us the strength to see the right,
let us strive on . . .
to do all which may achieve and cherish
a just and lasting peace,
among ourselves, and with all nations."

Lincoln at Gettysburg

GIRL: The flowery long oration
preceding his was through,
the spirited ovation,
and now . . . his speech was due.

He took it from his pocket—
two pages, that was all.
Would the crowd around him mock it?
He stood up, stooped but tall.

His voice was slow and steady,
at Gettysburg that day,
but few who heard were ready
for what he had to say:

BOY: "We here highly resolve
that these dead
shall not have died in vain;
that this nation, under God,
shall have a new birth of freedom,
and that government of the people,
by the people,
and for the people,
shall not perish from the earth."

GIRL: No wasted word or letter
to praise the honored dead:
Abe Lincoln said it better
than it was ever said!

Walt Whitman's Lincoln

WALT WHITMAN: I, Walt Whitman, was visiting my mother in Long Island when I heard the news. It was Saturday morning, the day before Easter, 1865. We were sitting at breakfast, but we ate nothing after we read, through misty eyes, the headlines in the newspaper. President Lincoln assassinated! Shot in his box at Ford's Theater on Friday night! What could we say?

I had come to visit my mother, exulting that the long, terrible war between the North and South was over. General Lee had surrendered to General Grant at Appomattox. But now . . .

BOYS (*Softly*):

"O, Captain! my Captain! our fearful trip is done,

The ship has weather'd every rack, the prize we sought is won,

The port is near, the bells I hear, the people all exulting,

While follow eyes the steady keel, the vessel grim and daring:

GIRLS (*Softly*):

"But O heart! heart! heart!

O the bleeding drops of red,

Where on the deck my Captain lies,

Fallen cold and dead."

WALT WHITMAN: All day my mother and I sat stupefied, silently passing the extra editions across the table to each other. And then I knew I must go back to Washington, where I had seen Lincoln so often riding to the White House on horseback from his summer lodgings at the Soldier's Home. Once he passed me very close, and I saw his face fully. Not one of the artists has caught its deep expression. They have caught only the surface. He bowed and smiled, but far beneath his smile I noticed something else in his face, out of this world and time.

ALL:

> "O how shall I warble myself for the dead one there I loved?
> And how shall I deck my song for the large sweet soul that has gone?
> And what shall my perfume be for the grave of him I love?"

WALT WHITMAN: And so I went back to Washington to hear first-hand about the foulest crime in history in any land or age. For days I walked alone brooding, or sat silently watching the Potomac flow on and on, as one could hope the life of such a man would flow. And as I walked and watched, my mind was full of Abraham Lincoln—whose love for freedom and democracy I shared.

BOYS:

> "O Captain! my Captain! rise up and hear the bells;
> Rise up—for you the flag is flung—for you the bugle trills,
> For you the bouquets and ribbon'd wreaths—for you the shore a-crowding,
> For you they call, the swaying mass, their eager faces turning;

GIRLS:

> "Hear Captain! dear father!
> The arm beneath your head!
> It is some dream that on the deck,
> You've fallen cold and dead."

WALT WHITMAN: I had first gone down to Washington late in the year 1862 to try to find my brother who had been wounded. I stayed there. There was so much to be done there, with fighting close by, and wounded soldiers being carried in by the hundreds and thousands. I took a little room at the top of a shabby rooming-house, and found part-time work in one of the government offices. That gave me time to visit the wounded and do what I could for them. President Lincoln used to visit them, too—and bend over their cots, and speak to them. And they loved him.

ALL:

"Hushed be the camps to-day
And soldiers, let us drape our war-worn weapons,
And each with musing soul retire to celebrate
Our dear commander's death.
No more for him life's stormy conflicts,
Nor victory, nor defeat—no more time's dark events,
Charging like ceaseless clouds across the sky. . . .
Sing of the love we bore him—because you, dweller in
   camps, know it truly."

WALT WHITMAN: It was lilac time in Washington that year when I walked along the Potomac brooding, brooding. The air was sweet with lilac fragrance, and, I wondered, how could such fragrance be companion of death? Lincoln and lilacs . . . the lost and the living. It was then I decided that on April the 14th of every year I would have a sprig of lilac in my room, in memory of him.

GIRLS:

". . . the lilac-bush tall-growing with heart-shaped
   leaves of rich green,
With many a pointed blossom rising delicate, with the
   perfume strong I love,
With every life a miracle . . . A sprig with its flower I
   break."

WALT WHITMAN: I could have met Mr. Lincoln, could

have shaken his hand, could have spoken to him of the things we both believed. But I never did. My friend, John Hay, assistant secretary to the President, could have arranged it for me. But I never asked him to. What could our tongues have said that our hearts didn't know already? We believed in a new time for the common man and woman, Mr. Lincoln and I. We believed in Emancipation and Union, in Democracy and Brotherhood. Whether he ever read my book of poems, first published ten years before he died, I'll never know. But it doesn't matter. He knew without reading.

BOYS:
"I was looking a long while for Intentions,
For a clew to the history of the past for myself . . . and
    now I have found it,
It is Democracy—(the purport and aim of all the past),
It is the life of one man or one woman to-day—the
    average man of to-day. . . ."

WALT WHITMAN: No, I never met the President. But during the summer of 1863 I saw him almost every day, as I happened to live where he passed, riding a good-sized, easy-going gray horse, dressed in plain black, somewhat dusty and rusty, looking about as ordinary in attire as the commonest of men. His face was grooved with deep lines, and his eyes seemed to be filled with a deep sadness. I never met the President . . . but now I would give my heart to hear him speak . . .

BOYS:
"My Captain does not answer, his lips are pale and
    still;
My father does not feel my arm, he has no pulse or
    will;

GIRLS:

"The ship is anchored safe and sound, its voyage
closed and done,
From fearful trip the victory ship comes in with object
won.

ALL:

"Exult, O shores, and ring, O bells!
But I with mournful tread,
Walk the deck my Captain lies
Fallen cold and dead."

WALT WHITMAN: The country mourned him as no man
was ever mourned before. From one end of America to
the other men stood, hat in hand, eyes moist, to pay
their respects. Because they knew he was one of
them. "Of the people, by the people, for the people,"
he said at Gettysburg. And everyone knew he meant
it. He wasn't one to speak words he didn't mean. "Of
the people, by the people, for the people . . ."

ALL:

"Underneath all, individuals,
I swear nothing is good to me now that ignores indi-
viduals,
The American compact is altogether with individu-
als. . . .
Sail, sail thy best, ship of Democracy!"

WALT WHITMAN: I lived in an agony of sounds those days
following Lincoln's death. To one whose ears are tuned
to hear grass grow and trees coming out in leaf, the
sound of a country weeping is almost more than a
human heart can bear. I walked with the sound of
tears like drum beats. I sat holding a sprig of lilac,
listening to a long continuous moan of grief like ele-
mental wind. America weeping.

GIRLS:

"Over the breast of the spring, the land, amid cities,
Amid lanes and through old woods, where lately the

violets peep'd from the ground, spotting the gray
debris,
Amid the grass in the fields each side of the lanes,
passing the endless grass,
Carrying a corpse to where it shall rest in the grave,
Night and day journeys a coffin."

WALT WHITMAN: And yet, through the depth of grief, I
could hear another sound emerging—like a sprig of
fragrant lilac bursting into bloom from varnished winter buds . . . like a young breeze testing the spring
sun. Slow at first, then gathering momentum. Lilacs
waiting through the cold of winter, waiting to open
their heart-shaped leaves! Lincoln living beyond his
mortal span into eternity! The momentum of now and
tomorrow. . . . For the first time since reading the
awful news of his death, I felt hope renewed within
me.

ALL:
"All the past we leave behind;
We debouch upon a newer, mightier world, varied
world. . . ."

WALT WHITMAN: Finally, I could lay my brooding aside
and look at my sprig of lilac with clear eyes. More than
the lilac is renewed from spring to spring! I could hear
America singing of the common man . . .

ALL:
"For we support all, fuse all,
After the rest is done and gone, we remain;
There is no final reliance but upon us;
Democracy rests finally upon us. . . .
And our visions sweep through eternity."

THE END

Young Abe Lincoln

NARRATOR: The time was Independence Day
in 1821,
the place, down Indianny-way,
the speaker almost done . . .

SPEAKER: "America! God bless her name,
is always well content
for any lad to rise to fame
and serve as President."

NARRATOR: A 12-year-old with shaggy hair
and arms and legs too long
stood heeding every word with care.
The speaker's voice was strong:

SPEAKER: The Gentry boys, Tom Lincoln's son,
might answer such a call.

NARRATOR: A hoot went up from everyone,
Abe Lincoln most of all.

Valentine's Day
(February 14)

Cupid in Earmuffs

Characters

CUPID
CUPID'S HELPERS, *6 boys and girls*
BOB ⎤
EDDIE ⎟
JANET ⎟
SUE ⎬ *schoolchildren*
MARGIE ⎟
LINDA ⎟
PAM ⎟
KATE ⎦

TIME: *Afternoon of Valentine's Day.*
SETTING: *A street near school. Cutout of tree is at one side of stage; bench at other side.*
AT RISE: TWO HELPERS *enter from opposite sides. They wear huge red paper hearts and carry spray-top bottles.*

57

Two Helpers (*Marching in step and chanting*): Hearts
. . . hearts . . . today is the heyday of hearts . . . hearts
. . . the gay day of hooray-day of hearts . . . hearts . . .
the jolly array-day of hearts . . . hearts . . . the grand
giveaway-day of hearts . . . hearts. (*They stop.*)

1st Helper (*Looking around*): Where's Cupid? Hasn't
he come back yet?

2nd Helper: I don't think so. I just got here myself.

1st Helper: And the others?

2nd Helper: I haven't seen them since this morning.
(*He tries to squirt his empty bottle.*) I ran out of the
love and friendship lotion.

1st Helper: So did I. Cupid didn't bring as much as
usual this time, because he caught cold down here on
earth last Valentine's Day, and he wasn't feeling too
friendly or loving.

2nd Helper: So that's why we ran out!

1st Helper: This year Psyche made Cupid wear red
wool underwear and an overcoat.

2nd Helper: With all that extra weight, I suppose he
had to cut down on his load of heart balm and lotion.
It's a long flight from Mt. Olympus to earth.

1st Helper: He didn't carry as many arrows in his
quiver as usual, either. And not enough splints for
heartbreak. (3rd *and* 4th Helpers *march in, chanting* "Hearts . . . hearts," *as before. Others join in,
marching around stage, then they stop.*)

3rd Helper: Where's Cupid?

1st Helper: Still splicing broken heart strings. Or
shooting love-tipped arrows, I guess.

4th Helper: It's been a busy day for us all. (*Tries to
squirt bottle*) I could have done with a bit more lotion.

3rd Helper: I just hope we didn't miss anybody. I used
most of mine spraying against hard-heartedness.
(*Looks around*) Cupid had better hurry up or he'll

58

miss the fun when school lets out. He always likes to listen to the children reading their Valentines.

1ST HELPER: It's lots of fun—one of the advantages of being invisible. (5TH *and* 6TH HELPERS *march in, chanting "Hearts . . . hearts."*)

5TH HELPER (*Looking around*): Everyone seems to be here now except Cupid.

6TH HELPER: I'll bet his overcoat slowed him down.

3RD HELPER (*Laughing*): I blame everything on those earmuffs. Did you ever see any like them?

4TH HELPER: Psyche put her heart into those earmuffs, all right! Red velvet hearts, one for each ear.

1ST HELPER (*Looking off*): Sh-h-h! Here comes Cupid! His quiver looks empty. So does his first-aid kit. (CUPID *enters, an amusing figure in oversized overcoat, heart-shaped earmuffs and red long underwear. He and* HELPERS *march around and chant again.*)

CUPID: Company halt, one, two. (HELPERS *halt.*) Front face. At ease. (HELPERS *turn to face* CUPID.) Well, I see you're all in good form this afternoon. Your hearts must still be in the right place.

HELPERS (*Quickly straightening their big paper hearts; together*): Yes, Cupid.

CUPID: Whew! I'm hot! I had to lug around this overcoat all day. (*Flaps it to cool himself*) And these earmuffs! Why did I ever promise Psyche I'd keep all bundled up like this? (*Lifts earmuffs partly off ears*) Well, how did you get along today? Did you put your hearts into your work?

1ST HELPER: I ran out of lotion.

2ND HELPER: So did I!

3RD HELPER: I needed more love potion . . .

4TH HELPER: And I'm worried that without it, there may be trouble.

CUPID (*Sighing*): I ran out of arrows (*Opens out empty*

pockets), and my supply of splices and splints is gone. All because Psyche insisted I weigh myself down with overcoats and red underwear. My normal supply would make me too heavy for the flight. (*Sound of children laughing and talking is heard offstage.*) Listen! School must be out. Let's move out of the way. We may be invisible, but we don't want to get stepped on. (CUPID *and* HELPERS *go to one side as* BOB, EDDIE, JANET *and* SUE *enter, holding Valentines and chatting happily.*)

BOB: I got ten Valentines this year!

EDDIE (*Reading one of his Valentines*):
Let's use the same umbrella,
Let's say the same lines.
Let's twine our hearts together—
Let's be Valentines!

JANET (*Holding up card*): Isn't this one cute: Look, a butterfly. It says, "I'm all a-flutter when I think of you."

SUE (*Reading a Valentine*):
A lot of peas are in a pod,
A lot of inches in a rod,
A lot of stars come out to shine,
But you're my *only* Valentine.
(BOB, EDDIE, JANET *and* SUE *exit.*)

CUPID: Looks as if we did a pretty good job, after all. (*Sound of crying is heard offstage.*) No, wait. (MARGIE *and* LINDA *enter.* MARGIE *is wiping her eyes.*)

LINDA: You shouldn't be crying on Valentine's Day, Margie.

MARGIE: But it's the first year I didn't get a Valentine from Pam. She won't even look at me. And I can't remember what we quarreled about. This is the worst Valentine's Day I've ever had!

HELPERS (*Ad lib*): We must have missed Pamela. Poor Margie! Poor Pamela! (*Etc.*)

60

MARGIE: Linda, you go with the others. Don't worry about me. I can't go home with my eyes all red.

LINDA (*Exiting*): All right, Margie. I'm sorry about what happened. Goodbye. (LINDA *exits. As* MARGIE *leans against tree,* PAM *and* KATE *enter.* PAM *is crying.*)

PAM: I . . . I wouldn't give her the satisfaction of looking at her, and now I feel awful! On Valentine's Day!

KATE: What happened between you and Margie, anyway?

PAM: I can't even remember. But it will take a miracle to patch it up now.

CUPID (*Shaking empty bottle*): Not a single drop of heart softener left!

PAM: It's the first year we didn't exchange hearts. Look, Kate, you go on home. I'll wait here until I calm down. (*Sits on bench*)

KATE: I'm sorry, Pam. Goodbye. (*She exits.*)

CUPID: This overcoat is such a bother! I could have carried a lot more heart balm if it hadn't been for the overcoat, and the wool underwear, and the earmuffs. (*Suddenly smiling*) I know! The earmuffs! (*Takes them off and looks at them*) They're perfect. Absolutely perfect! Thank heaven I'm invisible. (HELPERS *look baffled, as* CUPID *breaks wire that holds earmuff hearts together. He attaches a heart to* MARGIE's *coat, the other to* PAM's *coat, then returns to* HELPERS.) Quick! Help me unravel some of my wool underwear. (*Leaning down,* HELPERS *pull out yards of yarn from underwear.*) Psyche, maybe you weren't so wrong, after all! (*He ties one end of yarn to* MARGIE's *sleeve, other end to* PAM's *sleeve, and holds onto middle.*)

MARGIE (*Suddenly seeing heart*): Why . . . how did that get there? A beautiful red velvet heart!

PAM (*Seeing heart on her coat*): What's this? Where did it come from? I never saw such a beautiful heart before!

CUPID (*Aside*): I guess you didn't! (*He pulls on yarn, drawing the two girls together toward center stage. They stare at each other's hearts.*)

MARGIE (*Pointing*): Oh! It's just like mine. As if it came from the same place.

PAM: As if they belonged together.

MARGIE: Maybe they do. Pam, look! There's the same funny piece of wire at the top. They *do* belong together.

PAM: It almost makes you believe in Cupid, doesn't it? Oh, Margie . . . (CUPID *joyfully breaks yarn, and girls walk off arm in arm.*)

CUPID: Wait till I tell Psyche. I was just *looking* for a good excuse to get rid of those earmuffs! (*He marches around with* HELPERS, *as they chant.*) Hearts . . . hearts . . . today is the heyday of hearts . . . hearts . . . the gay day hooray-day of hearts . . . hearts . . . the jolly array-day of hearts . . . hearts . . . the grand giveaway day of hearts . . . hearts. (*Curtain*)

THE END

PRODUCTION NOTES
CUPID IN EARMUFFS

Characters: 6 female; 2 male; 1 male or female for Cupid; 6 male and female for Cupid's Helpers.

Playing Time: 15 minutes.

Costumes: Cupid wears oversized overcoat, red long underwear, and heart-shaped red earmuffs. Helpers wear huge red paper hearts. School children wear modern, everyday dress.

Properties: Six spraytop bottles; several valentines.

Setting: A street near school. Cutout of tree is at one side of stage; bench at other side.

Lighting and Sound: No special effects.

Valentines

FOUR BOYS AND GIRLS *enter, holding large Valentines, which they display when they speak their lines.*

1ST: Valentines plain
and Valentines fancy,
2ND: Gentle and quiet,
skippy and dancy.
3RD: Valentines comic,
turned on a pun,
4TH: Valentines given,
Valentines won . . .
ALL: Oh, aren't Valentines fun!
1ST: Valentines frank,
and sweetly appealing,
2ND: Valentines bright
with color and feeling,
3RD: Gaudy and lacy,
full of advice,
4TH: Pledges, endearments,
sugar and spice . . .
ALL: Oh, aren't Valentines nice!
1ST: Valentines signed
or leaving one guessing,
2ND: Full of devotion
friends are expressing,
3RD: Cupids with arrows
shooting our way,
4TH: Winning our hearts
on Valentine's Day.
ALL: Oh, aren't Valentines gay!

Valentine Fun

I thought I'd buy some gay designs
for all my friends for Valentines.

So off I hurried to the shops
to see what styles were Valentops.

How red the hearts! How gay the rhymes
in keeping with the Valentimes!

But oh, the prices . . . I could see
that I was up a Valentree.

"I wish that I could turn a trick,"
I said. "What makes a Valentick?

"The size? The colors front and back?
I'll try a *different* Valentack!"

So home I rushed with eager haste
to illustrate my Valentaste:

I mixed some dough and rolled it thin
and baked it in a Valentin,

But cut it first in shapely hearts . . .
for scads and scads of Valentarts!

I frosted them with "I Love You,"
which certainly is Valentrue.

And all my friends exclaimed, "How *sweet*
to think of such a Valentreat."

February Spelldown

TEN BOYS AND GIRLS, *wearing red and white, enter one by one and stand in line, showing large cardboard letters when they speak.*

> 1ST: V for verses quite extreme
> on a very tender theme.
> 2ND: A for all those artful arrows
> aimed at hearts instead of sparrows.
> 3RD: L for language full of love
> coo-y as a turtledove.
> 4TH: E for envelopes enclosing
> eager pledges, most imposing.
> 5TH: N for news that love is true
> signed by someone named Guess
> Who.
> 6TH: T for ten or twelve or twenty
> touching thoughts with vows aplenty.
> 7TH: I for inquiry intense:
> "Must you keep me in suspense?"
> 8TH: N for new and novel notions
> voicing whimsical emotions.
> 9TH: E for each and every one
> entering gaily in the fun.
> 10TH: S for symbols and for signs
> that, of course, spell . . .
> ALL: V A L E N T I N E S!

Washington's Birthday
(February 22)

A Dish of Green Peas

Characters

MATTIE
MISS FRAUNCES
ORDERLY
VAN STARN
THOMAS HICKEY

SCENE 1

TIME: *Mid-June, 1776.*

SETTING: *The kitchen of a large house on an estate near New York City, where General Washington has his headquarters.*

AT RISE: MATTIE *and* MISS FRAUNCES *are working in the kitchen, keeping busy at various tasks.*

MATTIE: Men have the only real chance to help their country, Miss Fraunces. Me, now. I'm dead set against the British—the way they think they can pull us around by the nose. But what can a girl do. Or a woman, either?

MISS FRAUNCES: It never was a woman's part to be obvious about her doings, Mattie.

MATTIE: It seems to me she never has a chance to *do* any doin's.

MISS FRAUNCES: I'd say you've done more than most right now, Mattie. There isn't another girl in America with your chance to make things comfortable for General Washington. As long as he's here at Mortier House we can feel we're doing our part.

MATTIE (*Sniffing*): Scrubbin' and cleanin' and cookin' and washin' dishes! Oh, I'm not complaining of the work, mind you. Only it's so piddling small, Miss Fraunces.

MISS FRAUNCES: I don't think it piddling that General Washington wanted me for his housekeeper.

MATTIE: After all the trainin' you got at your father's tavern, he's lucky to have you. Fraunces Tavern in New York City is famous. But, Miss Fraunces, if I was a man now . . . I could be learnin' how to take aim at a Redcoat.

MISS FRAUNCES: There may be more than one way to do that.

MATTIE: Not cleanin' and cookin'!

MISS FRAUNCES: I'm not so sure, Mattie. You know how strong the Tories are. Why, I've heard that a third of the colonists are loyal to England and King George. And New York is the very worst. We women may have a better chance than men to smell out the enemy.

MATTIE: How? Peelin' potatoes and shuckin' peas?

MISS FRAUNCES: We must keep our eyes and ears open and our courage up. (*There is a knock at inner door.*) Come in!

ORDERLY (*At door*): Oh, Miss Fraunces. General Washington asked me to tell you how much he enjoyed the green peas at dinner last night.

MISS FRAUNCES: I'm so glad. They are just in season now.

ORDERLY: Speaking on my own, I believe the General would enjoy them again. They are one of his favorite dishes.

MISS FRAUNCES: Of course, he shall have them again. As a matter of fact, I've already told Mr. Van Starn to bring us more as soon as he picks them.

ORDERLY: The General is grateful for all the things you do to make him comfortable.

MISS FRAUNCES: Thank you. I only wish we could do more.

MATTIE: But we don't get much chance.

ORDERLY: Oh, I'd say you do very well. (*He exits right. VAN STARN stands at open door left, knocks on door frame.*)

VAN STARN: Morning, Miss Fraunces. I've brought the turnips and potatoes you wanted, and some more peas.

MISS FRAUNCES: That's fine, Mr. Van Starn. Put the turnips and potatoes in the root cellar, will you, please? And bring the peas into the kitchen.

VAN STARN: Yes'm. (*Exits*)

MISS FRAUNCES: Now, Mattie, think what a service you can do for your country when you shell more peas for the General!

MATTIE: Fightin' the British with both hands!

MISS FRAUNCES: Cheer up, perhaps you will see that nice young man in the General's Guard again tonight.

MATTIE: Mr. Hickey? (*Bursts out*) Now, that's what I mean, Miss Fraunces. Here's Mr. Hickey, one of General Washington's bodyguard. Think of what *he's* doin' for the war, for the cause of freedom, compared to shellin' peas.

MISS FRAUNCES: It's a responsible job to be a bodyguard, all right. And a great honor.

MATTIE: Mr. Hickey's proud of it. Though he hasn't come right out and said so.

MISS FRAUNCES: He's very handsome, isn't he? (VAN STARN *re-enters with big basket of peas.*)

VAN STARN: Here are the peas, Miss Fraunces. (*Hesitates*) There's . . . a little matter I'd like to take up with you. Mind, I'm not blaming you . . . but it's hard on a poor farmer, money not being worth much at best . . .

MISS FRAUNCES: What is it, Mr. Van Starn? Haven't I been paying you enough?

VAN STARN: Enough, yes. Except that . . .

MISS FRAUNCES: What?

VAN STARN: I went to buy a new bridle, and what did the saddler tell me? Half the bills you gave me are counterfeit.

MISS FRAUNCES (*Shocked*): Counterfeit! How could that be?

VAN STARN: They tell me it's a trick of the British, making counterfeit bills and flooding them around, so the people will lose faith in our paper money. All I know is I didn't get my bridle.

MISS FRAUNCES: How dreadful. I'll make it up to you, of course, when I pay you the end of the week.

VAN STARN: Thank you, ma'am. They tell me you never know where these counterfeiters are with their packets of bills to circulate.

MATTIE (*Aside*): Packets of bills!

MISS FRAUNCES: As if we haven't enough troubles trying to finance the war.

VAN STARN: That's just it. (*Turns to go*)

MISS FRAUNCES: Oh, by the way, Mr. Van Starn . . . any time you have more peas, I'd like to buy them. General Washington is very fond of peas.

VAN STARN: Should be more in a day or two. I'll bring them. Good day to you. (*Exits*)

MATTIE (*Aside*): Packets of bills. No, it can't be. Not him!

MISS FRAUNCES: What are you mumbling about, Mattie?

MATTIE: They don't get a very big salary, do they?

MISS FRAUNCES: Who?

MATTIE: The soldiers. I mean, I'm specially thinkin' of the bodyguard.

MISS FRAUNCES: Oh, Mr. Hickey?

MATTIE: What's their pay, Miss Fraunces?

MISS FRAUNCES: I really don't know, Mattie. But it isn't high . . or regular, either.

MATTIE: Then he wouldn't be likely to have packets of bills, would he?

MISS FRAUNCES: What are you trying to get at, Mattie?

MATTIE: You said we had to keep our eyes open, remember?

MISS FRAUNCES: Go on.

MATTIE: It was when I was cleanin' the guards' room— the one Mr. Hickey and Mr. Green share. The upper drawer of the highboy was a little open, and I couldn't help seein', Miss Fraunces. . .

MISS FRAUNCES: Seeing what?

MATTIE: Packets of bills. They wouldn't be earning that much, would they?

MISS FRAUNCES: Hardly. Mattie! Maybe we've no right to be suspicious of a likely-looking young man. But this is war. We have to find out, in a quiet way, if Mr. Hickey is the patriot he poses as. The men are gone now . . . slip up and get one of the bills from the packet. You can put it back later. No one need ever know.

MATTIE (*Upset*): I can't believe he'd do a thing like that.

MISS FRAUNCES: Neither can I, but we must be sure. Run along, Mattie. (MATTIE *hurries out. There is a knock at the inner door.*) Come in!

ORDERLY (*At door*): I forgot to tell you, Miss Fraunces,

the General will be having five guests for dinner to-night.

MISS FRAUNCES: I will see to it that the places are set.

ORDERLY (*Seeing the peas*): More peas! You did that in a hurry.

MISS FRAUNCES: We have to thank Van Starn for the peas. Our only contribution is the shelling. Oh, that reminds me, sir. Van Starn says I gave him several counterfeit bills when I paid him last week. Do you know anything about counterfeit bills?

ORDERLY: Too much, unfortunately. The British figure if they can flood the market with counterfeit bills, our money won't be worth the paper it's printed on.

MISS FRAUNCES: Can you tell a counterfeit bill when you see one?

ORDERLY: I think so. I've examined them for the General.

MISS FRAUNCES: I've just sent Mattie for . . . a bill. Perhaps you can tell me . . . (MATTIE *enters, holding bill.*) Here she is now. Show the orderly the bill, Mattie.

ORDERLY (*Taking bill, holding it to light*): It does seem like a counterfeit.

MISS FRAUNCES: Good gracious! Next time I'm going to ask you to be present when I pay the weekly accounts. We must get to work now. Guests for dinner tonight . . . and fresh green peas. Mattie can't *wait* to shell those peas.

ORDERLY (*Exiting*): Mattie is a first-class patriot! (*Exits*)

MISS FRAUNCES (*Turning over bill*): I'm afraid that's more than can be said for your Mr. Hickey, Mattie. He's not a man to be trusted.

MATTIE (*Angrily*): Just wait till I see him!

MISS FRAUNCES: Now, Mattie, control yourself. We

must report Mr. Hickey immediately. (*Pause*) No, maybe not. Maybe we should try to find out what he is up to first. This may be your chance to do more than keep house for the General!

MATTIE (*Excitedly*): But how? What can I do?

MISS FRAUNCES: You and Mr. Hickey are on friendly terms. Perhaps if you lead him to think you are a Tory at heart, he will confide in you. Think hard, Mattie. Have you spoken out about our fight for liberty?

MATTIE: Nothing beyond mentioning I wished *I* could be holdin' an important post like bein' one of the General's Guard, and that I'd like to skin all the Redcoats alive.

MISS FRAUNCES: Mercy! Mr. Hickey would never confide in you. If he's plotting anything, he'd never breathe a word of it into *your* ear. (*Thinking*) We'll have to do it some other way. Have you ever mentioned *me* to Mr. Hickey, Mattie?

MATTIE (*Thinking hard*): No, I don't believe I have. No, I'm sure I haven't.

MISS FRAUNCES: Good. Then you must plant the idea this very night that you think I am with the British at heart . . . that I am opposed to the fight for freedom. You must say you are afraid that if I get hold of any information here at Mortier House, I'll pass it along to the British. But ask Mr. Hickey to keep your suspicions a secret until you get some real proof.

MATTIE: I'll plant more seeds than in a garden, Miss Fraunces, but how will it help the cause?

MISS FRAUNCES: If Mr. Hickey thinks I am loyal to the King, he will undoubtedly approach me. Then, by playing my cards carefully, I can find out what he has in mind . . . what sort of bodyguard he really is for our great General.

MATTIE (*Excitedly*): Oh, Miss Fraunces. And here I

thought there wasn't any way we could serve except sweepin' and shuckin' peas! (*Curtain*)

* * *

SCENE 2

TIME: *Several days later.*

SETTING: *Same as Scene 1.*

AT RISE: MISS FRAUNCES *and* MATTIE *are preparing dinner.*

MISS FRAUNCES: To think what a packet of counterfeit bills can lead to, Mattie!

MATTIE: And us in the thick of it. I never was so on edge in my life, Miss Fraunces. (*Beating bowl of batter*) It's a comfort to be beatin' something.

MISS FRAUNCES: You played your part well, planting those seeds about me. Mr. Hickey has been cultivating me for all he is worth.

MATTIE: You should have heard how I dropped them in his ear, innocent as a day-old lamb, you might say. (*Laughs*) And him takin' you for a Tory and tellin' you the whole plot and all!

MISS FRAUNCES (*Worriedly*): If only I'd hear from the General that he got my warning letter.

MATTIE: I've been like a cat on hot bricks for the past few hours.

MISS FRAUNCES: Why doesn't he answer? What if the Orderly forgot to deliver my letter?

MATTIE: Maybe you should have tried to see General Washington yourself.

MISS FRAUNCES: But how could I? With Mr. Hickey as the bodyguard? And goodness knows how many other spies are around. No, I couldn't take that chance. I had to write him instead.

MATTIE: You did it real clever-like. "A surprise for General Washington," you said.

MISS FRAUNCES: I couldn't come right out and say it was a matter of life and death, Mattie. What if the Orderly is a Tory, too? One can never be sure these days. (*Looks around nervously*) The very walls have ears.

MATTIE: "Something to do with a dinner party," you said. Oh, and what a dinner party! With that dish of green peas in front of the General! "A surprise for the staff, too," you said. No, there couldn't be anything suspicious about that.

MISS FRAUNCES (*Nervously*): But if General Washington got my warning, why doesn't he send word? How can we serve the peas to him if we aren't sure, Mattie?

MATTIE: How can we get out of it, either, without makin' Mr. Hickey suspicious? We *are* in a fix, Miss Fraunces. But remember what you told me. We women have to keep our hearts strong and our courage up.

MISS FRAUNCES: That was easy to say . . . before we were mixed up in this dreadful plot. The whole war depends on what happens tonight.

MATTIE (*Excitedly*): And we're in the thick of it, Miss Fraunces! When's Mr. Hickey plannin' to bring the poison?

MISS FRAUNCES: Any time now. I'll have to send you out when he comes.

MATTIE: And it's a good thing, or I'd be scratchin' his eyes out. (*Looks out window*) There he comes now, the traitor.

MISS FRAUNCES: Let's be talking commonplaces, in case he comes in without knocking. How did the pound cake turn out?

MATTIE: It fell again in the middle, like a sway-backed horse. It's the oven. I hope to live to see the day we make a perfect pound cake . . .

HICKEY (*At door*): So do I! Good evening, ladies. (*To* MATTIE) And how is the little Rose of Sharon today?

MATTIE: I'd thank you to be less flowery, sir.

HICKEY: Aren't you the quick one, though? But I like you the better for your spice. Come on, Mattie—how about a glass of nice, cool milk to take the edge off my thirst?

MATTIE: And where would I be gettin' a glass of cool milk in a hot kitchen on a June day?

MISS FRAUNCES: Run down to the milk-house and get some, Mattie. We'll need it for dinner, anyway. Take the large pitcher.

HICKEY: And don't run too fast, my little maid, on a June day! (MATTIE *takes pitcher and goes out, giving* HICKEY *a pert look.*) We have to hurry! (*Goes to inner door, closes it, locks it*) I brought the poison. Are the peas ready? Where are they?

MISS FRAUNCES (*Hesitating*): The General is having guests for dinner again tonight. Wouldn't it be better tomorrow?

HICKEY: We can't wait. You aren't backing out on me, are you, Miss Fraunces?

MISS FRAUNCES (*Firmly*): Of course not. What a question!

HICKEY: We can't wait because everything's all set. There was a meeting at the tavern again last night. Three hours from now our men will start blowing up the rebel ammunition dumps. The General must be out of the way before that happens. With their ammunition gone and their General gone, the rebel ranks will fall apart like a stack of jackstraws. We'll take over New York City in no time. Hand me the peas . . . (MISS FRAUNCES *fills dish from kettle and brings it to* HICKEY.) That was a stroke of genius, thinking of green peas. (*Stirs in poison*)

75

MISS FRAUNCES: The General's favorite dish. He can't get enough of them.

HICKEY (*With a sneer*): Here's one time he'll get enough . . . and to spare. Where can I set this dish to keep it from getting mixed up with the others?

MISS FRAUNCES: Here on the chimney-shelf above the oven, to keep warm.

HICKEY: We can't take a chance on a rattle-brained girl like Mattie. You must serve the peas to the General yourself. Understand?

MISS FRAUNCES: That I will, with my own hands.

HICKEY: You will be paid well for your part in this, Miss Fraunces.

MISS FRAUNCES (*Trying to be lighthearted*): In counterfeit bills, Mr. Hickey?

HICKEY: No sir-ee. In good British gold. (*Glancing out window*) Here she comes with the milk. (*Changes tone*) . . . that's what I say, too. There's a flavor to pork you don't get in lamb. And as for fowl, give me a piece of roast beef any day. (MATTIE *enters with pitcher.*)

MATTIE (*Filling glass*): Here's to your health, Mr. Hickey. May it flourish like a garden. (*Gives him glass*)

HICKEY: Mattie, you have a poetic tongue. (*Drinks*) Well, I must spruce up a bit before dinner. The General always expects his men to put their best foot forward.

MATTIE: Mind you don't trip on yours, Mr. Hickey (HICKEY, *chuckling, exits.* MATTIE *watches until it is safe to talk.* MISS FRAUNCES *unlocks inner door.*) Did he do it?

MISS FRAUNCES (*Pointing*): There are the peas, all poisoned. Oh, Mattie, how can I set them before the General not knowing . . . not being sure he won't eat them? It's getting so close to dinner time, if we don't hear soon . . .

MATTIE: I'm nervous as a hen, I am. (*Knock on inner door*)

MISS FRANCES: Yes? (*Opens door and* ORDERLY *enters*)

ORDERLY: The General was interested in your surprise, Miss Fraunces. (*Holds out note*) He asked me to give you this reply. When is the party to come off, may I ask?

MISS FRAUNCES (*Taking note without a show of emotion*): You'll know soon enough. If I told you, it wouldn't be a surprise. (*She casually puts note in apron pocket.*)

ORDERLY: Always glad to oblige when there's a surprise in the offing. (*Exits*)

MATTIE: Hurry, Miss Fraunces. Read it! Read it! (*She looks to see that the coast is clear.*) I'll keep watch.

MISS FRANCES (*Opening letter nervously*): Thank God he got my warning. (*Begins to read*) "My dear Miss Fraunces: I am, I must confess, greatly disturbed by your letter. That such treachery should be afoot in my own bodyguard stuns me. I am thankful for your quick thinking and acting that will soon bring this matter to a head."

MATTIE: Thomas Hickey's head! Hangin' by a rope!

MISS FRAUNCES (*Reading*): "You must by all means go through with the plot. Only in that way will we have the necessary evidence. Let the dish of green peas be served to me at dinner. I shall not eat them. As soon as the dishes are cleared from the table, have your maid throw most of the peas out to the chickens . . ."

MATTIE (*Excitedly*): That's me! That's me havin' a hand in it.

MISS FRAUNCES (*Reading*): "Let the balance be kept for evidence. I shall watch from the window and call for an explanation when the chickens die from the poison. You must then, with feigned reluctance, confess that the peas were poisoned, and in your confession implicate Mr. Hickey. And here I must ask your great indulgence, for occasionally great service to one's country must be attended with temporary disgrace."

MATTIE: Temporary disgrace, Miss Fraunces? Does he mean *you?*

MISS FRAUNCES (*Reading*): "You, as well as the traitor, will be thrown in prison . . ."

MATTIE: Prison! Why, that's almost as good as carryin' a gun!

MISS FRAUNCES (*Reading*): "Of course, your imprisonment will be short, for you will be jailed merely as a blind while other members of the plot are rounded up. I have often thought how those who serve in quiet ways are sometimes more our heroes than those for whom the drums roll and the bells toll. Believe me, my dear Miss Fraunces. Your grateful friend, George Washington."

MATTIE: Grateful friend . . . (*Sighs ecstatically*)

MISS FRAUNCES: Oh, I'm so relieved, Mattie. And so humble . . . to think we had the privilege of saving the General. Doing what soldiers in the field couldn't do.

MATTIE: And me thinkin' 'twas only men had a chance to serve their country. How right you were, Miss Fraunces. Women don't have to fight to be in the thick of things. They can stay right at home . . . and shell peas!

THE END

Historical Note: Thomas Hickey was the first Revolutionary soldier to be hanged for treachery to the cause.

PRODUCTION NOTES
A Dish of Green Peas

Characters: 3 male; 2 female.

Playing Time: 25 minutes.

Costumes: The Orderly and Hickey wear uniforms. Van Starn wears farmer's clothing. Mattie and Miss Fraunces wear plain long-skirted dresses, aprons, and caps.

Properties: Scene 1: Various pieces of kitchen equipment, including bowls, spoons, etc.; basket of peas; bill. Scene 2: Pitcher; dish of peas; bottle of green liquid; glass; letter.

Setting: A colonial kitchen. The room is furnished with a table, chairs, cabinets and cooking equipment. At one side is a large fireplace. A kettle hangs in the fireplace. In Scene 2, the kettle holds cooked peas.

Lighting: No special effects.

George Washington

His choice was not
to fight a war.
Mount Vernon held
his interest more.

His choice was not
to spend eight years
with troops and guns
and trials and tears.

His choice was not,
when worn and spent,
to serve two terms
as President.

Yet when he heard
his country's voice,
her *need* each time
became his choice.

79

Washington Marches On

Characters

CHORUS, *8 or more boys and girls*
AUGUSTINE WASHINGTON, *Virginia planter*
GEORGE WASHINGTON, *as a teen-ager*
BETTY WASHINGTON, *13*
SAMUEL WASHINGTON, *12*
MRS. MARY BALL WASHINGTON, *their mother*
LORD FAIRFAX
LAWRENCE WASHINGTON
ANNE FAIRFAX WASHINGTON
GEORGE WASHINGTON, *in his twenties*
GENERAL BRADDOCK
THREE SOLDIERS
JOHN ADAMS
GEORGE WASHINGTON, *as a mature man*
TWO SENTRIES
MESSENGER
MARTHA WASHINGTON
ORDERLY
MARQUIS DE LAFAYETTE
TWO NEWSBOYS
NELLY CUSTIS, *15*
CHANCELLOR LIVINGSTON
VOICES FROM AUDIENCE, *extras*
SCHOOLMASTER
BOYS AND GIRLS, *extras*

SETTING: *Two chairs and a table, holding paper, ink, and quill pen, are at center. Stage is bare.*

AT RISE: *Lights come up full on* CHORUS, *seated at rear on risers.*

CHORUS: When was he born, George Washington?
What was the place and date?

SOLO (*Holding up card or writing on blackboard: Born— 1732*):
Seventeen hundred thirty-two.
Virginia, the State.

(*Stage lights dim. Spotlight comes up center on a seated* AUGUSTINE WASHINGTON. *He appears greatly excited. He begins to write.*)

AUGUSTINE (*Reading with animation as he writes*):

Wakefield on the Potomac
February 22, 1732

Lawrence and Augustine
   Washington
Appleby School. England

My Dear Sons: It is with great pleasure that I inform you that you now have a half-brother, born this very day. The baby and his mother are doing well. We have decided, after some discussion, to name him George. Unfortunately it may be some years before you will be able to make his acquaintance.

I trust you are doing well in your studies and working diligently. I trust also that you are enjoying this acquaintance with our mother country. Enclosed you will find a draft of money for your use, over and above expenses, in celebration of the happy event that has taken place today. Your affectionate father, Augustine Washington. (*He nods with satisfaction, seals letter, rises, and hurries offstage. Spotlight fades out. Stage lights come up on* CHORUS.)

BOYS: Washington marches on!

CHORUS: How did he grow, George Washington?

SOLO: Strong as a sturdy tree.

CHORUS: Did he have hopes and youthful dreams?

SOLO (*Holding up card or writing on blackboard: 1746— To Sea?*): He wanted to go to sea! (*Stage lights dim. Spotlight comes up down left on* GEORGE WASHING-TON, *as a teenager, with* BETTY *and* SAMUEL. BETTY *is holding a packet of letters.*)

BETTY: Here is Uncle Joseph's letter to Mother. What will it say, I wonder, George, about your going to sea? I hope he doesn't say you should.

GEORGE: I want to go so badly, though, Betty.

BETTY: But I don't *like* to think of you going so far away. And it's so *dangerous*. That's what Mama says.

SAMUEL: George isn't afraid of danger. Are you, George?

BETTY: I wonder if Uncle Joseph knows how *anxious* we've been, waiting to hear from him? (*Takes up letter, tries to look through envelope*) It certainly takes a long time for a letter to get from London, England, to Fredericksburg, Virginia.

GEORGE: Too long. I've had my things packed for weeks. And Lawrence has the promise of a commission in the Navy for me. All I need is for Mother to say *yes*. (*Sighs*) I wish she'd listen to brother Lawrence, instead of asking Uncle Joseph.

BETTY: She thinks Lawrence is too young to give advice.

SAMUEL: He's twenty-eight. That's old!

GEORGE: And he's married to Anne Fairfax, and he's

been in the Navy fighting in the West Indies, and he's master of Mount Vernon, and . . .

BETTY: Still, Mama thinks Uncle Joseph knows best. You know how she has depended on him, ever since Father died.

GEORGE: Well, there's a good chance he'll say yes, anyway. (*Calls*) Mother! Mother! The letter has come from London. From Uncle Joseph.

MRS. WASHINGTON (*Hurrying in right, excitedly*): The letter! Did I hear you say the letter has come? At last. (*She takes it, hesitates.*) I *trust* your uncle's judgment is the same as mine. (*Opens letter*) Hmmmm. (*Reads to herself while others watch*)

BETTY: What does he *say*, Mama?

GEORGE (*Anxiously*): May I go?

MRS. WASHINGTON: Listen to this: "I understand that you have some thoughts of putting your son George to sea. I think he had better be put apprentice to a *tinker*. The common sailor has no liberties . . . they will use him like a dog." (*To* GEORGE) Do you hear, George? It is not only dangerous to go to sea, but they'd use you like a dog! So . . . it is decided. After this excellent advice from your Uncle, assuredly you must not go to sea. What else is there in the post, Betty? (*She and* BETTY *exit right, looking at mail.* GEORGE *and* SAMUEL *start out left.*)

GEORGE (*Obviously disappointed*): Want to drive stakes for me, Sammy? I suppose there's nothing to do now but practice with Father's surveying instruments. (*Brightens*) There's something like an ocean . . . an endless sea . . . about the wilderness. If I could be a surveyor in the wilderness, I wouldn't mind not going to sea . . . very much. (*They exit. Spotlight fades out.*)

GIRLS: Washington marches on!

CHORUS:
When did he help survey the lands
That rich Lord Fairfax had?

83

SOLO (*Holding up card or writing on blackboard: 1748–52—Surveyor*):
Seventeen hundred forty-eight . . .
When he was still a lad.
(*Spotlight comes up down right on* LORD FAIRFAX *and* LAWRENCE WASHINGTON. LAWRENCE *takes a paper from his pocket and holds it out.*)
LAWRENCE: What do you think of this, Lord Fairfax?
LORD FAIRFAX: What is it? (*Peers at paper, takes a small magnifying glass from pocket*) A map?
LAWRENCE: Do you recognize it?
LORD FAIRFAX (*Studying paper*): A map of the South Meadow here at Mount Vernon, is it not? Very carefully done. Neat. Accurate, as far as I can judge. Excellent workmanship. Did your younger brother, George, do it? I have seen him with his instruments, again and again.
LAWRENCE: Yes, George did it. Amazing, how serious he is about his maps. For a lad not quite sixteen . . .
LORD FAIRFAX: He has skill. Ambition. Patience. Self-discipline. I have been wondering, Lawrence, about the thousands of acres of wilderness I own west of the Blue Ridge Mountains. Settlers are moving in, taking what land they want, cutting timber, building cabins. I feel I should have my boundaries marked, to establish ownership. Do you think George would care to help?
LAWRENCE: Do I think . . . ! There he comes now, Lord Fairfax, over the hill. I am sure he can answer your question better than I. (*Calls*) George! Over here, George!
LORD FAIRFAX (*Looking at map again*): A nice piece of work. Very nice indeed. (GEORGE WASHINGTON, *as a teen-ager, enters with tripod.*)
GEORGE: Good morning, Lawrence. And Lord Fairfax, sir.

LAWRENCE: Lord Fairfax has a question to ask you, George.

GEORGE: To ask *me?*

LORD FAIRFAX: And not about foxhunting, either. Or horses. (*Clears throat*) You are interested in surveying, I notice . . .

GEORGE: Yes, sir. Very much, sir.

LORD FAIRFAX: And how far along are you?

GEORGE: I still have a great deal to learn. But I'm not *too* bad, am I, Lawrence?

LORD FAIRFAX: Would you be able to start in three weeks? On March 11, say?

GEORGE: Start what, sir?

LORD FAIRFAX: I am planning to have my wilderness lands surveyed. Would you care to be one of the party? I will pay you well.

GEORGE (*Eagerly*): Would I! Would I, sir! Oh, let me get some of my maps to show you . . . (*He runs out.* LAWRENCE *and* LORD FAIRFAX, *amused, follow. Spotlight fades out.*)

BOYS: Washington marches on!

CHORUS: When did Mount Vernon come to him—
His brother's large estate?

SOLO (*Holding up card or writing on blackboard: 1752—Gets Mt. Vernon*):
Seventeen hundred fifty-two,
Dropped from the hands of fate.
(*Spotlight comes up, down left, as* ANNE FAIRFAX WASHINGTON *and* GEORGE WASHINGTON, *now in his twenties, enter and walk into spotlighted area.*)

ANNE: I need your help, George.

GEORGE: You know I will do anything I can, Anne. But I cannot bring Lawrence back . . . or your little daughter. To think of losing them both, so close together!

ANNE: Within a few weeks of each other. That was July. Now it is November, and the ache is still in my heart.

They say that time heals all sorrows. But, oh, how slowly, George.

GEORGE: I know. I miss Lawrence too, more than I can say. He was so much more to me than a half-brother. Had he been full brother and father combined, I could not have loved him more.

ANNE: I am glad you had those months with him in the Bahamas last winter . . . though I missed him terribly at the time.

GEORGE: We were so hopeful the mild air would help him. And for a while it did, you know. But (*Giving gesture of despair*) . . . And so young, only thirty-four.

ANNE (*After a pause*): George, I want your advice—as a brother-in-law, not as one of the executors of the estate. Lawrence left you a large interest in Mount Vernon, and you have always loved the place. Don't you think you should take it over? I have no wish to be burdened with so many acres of farm land. I know nothing about farming.

GEORGE (*Figuring on back of envelope*): No place in the world means more to me than Mount Vernon. But, as Lawrence's wife, you must have a fair return. (*Figures*) How would it be if I paid you eighty thousand pounds of tobacco yearly?

ANNE: Isn't eighty thousand pounds of tobacco a great deal, George?

GEORGE: I would gladly pay it.

ANNE: You are more than fair. You are generous! And it will be such a load off my mind to know you are here, carrying on as master of Mount Vernon. You will be very busy, George . . . with all those acres, and Lawrence's wish for you to enter the militia . . . and the House of Burgesses.

GEORGE: Yes, I shall be very busy. But that is exactly what I like. And now, shall we go check the accounts?

86

(*They leave spotlight and exit. Light fades out.*)

GIRLS: Washington marches on!

CHORUS: When did he fight in The French and Indian War?

SOLO (*Holding up card or writing on blackboard: 1754–58, French & Indian War*):

Seventeen fifty-four to eight,

With hardships by the score.

(*Spotlight comes up down right.* GENERAL BRADDOCK, *brandishing his sword, enters excitedly and crosses stage to spotlighted area.*)

BRADDOCK (*Shouting as if to soldiers nearby*): Hold ranks! Hold ranks! Take the fire of the enemy like men. I command you to hold ranks. (GEORGE WASHINGTON *rushes in to catch up with* GENERAL BRADDOCK.)

WASHINGTON: General Braddock! General Braddock . . . if you will order the men to scatter, sir. . . . Let them meet the enemy under cover instead of out in the open. I know how these Indians and French fight, from behind trees . . .

BRADDOCK (*Striding out*): My men will stand in ranks, Washington, as they are bidden, without breach of discipline. (*Exits*)

WASHINGTON: But, sir . . . (*Exits after* BRADDOCK. *Spot remains on.* THREE SOLDIERS *stagger into lighted area.*)

1ST SOLDIER: Let's get out of here, anywhere. Anywhere!

2ND SOLDIER: Where did the shots come from? Did you see the enemy?

3RD SOLDIER: The shots come from all directions. No one sees the enemy.

1ST SOLDIER: We make easy targets in our red coats.

2ND SOLDIER: Did you see Braddock's aide-de-camp,

Colonel Washington? He strode among us soldiers, calm as ice, trying to get us to retreat in orderly fashion. His horse was shot out from under him.

1ST SOLDIER: Aye, and he mounted another.

2ND SOLDIER: Men were slaughtered all around him, but he wasn't even wounded.

3RD SOLDIER: I could follow a man like that! Would to heaven he were in charge here. (*They stagger out. Spot fades out.*)

BOYS: Washington marches on!

CHORUS:
When did he marry, settle down
On the land he loved so well?

SOLO (*Holding up card or writing on blackboard: 1759–75, Farmer*):
Seventeen hundred fifty-nine,
A happy date to tell.
(*At center, spotlight comes up on* MRS. WASHINGTON, *seated, sewing. Soon* BETTY, *now in her twenties, hurries in with newspapers. She greets her mother affectionately, and takes off wraps as she talks.*)

BETTY: Oh, Mama, have you seen the papers—from Fredericksburg and Alexandria? I was afraid you hadn't, so I took the ferry over . . . I couldn't wait to show you.

MRS. WASHINGTON: About George's wedding?

BETTY: Yes, look! (*Shows a paper*) A long account, and so glowing, Mama. The charming and beautiful young widow, Martha Custis, and the handsome and gallant young officer, George Washington!

MRS. WASHINGTON (*Looking at paper*): She will be a great help to George in many ways. Perhaps I should not say it out loud . . . but I can't help thinking that her fortune will not come amiss. I hear it is a large one.

BETTY (*Sitting*): And, imagine, a ready-made family for George! Jacky six, and Patsy four. I can imagine how he loves them.

MRS. WASHINGTON (*Reading*): "In the church where the wedding was solemnized there was a bright show of resplendent uniforms with their gold lace and scarlet coats. Later the bridegroom, himself clad in shining blue and silver and scarlet, rode beside the coach that bore his bride homeward . . ." (*Looks up*) George has done well, Betty. I always knew he would.

BETTY: And remember how he wanted to go to sea? And how Uncle Joseph agreed with you that he shouldn't?

MRS. WASHINGTON: Indeed I remember. How different his life would have been! Come, let us move closer to the grate. There is a January chill in the air today. (*They exit. Spot fades out.*)

GIRLS: Washington marches on!

CHORUS:
When did the Revolution start—
That placed him in command?

SOLO (*Holding up card or writing on blackboard: 1775–83, Commander-in-Chief*):
Seventeen seventy-five. In June
He took the task in hand.
(*Spotlight comes up center. JOHN ADAMS enters and takes place behind table.*)

VOICE FROM AUDIENCE: Sh! John Adams is about to speak. Sh!

ADAMS: Gentlemen of the second Continental Congress—We are agreed that we must prepare to defend ourselves against British tyranny immediately. To my mind the choice of commander of the Continental armies is easy enough. There is no soldier in America to be compared with Colonel George Washington of Virginia, either in experience or distinction. He is gallant, straightforward, earnest. (*Looks up*) Did I glimpse the Colonel leaving the room in confusion just now? Run after him, attendant. Bring him back! (*Resumes speech*) I move that Congress, meeting here in solemn assembly in Philadelphia, put the gentleman from Virginia in charge of the Colonial army! (*Cheers, shouts of approval from audience*) With his skill and experience as an officer, his independent fortune, great talents, and excellent universal character, he would unite the Colonies better than any other person in the union. (*More cheers from audience*)

VOICES FROM AUDIENCE: Washington! Colonel Washington! (WASHINGTON, *as a mature man, enters slowly.* JOHN ADAMS *steps up, escorts him to table, then sits.*)

WASHINGTON: I beg it to be remembered by every gentleman in this room, that I this day declare with the utmost sincerity I do not think myself equal to the command I am honored with. I cannot refuse a call to serve my country. As to pay, I will have none of it. I do not wish to make any profit from the war. I shall keep an accounting of my expenses, and that is all I desire. (*Cheers from audience.* JOHN ADAMS *grasps* WASHINGTON's *hand, and they exit together. Center spot fades out.*)

BOYS: Washington marches on!

CHORUS:
Month after month the army fought, and often on the run!
Month after month of toil and trial, and never a battle won.

SOLO (*Holding up card or writing on blackboard: 1776, Crosses Delaware*):
Then on a bitter Christmas night
Washington staged a famous fight.
(*Spotlight comes up down left on* TWO SENTRIES, *pacing back and forth.*)

90

1ST SENTRY: No morning ever has gone more slowly. (*Slaps arms to keep warm*) How soon do you think they will send back news?

2ND SENTRY: For the hundredth time, don't expect news till noonday, at the earliest. (*Looks at watch*) Eleven o'clock. Calm down, brother.

1ST SENTRY: If only I could have gone along.

2ND SENTRY: Someone had to stay behind to guard the camp. You and I are as good as the next. (*Stomps feet*) It's blasted cold.

1ST SENTRY: Noonday at the earliest?

2ND SENTRY: Look here. They didn't leave till after midnight. (*He shudders*) And *what* a Christmas midnight! Sleet. Bitter cold. The Delaware choked with cakes of floating ice. Do you think it a quick and easy task to transport 2400 men across the river on such a night? Even with the best planning?

1ST SENTRY: They say General Washington had it all worked out to the smallest detail.

2ND SENTRY: Naturally. Still, after the crossing, they had to march nine miles through snow and cold to Trenton. Think that can be done in a moment, do you?

1ST SENTRY: No.

2ND SENTRY: I say if they arrived at Trenton an hour after sunrise they did well. And *then.* Do you expect they could march right in and take the town? Against those well-armed German soldiers the British hired to guard it? (*Pounds hands together*) You expect too much.

1ST SENTRY: I am counting on Christmas. I am counting on those Hessians drinking too much, and celebrating too much, last night.

2ND SENTRY: Even so, taking a town is not easy. And have you reason to suppose our luck has changed? Retreat. Retreat. Retreat. That has been our record. Have we won a battle yet? Answer me that!

91

1ST SENTRY (*Grudgingly*): No. . . . But this! We are all fired with the wish to give General Washington a Christmas present. A victory—at last.

2ND SENTRY: A wish! That's all very well. But wishes don't win battles. Though heaven knows a victory is a Christmas present that would warm all our hearts. (*Bitterly*) They need warming. (*Stomps*) And not only our hearts.

1ST SENTRY: Noonday!

2ND SENTRY: Remember, a messenger would have to get back the nine miles from Trenton, and cross the river again. After the battle.

1ST SENTRY (*Stubbornly*): If the victory were a quick one . . . (*They pace back and forth in silence. In a few moments a* MESSENGER *enters spotlighted area.*)

SENTRIES (*Challenging him*): Halt! Who goes there?

MESSENGER (*Saluting*): Messenger from General Washington in Trenton.

SENTRIES (*Eagerly*): Speak up, lad. What news?

MESSENGER: We crossed the river on the barges without mishap, in spite of the sleet and bumping ice.

1ST SENTRY: Yes, yes, you crossed the river. But the battle? Do we hold Trenton?

MESSENGER: We marched the nine miles without mishap, arriving after sun-up, deploying to enter by different roads.

2ND SENTRY: Naturally, by different roads. We know the General had it all planned. But the Hessians? Did they put up a good fight?

MESSENGER: There was no place for them to run. They were dazed, drugged from too much celebrating last night. We had no losses to speak of.

SENTRIES: And the Hessians?

MESSENGER: They lost their commander and forty-one others—dead. It was all over in less than an hour. We captured thirty officers and more than a thousand men.

SENTRIES (*Throwing up their hats*): A victory! A victory! A Christmas present for General Washington! Come, let's tell the others. (*As they exit with* MESSENGER) Our first victory in the war . . . (*Spotlight fades out.*)

GIRLS: Washington marches on!

CHORUS:
Success was brief. Then more retreat
Through countryside and gorge.
What was the time that tried men's souls?

SOLO (*Holding up card or writing on blackboard: 1777–78, Valley Forge*):
The winter at Valley Forge.
(*Spotlight comes up center, as* MARTHA WASHINGTON *enters, crosses into spotlighted area and sits, knitting busily.* GEORGE WASHINGTON *enters and paces back and forth, deep in thought.*)

MARTHA: You are worried, George. (*Pause*) Are you angry with me for coming? You wrote that I would be much more comfortable at Mount Vernon.

WASHINGTON (*Going to her affectionately*): No. No. I am not angry with you, Martha. Assuredly you *would* be more comfortable at Mount Vernon. Valley Forge is not renowned for its comforts! But you have been a cheering note in a bleak landscape ever since you came, my dear. The soldiers feel it. Especially the sick and wounded you so kindly visit.

MARTHA: Oh, I'm glad.

WASHINGTON: And the ones who get the socks you knit think you are an angel from heaven! I wonder if you realize how much a pair of warm socks means in Valley Forge?

MARTHA: Yes, I do, George.

WASHINGTON (*Bursting out impatiently*): Socks . . . mittens . . . coats . . . shoes . . . uniforms . . . *why* don't we get our supplies? Bread . . . meat . . . ammunition . . . guns . . . we need everything, Martha. Everything! That's why I am worried. Congress is so disorganized and inefficient. Why, these days, we scarcely have what can be called a government.

MARTHA: I suppose the movement of the British into Philadelphia didn't help matters. You say Congress is in exile at York. It has probably lost heart. (*Hastily*) Though, of course, I understand nothing about politics.

WASHINGTON: Lost heart! Lost head, I should say. (*Paces angrily*) And to think that just twenty miles from here General Howe and his officers are having a gay winter social season in Philadelphia! His men are warm and well-fed. They live in ease and comfort. While my men starve and freeze! Yet suffering as they are, Martha (*There is a catch in his voice.*) . . . they show incomparable patience and loyalty. Ah, Thomas Paine is right . . . this is indeed a time that tries men's souls. Mine included.

MARTHA: Is there no way out?

WASHINGTON: None that I can see at the moment, unless Congress can pull itself together. How can we have an army without supplies? And the men have not been paid for months! (ORDERLY *enters, salutes.*)

ORDERLY: The Marquis de Lafayette to see you, sir.

WASHINGTON: Lafayette! Show him in immediately.

MARTHA (*Rising*): Perhaps I should leave . . .

WASHINGTON: Not until you have greeted our young friend, Martha. He, too, is a bright light on a bleak horizon. (LAFAYETTE *enters, salutes. He and* GENERAL WASHINGTON *greet each other affectionately.*) My dear Lafayette!

LAFAYETTE: General Washington!

WASHINGTON: You have met my wife once before. (*She and* LAFAYETTE *bow.*) The soldiers here call her Lady Washington.

MARTHA (*Smiling at* LAFAYETTE *as she exits*): It is my reward for darning their socks, Marquis!

LAFAYETTE: I could not wait to bring you the news, sir.

WASHINGTON: News?

LAFAYETTE (*Taking letter from inner pocket*): A secret letter, from friends in France. There is every reason to believe that France will soon declare war on England, and support our cause with money and supplies.

WASHINGTON: Can it be true! Soon, you say?

LAFAYETTE (*Showing letter*): Very soon. Indeed, I am informed that a handsome sum of money is already on the way.

WASHINGTON (*Much relieved*): What is it they say . . . that it is always darkest just before the dawn? Come, we must tell Martha. (*They exit. Spot fades out.*)

BOYS: Washington marches on!

CHORUS:
Year after year the war dragged on, the verdict still not won.
And then the battle of Yorktown came.

SOLO (*Holding up card or writing on blackboard: 1781, Yorktown*): Seventeen eighty-one.
(TWO NEWSBOYS *run across stage and into lighted area, right, waving papers.*)

1ST NEWSBOY: Extra! Extra! Cornwallis surrenders after three-week siege. Washington takes 8000 men. Victory! Victory!

2ND NEWSBOY: The most decisive battle of the war. Washington wins at Yorktown. The war is over!

NEWSBOYS (*Together*): Washington marches on! (*They exit, as spotlight fades out.*)

CHORUS:
But still a treaty to be signed
Before our land was free!

SOLO:
The General had to keep command
Till seventeen eighty-three.

CHORUS:
And then, at Christmas, home again!
Mount Vernon. Home, at last.

SOLO (*Holding up card or writing on blackboard: 1784–88, Farmer*):
Seventeen eighty-four to eight.
And, oh, the time went fast.
(*Spotlight comes up on center area, revealing WASHINGTON, seated, writing.*)

WASHINGTON (*Reading*): To the Marquis de Lafayette, many greetings. At length, my dear Marquis, I am become a private citizen on the banks of the Potomac; and under the shadow of my own vine and my own fig-tree, free from the bustle of a camp and the busy scenes of public life, I am solacing myself with those tranquil enjoyments of which a soldier can have very little conception. I have not only retired from all public employments, but I am retiring within myself . . . (*NELLY CUSTIS comes into spotlight a little tentatively.*)

NELLY: Grandfather. Grandfather, you promised to show me the new little colt . . . (*WASHINGTON smiles, puts down quill, and goes out with NELLY. Spot fades out.*)

GIRLS: Washington marches on!

CHORUS:
When was he called to serve again?
Washington, President!

SOLO (*Holding up card or writing on blackboard: 1789–97, President*):

Seventeen hundred eighty-nine.

Two terms, eight years, he spent.

(*Spotlight comes up, down left, revealing* CHANCELLOR LIVINGSTON, *carrying a Bible, and* GEORGE WASHINGTON.)

LIVINGSTON (*Holding out Bible*): Do you solemnly swear that you will faithfully execute the office of President of the United States, and will, to the best of your ability, preserve, protect, and defend the Constitution of the United States?

WASHINGTON: I do solemnly swear that I will faithfully execute the office of President of the United States, and will, to the best of my ability, preserve, protect and defend the Constitution of the United States. (*Bends to kiss Bible. Then, solemnly, with bowed head . . .*) So help me, God.

LIVINGSTON (*To audience*): Long live George Washington, President of the United States!

VOICES (*Cheering*): Long live George Washington. Long live the father of our country. Hail to the first President of the United States. (WASHINGTON *and* LIVINGSTON *exit. Spotlight fades gradually.*)

1ST VOICE FROM AUDIENCE: Did you hear? He won't accept a salary as President.

2ND VOICE: Nor did he take a salary all those years he was commander-in-chief.

3RD VOICE: Imagine, he fears he is not good enough for the post!

4TH VOICE: Who *would* be good enough if he isn't?

SEVERAL: No one. No one in our thirteen States.

5TH VOICE: Poor man, we snatch him away from Mount Vernon again. We demand much of him.

VOICES: We need him. We need him! Long live George

97

Washington, President of the United States!

BOYS: Washington marches on!

CHORUS: When did he die, George Washington?

SOLO (*Holding up card or writing on blackboard: 1799— Died*): Seventeen ninety-nine.

CHORUS: But he still lives on in our minds and hearts,
And will till the end of time!

(*Spotlight comes up, down right, as* SCHOOLMASTER, *carrying books, enters, walking sadly into spotlighted area.*)

SCHOOLMASTER: Boys of the Latin School of Fredericksburg, sad news has just reached us from Mount Vernon, this December day. George Washington is dead! The father of our country is dead.

He was our friend . . . almost our neighbor, when he lived across the river at Ferry Farms years ago. And many of you remember his mother when she lived on Charles Street next door to her daughter and grandchildren.

George Washington is dead. In him were united such qualities of greatness as seldom appear in one man. How long he served our country! How well he served it—as soldier, patriot, statesman, citizen!

Boys, open your copy books and write these words on the title page where you will see them often: "George Washington—first in war, first in peace, and first in the hearts of his countrymen."

Our beloved commander-in-chief, our first President, is dead. But he will never be forgotten. Other heroes, other statesmen, will come and go, but the memory of George Washington is here to stay. (*Nods solemnly, and exits; spotlight fades out. Stage lights come up full.*)

CHORUS: Washington marches on! (*Procession of* BOYS AND GIRLS *of the present generation march across stage, carrying flags.*)

BOYS AND GIRLS (*Chanting*): Washington marches on! (*Etc.*)

THE END

PRODUCTION NOTES
WASHINGTON MARCHES ON

Characters: 25 male; 9 female; male and female extras. (This is a maximum cast; many of the parts may be doubled.)

Playing Time: 25 minutes.

Costume: If costumes are used, all the characters should wear costumes appropriate for the time and place of their particular scenes.

Properties: Paper, ink, quill pen, packet of mail, map, magnifying glass, tripod, sewing, newspapers, knitting, letters, Bible, books, flags.

Setting: On stage are two chairs and a table holding paper, ink and quill pen. If a blackboard is used, it should be placed at a downstage corner of the stage.

Lighting: Spotlight, as indicated in text.

How to Spell a Patriot

Characters

SIXTEEN BOYS *and* GIRLS

SETTING: *Across the front of the stage is a chalk line with places marked with letters, in order, spelling* GEORGE WASHINGTON, *where Boys and Girls will stand when they say their lines.*

AT RISE: BOYS *and* GIRLS *are at back of stage in small groups. Each carries one of the letters that spells out* G-E-O-R-G-E W-A-S-H-I-N-G-T-O-N. *In the beginning the letters are all mixed up. Each child leaves the group and stands on the letter indicated to say his lines.*

ALL: We can spell a patriot!
　　　We needn't ask our betters.
　　　We can spell a patriot
　　　By using sixteen letters!

H: 　Take H to stand for honor
　　　In peace as well as war,

W: 　Take W for wisdom
　　　And watchfulness, what's more.

G: 　Take G to stand for greatness
　　　In planning and in deed,

G: Take G for goodness also,
     Which even heroes need!

O: Take O for optimism
     When fortune seems to frown,

R: Take R for real resistance
     When trouble presses down.

I: Take I to stand for insight
     In doing what is best,

S: Take S for strength in service
     To meet the grimmest test.

T: Take T to stand for talent,
     And also truth and trust,

O: Take O for opposition
     To everything unjust.

N: Take N for noble nature—
     Not seeking fame or power,

E: Take E for great endurance
     In every crucial hour.

N: Take N for nerve to tackle
     Whatever must be done,

E: Take E for extra effort
     When battles must be won.

A: Take A for ardent action
     To make injustice cease,

G: Take G to stand for guidance
     In war as well as peace.

ALL (*Holding letters high*):
     There, we spelled a patriot
     In letters big and tall—
     A patriot, GEORGE WASHINGTON,
     The greatest of them all!

Washington at Valley Forge

ALL:
A wooded valley and a frozen creek,
the hills surrounding, high and cold and bleak;
a little forge for melting metal down,
a valley forge—the kernel of a town,
a dreary place with Christmastime so near . . .

1ST BOY:
The General called a halt: "We're camping here.
We'll need some huts as shelter from the cold.
Work quickly, men, the year is growing old."

ALL:
The General watched his soldiers chop and saw.
Their feet were bleeding and their hands were raw.
They lacked supplies and clothes and shoes and food,
but, like their leader, they had fortitude.

2ND BOY:
The General stood upon a rise of ground.
His heart was heavy as he looked around:
"My unpaid men are weary, hungry, cold,
while twenty miles away the Redcoats hold
fair Philadelphia and live in state,
and sit in comfort near a blazing grate!"

ALL:
The General thought of home—Mount Vernon's charm.
His soldiers wintered, what would be the harm
in going home? The cold had months to run!
He turned and looked into the puny sun,
and chose the hardship—as he'd always done—
the General by the name of Washington.

102

MARCH

Wearing of the Green

It ought to come in April,
or, better yet, in May
when everything is green as green—
I mean St. Patrick's Day.

With still a week of winter
this wearing of the green
seems rather out of season—
it's rushing things, I mean.

But maybe March *is* better
when all is done and said:
St. Patrick brings a promise,
a four-leaf-clover promise,
a green-all-over promise
of springtime just ahead!

St. Patrick's Day

1ST GIRL: 'Tis the luck of the Irish
          to have an easy smile.

1ST BOY: That's from the sparkly sun that shines
          upon the Emerald Isle.

2ND GIRL: 'Tis the luck of the Irish
          to have a lilting song.

2ND BOY: That's from the gladsome birds that sing
          the Irish summer long.

3RD GIRL: 'Tis the luck of the Irish
          to have a ready wit.

3RD BOY: That's from the Blarney Stone they kiss,
          and wink while doing it!

4TH GIRL: 'Tis the luck of the Irish
          to have a patron saint.

4TH BOY: St. Patrick drove the serpents out
          and no one voiced complaint.

ALL: 'Tis the luck of the Irish
          to have a day apart
          when Ireland's green is on their coat,
          a song within their heart.
          (All sing Irish song, if desired.)

Spring
(First Day, March 21)

Sing the Songs of Springtime

Characters

SPIRIT OF SPRING
TWO HARBINGERS
APRIL
APRIL FOOL
ARBOR DAY
EASTER
QUEEN OF THE MAY
CHILDREN
FIVE MAYPOLE DANCERS
CUCKOO BIRD, *offstage voice*

TIME: *A spring day.*
SETTING: *A meadow.*
AT RISE: SPIRIT OF SPRING *enters, looks around, and listens.*

CUCKOO BIRD (*Offstage*): Cluck, chuck, cuckoo!

SPRING: It's spring! It's spring! The cuckoo is calling. Where are my harbingers?

CUCKOO (*Offstage*): Cluck, chuck, cuckoo! (SPRING *sings first stanza of "The Cuckoo."*)

SPRING (*Singing*):
"The cuckoo is a funny bird,
She sings as she flies.
She'll bring you glad tidings,
She'll tell you no lies.
She sips from the pretty flowers
To make her voice clear,
And she'll never sing, 'Cuckoo,'
Till the spring of the year."

CUCKOO (*Offstage*): Cluck, chuck, cuckoo.

SPRING (*Clapping hands*): Where's everyone? Come, dance and sing! It's spring.

HARBINGERS (*Dancing in*): Greetings, Spring.

SPRING: Where have you been? Haven't you broadcast the news that winter is over, that the earth is stirring with life, that the air is warm with sun, and the cuckoo is singing?

1ST HARBINGER: Spirit of Spring, we broadcast the news far and wide. Surely April will be here in a few minutes.

2ND HARBINGER: Bringing April Fool and Arbor Day and Easter.

SPRING: Good. And what about May and June? You brought the news to them, too?

1ST HARBINGER: Yes. But you know June. She always takes her time about coming. And May—(*Hesitates*) Unfortunately the Queen of the May—has, you might say, gone into decline. She doesn't think she'll be able to come to the reunion. She's hobbling around with a cane.

SPRING: A cane!

2ND HARBINGER: The poor Queen has been having a hard time.

SPRING: That will never do! Spring is the time to dance and sing. We can't have May limping around. Why, see how brightly the sun shines, how the puddles sparkle, how the buds glisten, how the birds sing!

CUCKOO (*Offstage*): Cluck, chuck, cuckoo!

SPRING: It won't do for the Queen of the May to be under the weather when so much depends on her. (APRIL, APRIL FOOL, ARBOR DAY, EASTER *dance in, singing. They join hands with* SPRING *and* HARBINGERS *and circle around, singing "Spring Carol."*)

ALL (*Singing*):
"Spring is here with all her joys,
Serving to remind us
Summer days will follow soon,
Winter lies behind us.
Flowers show their tender buds,
Lightly colored petals
Beckon, as the gentle breeze
On the meadow settles." (*Etc.*)

SPRING: Welcome, welcome, my dear friends. It's wonderful to see you after such a long, cold, lonesome winter. April, you always remind us of rhymes—flowers and showers, buds and floods, roots and boots . . .

OTHERS: And bumbershoots!

SPRING (*Laughing*): Yes, bumbershoots. What do you have to say for yourself, April?

APRIL: I never seem to be able to make up my mind. Folks say I blow hot or cold at the drop of a hat. April Fool is going to speak for me this year.

APRIL FOOL: I'm perfectly willing to speak, but don't ask me to sing with this *frog* in my throat. (*Takes stance and recites*)

108

April, April, aren't you queer,
April, aren't you funny?
You pout and weep and shed a tear,
Then smile and look all sunny!
Now you send a warming breeze . . .
Now your breeze is cooling . . .
April, April, you're a tease,
You're always April-fooling!
OTHERS:
April, April, you're a tease,
You're always April-fooling!
SPRING (*Looking around*): Let's see who else is here for
our spring reunion. Ah, Arbor Day. We're always glad
to see you. (ARBOR DAY *curtsies.*) Why, a hundred
years ago when pioneers were moving west, some of
the prairie states had hardly any trees at all. Now,
thanks to you, millions of trees are growing on the
prairies, holding moisture in the soil, breaking the
wind, making America beautiful. What do you have to
say to us, Arbor Day?
ARBOR DAY: Just what I've always been saying . . . in
three words. Trees. Trees. Trees. (*Begins to sing
"The Tree in the Wood"*)
"All in the wood there was a tree,
The prettiest tree that you ever did see.
And the green grass grew all around, all around,"
ALL (*Singing*):
"And the green grass grew all around."
ARBOR DAY (*Singing*):
"And on that tree there was a branch,
The prettiest branch that you ever did see.
Branch on the tree,
And the tree in the wood
And the green grass grew all around, all around,"

ALL (*Singing*):

"And the green grass grew all around."

(*This song can keep going as long as desired, adding a nest, an egg in the nest, a bird on the egg, a feather on the bird, etc.*)

SPRING: All that because there was a tree!

ARBOR DAY: Trees. Trees. Trees.

APRIL: We should remember to ask Johnny Appleseed to come join us some time. He was one of the greatest planters of trees in America. Apple trees. He went all over Ohio in the early days, and even into Kentucky and Indiana, planting orchards for the new settlers, making the wilderness look more like home.

APRIL FOOL (*Cavorting around*):

Oh, planting trees on Arbor Day

Is fine, we are agreed,

But *every* day was Arbor Day

For Johnny Appleseed!

(EASTER *enters, crosses to* SPRING.)

SPRING: And here's Easter, to speak to us of renewal, and rebirth, and joy in living.

EASTER (*Singing*):

Welcome, Sweet Springtime,

We greet thee in song!

SPRING: I always marvel at how young you look, Easter. And you've been in the world such a long time.

EASTER: Isn't everything young in spring—fresh and new and eager?

SPRING: Everything should be. But . . . slip-ups do happen. (*Looks around*) The Queen of May hasn't come, has she? Harbingers, run tell her we're waiting for her, we need her. What's spring without the May Queen? Tell her our reunion won't be complete without her. Tell her to come, cane and all. (HARBINGERS *run out.*)

110

APRIL FOOL: Cane and all?

EASTER: Is something wrong with the Queen of the May?

SPRING: She's gone into decline, they tell me. She's not like her old self at all.

EASTER: But how *can* anything be wrong? May is a month of joy and gladness, a time of wonder and surprises, quite as much as April. Remember how she always used to come in singing "The May Carol?"

APRIL FOOL (*Dancing around, mimicking*): Yes. Hand me my crown, Arbor Day. (*Gives* ARBOR DAY *his fool's cap and puts on garland, half singing and half chanting "The May Carol."*)
"This morning is the month of May,
the finest of the year.
Good people all, both great and small,
I wish you joyful cheer."

OTHERS (*Joining in*):
"I've wandered far, through all the night,
And also through the day.
And when I come your way again,
I'll bring a branch of may."

SPRING: I doubt if she'll sing it this year.

EASTER: Poor May, whatever is the trouble?

APRIL FOOL (*Looking offstage*): Shall I help find her? (*He has put his fool's cap back on.*)

SPRING: No. She might think we're fooling if she sees you, April Fool, and this is a serious matter.

ARBOR DAY: I remember the Queen used to love the rousing old English country songs. Perhaps if we sang one it would encourage her. What about "Hey Ho to the Greenwood"?

SPRING: To the greenwood let us go!

APRIL FOOL (*Peering offstage*): Here she comes. And she's not singing her May carol.

111

EASTER: She's hobbling along with a cane.

SPRING: Let's give her a rousing welcome . . . three cheers and a song.

ALL: Hooray, hooray, hooray, for the beautiful Queen of the May! (SPRING *leads the singing of "Hey Ho to the Greenwood."*)

"Hey ho, to the greenwood now let us go,
Sing heave—and ho,
And there shall we find both buck and doe,
Sing heave—and ho . . ." (*Etc.* QUEEN OF THE MAY *hobbles in with cane, a* HARBINGER *on each side.*)

SPRING: What in the world has happened to you, my dear? Did you have a fall?

QUEEN: A fall? Well, yes, you might put it that way.

SPRING: It's the first time you haven't come in singing.

QUEEN (*Sighing*): I haven't felt much like singing lately. (*Takes out handkerchief*) Nobody loves me any more.

EASTER: Why, what do you mean—nobody loves you? We all do.

QUEEN: I mean . . . I mean nobody else does. In olden times in England, I really *was* somebody. May Day was the great public holiday of spring.

APRIL FOOL: Nobody ever made a holiday of me, but I have a lot of fun slipping in edgewise.

QUEEN: People used to get up early on the first day of May to gather flowers and branches, and to dance and sing. They carried the Maypole to the village green and set it up with great ceremony and danced around it. Now who remembers May Day and the Queen of the May? Where are the dancers? The garlands? The Maypoles? The ribbons? (*Wipes her eyes*) Nobody remembers me any more.

SPRING: Oh, I'm sure many people remember you.

OTHERS: We do! (SPRING *beckons to* HARBINGERS,

112

whispers to them. They smile and nod and go out.)

QUEEN: Ever since the time of the Pilgrims, I've been out of things. Maybe you don't remember, but when the people of Plymouth town set up the first Maypole to celebrate spring, the Pilgrim fathers made them take it down. They didn't believe in having May games or Maypoles. They didn't believe in *me*.

EASTER: It doesn't seem possible.

QUEEN: I'm not saying they weren't good and upright and all. But they never made me feel welcome. I never really had a chance to get a foothold in America. And time doesn't seem to improve matters. (*Wipes her eyes*) Oh, the beautiful flowers and streamers of old England!

SPRING: Come, come, my dear, it can't be as bad as that.

QUEEN: May Day just isn't important any more. (*There is the sound of singing offstage.* QUEEN *is suddenly alert.*) Why, that's my song! "The May Carol." I didn't think anyone remembered . . .

CHILDREN (*Running in with May baskets; singing*):
"This morning is the month of May,
The finest of the year.
Good people all, both great and small,
We wish you joyful cheer."
(*They curtsy to* QUEEN, SPRING, *etc., in turn.*)

SPRING: What do you have in your baskets, may I ask?

CHILDREN: Mayflowers.

BOY: We got up early to pick them, so we wouldn't be late for school.

QUEEN (*Hopefully*): And are you going to make a garland for a Maypole?

GIRL: No. We're going to hang our baskets on doorknobs when nobody's looking. Then we'll ring the bell and run away. Whoever comes to the door will be surprised to see it's May Day.

113

QUEEN: What a charming idea! (*Steps forward eagerly to look into baskets letting go of her cane.* APRIL FOOL *catches it just in time to keep it from falling.*) Mayflowers. Spring beauties. Daffodils. Cherry blossoms. Apple bloom. Candytuft. And how did you get this delightful idea for May Day?

GIRL: Why, we do it every year in our town.

BOY: Doesn't everybody? It's fun.

GIRL: And people are always so surprised to get a May basket.

QUEEN: Well, I should think so. I would be, too.

GIRL: Doesn't everybody do it on the first of May?

QUEEN: I'm afraid not. (*She sighs, then suddenly remembers her cane. Takes it from* APRIL FOOL.)

CHILDREN: They *should.* (*They skip out singing "The May Carol."*)

SPRING: There, my dear, you see everyone hasn't forgotten May Day. (HARBINGERS *come running in.*)

HARBINGERS: Make way! Make way!

SPRING: What is it, Harbingers?

HARBINGERS: Something we found in the park. Make way! (*They wave everyone toward back of stage.*)

1ST HARBINGER: They were one dancer short, so we told them to come here.

QUEEN: Who were?

APRIL FOOL (*Stepping up*): If they're one dancer short, what about me? *I'm* short. (SPRING *waves him aside.*) I can dance and sing. (*He ducks under* SPRING's *arm and prances forward, singing fifth stanza of "'Twas May Day in the Morning."*)

"There was a man who grew so fat
He always stuck in his rocking chair,
It doesn't rhyme but I don't care—
'Twas May Day in the morning."

(*Others laugh and push him aside as* DANCERS *enter*

carrying a Maypole and singing, "Now Is the Month of Maying.")

DANCERS:
"Now is the month of maying,
When merry lads are playing,
Fa la la . . ." (*Etc.*)
Each with his bonny lass,
A-dancing on the grass.
Fa la la . . ." (*Etc.*)

QUEEN: That's one of the songs they used to sing in England years ago! (*Excited*) Where did you learn it? Where did you come across it?

1ST DANCER: Why, it's in one of our songbooks at school.

2ND DANCER: If we had one more dancer, we'd do an English country dance, and then weave the Maypole.

QUEEN: One dancer short! (*She drops her cane as she steps forward eagerly.* APRIL FOOL *catches cane just in time.*) Would I do? I know the song. I know all the May Day songs and dances.

DANCERS: You *do!*

5TH DANCER: Then you're just the one we need.

SPRING: It's spring, it's spring. Come, dance and sing! (QUEEN *joins dancers, and they quickly set up the Maypole. It may be placed in a strong Christmas tree holder. As they sing "Now Is the Month of Maying," they pick up streamers and dance around pole until weaving is completed.*)

SPRING (*Rushing up to* QUEEN *at end of song*): My dear, are you all right? After all that dancing and exertion?

1ST DANCER: She's wonderful—and she didn't even practice!

QUEEN: I haven't felt so well in years. Not since the seventeenth century. I'm so excited to know that these things are going on in America.

2ND DANCER: We would like to crown you Queen of the May. May we?

OTHERS (*Amused*): The Queen of the May! The Queen of the May!

SPRING (*Laughing*): Do you think you could fill the role, my dear?

QUEEN (*Laughing*): I could try.

2ND DANCER (*Urgently*): Will you be our May Queen, please? (APRIL FOOL *mischievously bows before* QUEEN, *and holds out cane to her.*)

QUEEN: Be done with your fooling. What do I want with a cane! (*She does a little dance.*) Don't you know it's spring, when everything is young and happy?

1ST DANCER: Then you *will* be our May Queen?

QUEEN: Be your May Queen? Indeed I will, dear friends. There's nothing in the whole wide world I'd rather be. (*All sing "Now Is the Month of Maying" as curtain falls.*)

THE END

PRODUCTION NOTES
SING THE SONGS OF SPRINGTIME

Characters: 2 male; 4 female; 2 male or female; 11 or more male or female for Children and Maypole Dancers.

Playing Time: 20 minutes.

Costumes: Characters wear costumes which suggest their names: Spirit of Spring, April, Easter and Queen of the May wear flowing dresses; April Fool wears a jester's suit and cap, and Arbor Day wears green tights with cloth leaves sewn on it. Harbingers may wear tights. Children and Maypole Dancers wear spring dresses or shirts and slacks.

Properties: Garland, cane, May baskets, flowers, Maypole.

Setting: A meadow. The stage may be decorated with flowers, shrubs, etc.

Lighting: No special effects.

Music: Appropriate songs may be found in various songbooks, if those indicated are unfamiliar or unavailable.

Benjy and His Red Flannels

On March twenty-first spring arrived at its worst,
Floods rushed down the rivers and channels.
But Benjy contended, "Since winter has ended,
I'm shedding my itchy red flannels."

His wife cried, "Now truly, don't be so unruly!
Today is no time to act silly:
I'm fearful you may go and catch the lumbago—
The weather's decidedly chilly."

But Ben was vivacious: "It's spring, goodness gracious!"
So after his wife went away,
He draped his red flannels across the bed panels
And dressed himself springlike and gay.

Then clang-ity-clang, the telephone rang,
And a voice cried, "Help, help! Hurry, hurry!
The bridge has crashed through, the streamliner's
    due . . ."
And Benjy was off in a flurry.

He grabbed his red britches and jumped over ditches;
they served as a beautiful flare.
By now, can you guess? Yes, he flagged that express
With never a moment to spare.

Well, Ben was rewarded: His deed got recorded
In all the historical annals,
And his wife now in spring doesn't murmur a thing
When he takes off his itchy red flannels!

Spring Pictures

BOY: Spring's an artist—she has fun
painting pictures in the sun.
GIRL: She likes watercolors best,
greens and yellows oftenest.
BOY: She daubs color on the hills
(doesn't worry if it spills),
runs her brush along the valleys,
up the streets, and down the alleys.
GIRL: She especially likes trees,
draping lace on some of these,
painting waves of golden hair
in the willows everywhere.
BOTH: What a blue she gives the sky,
with its sparkling golden eye!
Spring's an artist—having fun
painting pictures in the sun.

A March Question

GIRLS: We know someone—
try to guess!
1ST CHILD: She wears a gold hat.
2ND CHILD: She wears a green dress.
3RD CHILD: She wears glass slippers
the color of rain.
4TH CHILD: And around her neck
is a dandelion chain.
5TH CHILD: She scatters flowers
over the hills,
some of them plain
and some with frills.
6TH CHILD: She listens when robins
and blackbirds sing.
7TH CHILD: And she laughs at winter,
because she's . . .
BOYS: SPRING!

APRIL

April Fool's Day
(April 1)

Benjamin's April Fool

One sunny spring morning Ben's wife said, "Take warn-
   ing,
Don't be absent-minded today:
It's April the first, be expecting the worst,
Remember the pranks people play . . .

"Don't pick up a wallet—no good can befall it.
Don't act like a dumbbell. Beware!"
And Benjy said, "Dearie, I'll surely be leery—
I'll take most exceptional care."

Well, Benjy went shopping, his coat-tails a-flopping,
His mind full of robins and spring,
His heart all a-flutter . . . "What's that in the gutter?
A purse! What a fortunate thing."

He reached for the purse. (Oh, what could be worse?)
"Ha. Ha. April Fool!" came the cry.
"A purse . . . April Fool!" laughed the children from
   school,
Who'd giggled and passed it right by.

Poor Benjy felt silly. His spine got all chilly.
But like a good fellow, he cried:
"I'll open the buckle." He did . . . with a chuckle.
He found fifty dollars inside!

Surprised by this hoard, "April Fool!" Benjy roared.
"I have a proposal to make:
You children admit that I fooled *you* a bit,
And I'll treat you to ice cream and cake."

Easter
(April)

Easter Daisies

Scurry, Rabbit,
hurry, Rabbit,
sleek and gray and furry Rabbit
with your puff of tail.
Find the daisies still in hiding
on the hill where Spring is striding,
tell them without fail:

"Hurry, daisies,
scurry, daisies,
willow cats are purry, daisies,
Winter's really done.
Easter's coming! Every bonnet
should have Easter trimmings on it!"
Tell them, Rabbit.
RUN!

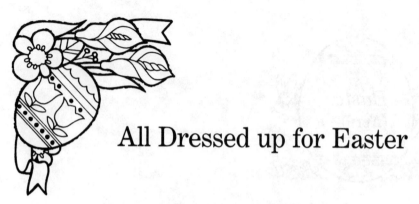

All Dressed up for Easter

All dressed up for Easter
in yellow, green and white—
but I've got a blister
'cause my shoes are tight!

Easter in the Air

It isn't on the calendar,
but every other Where
a new year is beginning now,
as everyone's aware:
new grass showing, new buds growing,
winter gone, and soft wind blowing . . .
Easter's in the air.

Arbor Day and Earth Day
(April)

Johnny Appleseed's Vision

Characters

LIDDY
JANE
JOHNNY APPLESEED
FATHER
BENJY
MOTHER

TIME: *Spring, about 1810.*
SETTING: *Outside a log cabin on a pioneer farm in Ohio.*
AT RISE: LIDDY *and* JANE *are sitting on a big log, talking earnestly. They keep glancing back at the cabin, as if to be sure their mother can't hear.* LIDDY *holds an old rag doll of which she is obviously fond.*

LIDDY:
Does Papa know what day it is?
JANE:
He's busy with that work of his—
Cutting trees and burning brush
And plowing land in such a rush!
I didn't ask for fear he'd say
He couldn't help it, anyway.

LIDDY:
And Benjy? He'll be full of sorrow
If he forgets about tomorrow.
JANE:
I asked him and he answered, "What!
Birthday? Why, I plumb forgot."
LIDDY (*Sadly*):
None of us has any present.
Mama's birthday won't be pleasant.
JANE:
Benjy found an arrowhead,
A perfect kind of one, he said.
He'll wrap it up with several others.
LIDDY:
Arrowheads aren't gifts for mothers!
(*She looks at her doll fondly, then suddenly seems to
have an idea.*)
I could give her Mary Lou—
For company . . . for talking to!
JANE:
Mama misses company. (*Shakes her head*)
What comfort would a rag doll be?
LIDDY:
She's company! I ought to know.
JANE:
Not for grown-up people though.
LIDDY:
What *can* we find or make or borrow
For Mama's birthday for tomorrow?
JANE (*Thinking hard*):
Let's pick a bunch of new spring flowers.
There are some along that path of ours.
LIDDY:
They're wild, and Mama likes things tame.
It's *all* been wild here since we came,

124

And Mama's lonesome through and through
For old familiar things she knew.

JANE:

A sprig of apple bloom, or peach—
Or, even better, some of each.

LIDDY:

And company to stay for dinner!

BOTH:

A day like that would be a winner.

(JANE *grasps* LIDDY's *arm and points offstage, much excited.*)

JANE:

That's not Papa. That's not Ben.
Or any of the Johnson men.

LIDDY:

'Way off there—who can it be?
Some "birthday-present" company!
Let's talk where Mama cannot see.

(*They go to clump of bushes and wait for stranger.*)

JANE:

We've got to find or make or borrow
A place to hide him till tomorrow!

(JOHNNY APPLESEED *enters. He has a knapsack on his back and a smile on his face, and carries a bundle of seedlings.*)

LIDDY (*Politely*):

Sir, you're just the one we need.

JANE:

A gift from heaven, yes, indeed.

JOHNNY:

You mean old Johnny Appleseed?
(*He laughs heartily.*)
I'm no gift, but, ah, I pack
A hundred thousand in my sack.

125

JANE:

A hundred thousand! Sir, our schooling
Isn't much—but aren't you fooling?

JOHNNY (*Chuckling*):

I'm no gift, but with this hand
I plant my gifts throughout the land.

LIDDY (*Puzzled*):

Plant them? Do they really grow?

JOHNNY:

Well, I guess. And I should know:
I've planted them for years, and I
Will go on planting till I die.
Some folks call me queer, benighted,
But perhaps I'm just farsighted.
(*He fumbles at his knapsack, and takes out several
small pieces of flowered cloth and hands them to*
JANE.)
Meanwhile, here's a gift for you—
Some in pink and some in blue.

JANE (*Puzzled*):

To plant? Oh, sir, it can't be true.

JOHNNY (*Handing a bright ribbon to* LIDDY):

And here's a gift for you, young lady,
To brighten hours that might be shady.
It's not for planting, though— beware,
Unless you plant it in your hair!

JANE *and* LIDDY: Thank you.

JANE (*To* LIDDY):

Liddy, in a day
We can sew a gift that's gay.

LIDDY (*Eagerly*):

Yes, we can, in several hours.
(*To* JOHNNY)
It's *Mama's* birthday, sir, not ours.
We were yearning for a present. . . .

126

JOHNNY:
    Ho, I'll make her birthday pleasant
    By giving her some gifts to plant.
    (*He shakes his finger at the girls*)
    Don't look at me as if I can't.
JANE:
    Gifts to plant—that sounds so funny.
    Do they cost a lot of money?
JOHNNY:
    A glass of milk, a crust of bread,
    Some talk, a place to lay my head—
    Why, they hardly cost a thing . . .
    And what a lot of joy they bring.
    (*There is a shout offstage, and in a moment* FATHER
    and BENJY *come in.*)
FATHER (*Holding out hand*):
    I thought I saw a stranger here.
    We've not seen many folks this year.
JOHNNY:
    They told me at the settlement
    You asked about me when you went
    To get supplies some months ago.
    I just got back this way, and so . . .
FATHER (*Excited*):
    You're Johnny Appleseed, I swear!
    A gift from heaven, I declare.
    You're just in time to help me out.
BENJY (*Baffled, to* LIDDY):
    Liddy, what's this all about?
FATHER:
    Just in time to ease my sorrow . . .
    There's a birthday here tomorrow.
LIDDY (*To* JANE):
    He *isn't* absent-minded, is he,
    Even though he's been so busy?

127

FATHER:
  I had no gift, but now you're here
  With gifts that live from year to year.
BENJY:
  Will someone kindly make this clear?
LIDDY *and* JANE:
  Don't look at us, because we can't.
JOHNNY:
  I carry riches here to plant.
  (*He shows bundle of seedlings, then puts them down and takes a tiny buckskin bag from his knapsack. All watch him curiously.*)
FATHER:
  I've heard of you, and know my wife
  Will like these gifts that last—for life.
BENJY:
  Appleseeds! And seedlings, too.
  You mean you'll let us have a few?
JOHNNY:
  I plant wherever I may roam . . .
  To give the wilds the look of home,
  And raise the settlers' hearts from gloom
  By looking at some apple bloom.
  (MOTHER *calls from offstage, then comes in.*)
MOTHER (*Pleased*):
  What's this? What's this? It looks to me
  As if we have some company.
FATHER:
  A welcome guest is here, indeed.
  My dear, meet Johnny Appleseed.
  Tomorrow is quite a special date—
  He's come to help us celebrate.
BENJY (*To* MOTHER):
  Your birthday's going to be a winner,
  With company to stay for dinner!

FATHER:
  Before the company's departed,
  An apple orchard will be started!
JANE *and* LIDDY:
  And something made of pink and blue
  Will be a birthday present, too.
JOHNNY:
  Some folks call me queer, benighted,
  But maybe I am just farsighted:
  A seed may seem a little thing,
  But it's a birthday every spring.
MOTHER (*Happily*):
  I little thought last week, last fall,
  When I felt lonely here, and small,
  This birthday would be best of all!
  (*Curtain falls.*)

THE END

PRODUCTION NOTES
JOHNNY APPLESEED'S VISION

Characters: 3 male; 3 female.
Playing Time: 10 minutes.
Costumes: Johnny Appleseed, Father and Benjy are dressed in working clothes. Johnny's costume should be composed of strange odds and ends. Liddy, Jane and Mother wear plain long-skirted dresses.
Properties: Rag doll for Liddy; knapsack containing flowered goods, hair ribbons, and buckskin bag of seeds for Johnny; seedlings for Johnny.
Setting: Outside a log cabin. There is a log for a seat. Toward one side of the stage is a clump of bushes.
Lighting: No special effects.

An Up-and-Doing Day

Characters

TEACHER
PUPILS, *any number*
8 BOYS AND GIRLS *with letters*

TIME: *An April day.*

SETTING: *A schoolroom. At the center of the stage is a screen (or screens) arranged to represent a closed spelling book. In front of the "book," the numbers 1–8 are written on the floor in chalk. These numbers are spaced out evenly across the stage.*

AT RISE: TEACHER *is at desk up front,* PUPILS *are in their seats.* 8 BOYS AND GIRLS *with large cardboard letters* (A,Y,R,A,B,D,O,R) *are hidden behind the "spelling book."*

TEACHER: Let's see how wise you are today,
   how full you are of learning:
   Who can spell a spring-like day
   that stands for spring returning?

PUPILS (*Puzzled*): Who can spell a spring-like day
   that stands for spring returning?

TEACHER: A day for looking far ahead, when vision is
   the rule . . .

1ST BOY (*Holding up hand*): I bet you spell it A-P-R-I-L
   . . . F-O-O-L!

1ST GIRL: We must keep looking far ahead—
that day is full of fooling!
TEACHER: No, no, I don't mean April Fool.
Dear me, where is your schooling?
I'm thinking of a spring-like day
when faith and hope are ruling.
PUPILS (*Puzzled*): Who can spell a spring-like day
when faith and hope are ruling?
TEACHER: A day when shoots and stalks and roots
are stretching necks and legs . . .
2ND GIRL: Do you mean *Easter*, full of hope
for flowers and Easter eggs?
PUPILS (*Nodding*): Easter is a spring-like day
that stands for spring returning.
2ND BOY: When stalks and roots and little shoots
are full of life and yearning,
3RD GIRL: When we have faith that winter's gone
and spring is quickly learning.
TEACHER: No, no, not Easter. Not this time,
but quite another day.
It comes much earlier down south,
and sometimes not till May . . .
a day when we are full of hope
and full of plans a-brewing.
Who can spell a spring-like day
when we are up and doing?
PUPILS (*Puzzled*): Who can spell a spring-like day
when we are up and doing?
3RD BOY: Give a hint!
4TH GIRL: Yes, give a hint.
PUPILS: The question isn't easy.
TEACHER: The spring-like day I'm thinking of
is very, very trees-y.
PUPILS: Trees-y, trees-y?

TEACHER: Full of trees!
Come, open up your spelling book and spell it, if you
please. (4TH BOY *and* 5TH GIRL *go forward and open
the "Spelling-book" screen, then return to their seats.
Letter* A *comes out, stands on space marked Number
1.*)

A: A for apple . . . apple tree,
and Johnny Appleseed
who planted orchards right and left,
for planting was his creed. (*Letter* Y *comes out, stands
on space Number 8.*)

Y (*Turning over card to show sketch of yew branch with
flat sharp-tipped needles, with "yew" printed beneath;
then turning card back to* Y): Y for yew . . . an evergreen
with branches sweeping down.
Plant a yew and you will have
the rarest tree in town. (*Letter* R *comes out, stands on
space Number 2.*)

R: R. for redbud—bright with blooms
before its leaves are out,
a tree George Washington admired
and planted roundabout. (*Letter* A *comes out, stands
on space Number 7.*)

A: A for aspen—commonest
of all the trees we know,
with shaky leaves and quaky leaves
that twinkle to and fro. (*Letter* B *comes out, stands on
space Number 3.*)

B: B for balsam, buckeye, birch,
and butternut and bay,
beech and basswood . . . take your pick
to plant this spring-like day. (*Letter* D *comes out,
stands on space Number 6.*)

D: D for dogwood—hold your breath
when starry blooms abound.

Jefferson and Washington
both loved that tree around. (*Letter O comes out,
stands on space Number 4.*)

O: O for oak, the king of trees,
that lives for years on end.
Plant an oak and you will have
a sturdy lifetime friend. (*Letter R comes out, stands
on space Number 5.*)

R: R for redwood—nature's giant,
the longest-lived of all.
And yet each mighty tree was once
a seedling, thin and small. (*The letters spell Arbor
Day*)

PUPILS (*Excited*): That spells Arbor Day. Just look!

TEACHER (*Laughing*): Just think of all you're learning.

5TH BOY: It surely is a trees-y day
that stands for spring returning.

6TH GIRL: A day for looking far ahead—
from acorns clear to oaks.

6TH BOY: From seedlings way to spreading trees
that shade the yard for folks.

TEACHER (*Nodding*): A day of vision and of faith,
a day of plans a-brewing.

PUPILS (*Eagerly*): Let's hurry up and plant some trees.
Let's all be up and doing!

THE END
PRODUCTION NOTES
AN UP-AND-DOING DAY

Characters: 8 male and female; 1 male or female for teacher; male and female extras to be pupils.

Playing Time: 5 minutes.

Costumes: Modern, everyday dress.

Properties: Eight large cardboard letters spelling Arbor Day.

Setting: A classroom. There are desks or chairs for the pupils placed at the sides of the stage. At downstage left is the teacher's desk. At the center of the stage is a screen (or screens) arranged to represent a closed spelling book. In front of "book," the numbers 1–8 are written on the floor.

Lighting: No special effects.

The Rescuers

Characters

NARRATOR
MOTHER NATURE
FATHER TIME
BOYS AND GIRLS

SETTING: *Stage is bare except for pile of litter at one
side.*
AT RISE: NARRATOR *stands up right.* MOTHER NATURE
and FATHER TIME *stand center.*
NARRATOR:
Said Mother Nature
to Father Time:
MOTHER NATURE:
My life isn't smooth
as a nursery rhyme.
I'm always working.
I probe and plan—
as I have done
since the world began—
to run the planet
with skill and grace,
with everything properly
in its place.
But I so frequently
go unheeded,

I frankly question
if I've succeeded.
NARRATOR:
  Said Old Father Time
  to Mother N.:
FATHER TIME:
  I marvel at you,
  again and again—
  the way you weave
  all things together—
  plants and animals,
  soil and weather.
  I think you've shown
  remarkable taste,
  working with care
  and never in haste,
  doing so much
  with so little waste.
NARRATOR:
  Said Mother Nature
  to white-haired Time:
MOTHER NATURE:
  Waste, I believe,
  is a dreadful crime.
  I've made it a rule
  which I seldom abuse:
  What one thing rejects
  another can use.
  Take carbon dioxide
  that people breathe out.
  Plants all need it,
  without a doubt.
  And as for the oxygen
  plants expel:
  Humans must breathe it
  wherever they dwell.

NARRATOR:
  Said Old Father Time:
FATHER TIME:
  You planned it well.
MOTHER NATURE:
  But now . . .
NARRATOR:
  Mother Nature
  looked around . . .
MOTHER NATURE:
  People with wasteful
  ways abound.
  I'm quite discouraged.
NARRATOR:
  She sighed and frowned.
  Said old Father Time
  with a matching sigh:
FATHER TIME:
  People are slow
  as the years go by,
  to put into practice
  your simple rules.
  They waste the land
  and the fossil fuels,
  pollute the air
  and the lakes and streams,
  poison the birds
  and spoil your dreams.
NARRATOR:
  Said Mother Nature:
MOTHER NATURE:
  And all this litter!
  These cans and bottles
  and foil that glitters,
  and trash and papers . . .

I'm not a quitter,
but all this rubbish
makes me bitter.
There's no such waste
from *wildwood* critters.
NARRATOR:
Said Old Father Time:
FATHER TIME:
I only hope
we both aren't reaching
the end of our rope!
NARRATOR:
Said Mother Nature:
MOTHER NATURE:
There must be a way
for the two of us
to save the day;
to save this world
of life and beauty!
It isn't that I have
forgotten my duty,
but I see little hope,
I'm sad to tell.
I haven't much cause
to be feeling well.
NARRATOR:
Then Father Time,
a hand to his ear,
said:
FATHER TIME:
Somebody's coming.
What's that I hear?
The voices of children!
They're coming near.
Let's see what they're doing,
then disappear.

(BOYS *and* GIRLS, *carrying trash bags, enter and begin picking up litter.*)
NARRATOR:
  Cried Mother Nature:
MOTHER NATURE:
  They're picking up litter!
  And I was tempted
  to be a quitter.
  They're shouting something
  that sounds like news.
BOYS *and* GIRLS (*Chanting*):
  Recycle!
  Conserve!
  Reuse!
MOTHER NATURE:
  These boys and girls
  are informed and clever.
  I trust they'll act
  on those words forever.
BOYS *and* GIRLS (*Together*):
  To make nature smile
  is our endeavor!
MOTHER NATURE:
  There's hope, Father Time,
  for me and you.
  (*They exit.*)
NARRATOR:
  So come along, everyone,
  let's lend a hand.
  You see, it's quite simple
  to clean up our land!
  (BOYS *and* GIRLS *continue to pick up litter as curtain closes.*)

THE END

Characters: 1 male; 1 female; 1 male or female; as many extras as desired
for Boys and Girls.
Playing Time: 5 minutes.
Costumes: Mother Nature, long, flowing dress, flowers in her hair; Father
Time, white hair and beard. All others, modern dress.
Properties: Trash bags.
Setting: Bare stage, except for pile of litter at one side.
Lighting: No special effects.

Johnny Appleseed

BOYS: He walked the wilderness unarmed
in days when few men dared it,

GIRLS: He sowed his seeds where poor folk farmed—
he had a dream and shared it.

ALL: Johnny Appleseed!

BOYS: Whatever weather blew his way
good-naturedly he'd brave it,
and dig and tramp and plant all day.

GIRLS: He dreamed a dream and gave it.

ALL: Johnny Appleseed!

BOYS: He led a life of lack and toil
and cheerfully he led it.

GIRLS: His roots were deep in seeds and soil—
he had a dream and spread it.

ALL: Johnny Appleseed!

BOYS: And even yet folks speak his name,
and glad we are to hear it.

GIRLS: His dream bore fruit, and those who came
long after still revere it.

ALL: Johnny Appleseed!

The Fable of Three Brothers

Characters

NARRATOR
FATHER
ELDEST BROTHER
2ND BROTHER
YOUNGEST BROTHER

NARRATOR: Once there were three brothers
    whose father had great wealth.
    He owned a thousand acres,
    but suffered from ill health.
    He called his sons together, and said:
FATHER: My work is done.
    I'll give you each a portion
    of my estate to run.
    Whoever shows most wisdom
    three years from now, come fall,
    in working on his acres,
    will then inherit *all*.
NARRATOR: The eldest son was favored:
    The eldest had first choice.
ELDEST: I'll take the wooded hillsides!
NARRATOR: He spoke with boastful voice.
2ND BROTHER: *I'll* take the rolling meadow
    that's watered by the stream.
NARRATOR: The second son spoke eagerly,
    his greedy eyes agleam.
YOUNGEST: I'll take what's left.

140

NARRATOR: The youngest remarked,
　　with a modest glance.
YOUNGEST: I'd gladly pry out boulders.
　　I'm pleased to have this chance.
NARRATOR: And so at once the brothers
　　set forth to start the test,
　　to show their ailing father
　　whose work would prove the best.
　　The eldest thought:
ELDEST: I'm wisest.
　　How simple it will be!
　　Before three years are over
　　I'll cut down every tree.
　　I'll sell them all for lumber.
　　My profit will be great.
　　I'll so impress my father,
　　I'll win the whole estate.
NARRATOR: The second son stood gazing
　　across his meadow land.
　　He watched the cattle grazing, and murmured:
2ND BROTHER: I'll expand.
　　I'll raise three times more cattle
　　and have more beef to sell.
　　I'll show that I can manage
　　my portion very well.
YOUNGEST: *I'll* dig out brush and boulders
　　and plant some windbreak trees.
　　I'll start a little orchard,
　　and maybe have some bees.
NARRATOR: So when three years were over,
　　the father took account.
　　The eldest waved his money—
　　a very great amount.
　　His father then inspected
　　the hillsides shorn of trees.
　　He frowned and fumed . . .

FATHER: I don't approve such practices as these.
   Without a web of rootlets
   to hold the soil in place,
   a hillside crumbles quickly
   and gullies scar its face.
   You failed from start to finish
   to treat your portion well.
NARRATOR: The second son stepped forward.
2ND BROTHER: Just see how *I* excel.
NARRATOR: He showed a bag of money . . .
   His father shook his head.
FATHER: I rue the way you earned it—
   Your senses must have fled!
   You put too many cattle
   to graze upon the land.
   They stripped it bare. Disaster
   is rife on every hand.
   You left the soil unshielded,
   to wash and blow away.
   The plan you had was foolish—
   such tactics do not pay.
NARRATOR: He then addressed the youngest:
FATHER: And what have *you* to say?
YOUNGEST: My soil was poor to start with.
   My earnings have been small.
   If you inspect my pockets,
   you won't find much at all.
   But I've enriched the acres
   and cleared the stones away.
   Have you observed the garden,
   the orchard, and the hay?
FATHER: I have! I praise your foresight.
   Your way is best by far:

You made the soil productive,
you did not leave a scar.
You tended it most wisely,
my son. You weren't misled
by hopes for present profit.
You planned for years ahead.
I'll rest content now, knowing
the future of these lands—
these hillsides, fields, and meadows—
is in such worthy hands.

Let's Plant a Tree

ALL: It's time to plant a tree, a tree.
　　　What shall it be? What shall it be?
1ST: Let's plant a pine—we can't go wrong:
　　　a pine is green the whole year long.
2ND: Let's plant a maple—more than one!—
　　　to shade us from the summer sun.
3RD: Let's plant a cherry—you know why:
　　　there's nothing like a cherry pie!
4TH: Let's plant an elm, the tree of grace,
　　　where robins find a nesting place.
5TH: Let's plant an apple—not too small,
　　　with flowers in spring and fruit in fall.
6TH: Let's plant a fir—so it can be
　　　a lighted outdoor Christmas tree.
7TH: Let's plant a birch, an oak, a beech,
　　　there's something extra-nice in each.
ALL: It's time to plant a tree, a tree.
　　　What shall it be? What shall it be?
　　　It doesn't have to matter much—
　　　they all have special charms and such
　　　in winter, summer, spring or fall.
　　　Let's plant a . . .

　　　　　　　　look, let's plant them *ALL*.

Patriot's Day
(April 19)

The Many Rides of Paul Revere

NARRATOR:
  Listen, my children, and you shall hear
  of the *many* rides of Paul Revere,
  the silversmith whose horse's feet
  pounded many a road and street
  in days when the colonists had cause
  to chafe and fret under British laws.
CHILDREN:
  You mean to say that the midnight ride
  over the April countryside
  in seventeen hundred and seventy-five
  wasn't the *only* ride he took?
  It's famous in every history book.
NARRATOR:
  On *many* a night or noon or morning
  he rode to carry some news or warning.
  Listen, my children, in seventy-three

Paul Revere helped dump the tea
from British ships into Boston's port.
In a patriotic attempt to thwart
the British passion to levy taxes,
the colonists swung their battleaxes!
Then Paul Revere and his trusty horse
carried the news along a course
more than two hundred miles in length,
in winter. It needed a man of strength.
He reached New York with the news to share
with Sons of Liberty active there.

CHILDREN:

All those miles in wintry weather
to bind the patriots together!

NARRATOR:

That isn't all . . . it's just the start.
Paul Revere played a worthy part
in getting relief for Boston Town
when, early in spring, the British crown
as punishment closed the harbor down.
Off to New York he rode again,
enlisting the help of fellowmen;
then on to Independence Hall
in Philadelphia, to call
upon the patriots there to heed
Boston's plight in its time of need.

CHILDREN:

He covered many a mile indeed.
And did he travel again before
the shot was fired that sparked the war
in seventy-five?

145

NARRATOR:

Through seventy-four
he went on missions again and again
with news for freedom-devoted men . . .
all for the sake of the cause, of course—
a middle-aged man on a sturdy horse.
He won a certain amount of fame:
"official courier" he became.
Even the British knew his name.

CHILDREN:

Then came the time he spread the warning
in the early hours of an April morning!

NARRATOR:

He watched to see what the light would be
in the belfry tower that crucial night:
one, if by land; two, if by sea.
He saw two lanterns burning bright,
and off he sped to cry the alarm
to every Middlesex village and farm.

CHILDREN:

"The British are coming! They're on the way."

NARRATOR:

The war for freedom began that day.
The war for freedom! The call was clear.
Patriots fought for many a year
and, thanks to stalwarts like Paul Revere,
we won the freedom we hold so dear.

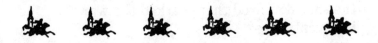

MAY

May Day
(May 1)

All on a Day in May

Characters

Two Girls
Two Boys
Four Wood Sprites

Time: *May Day morning.*
Setting: *The edge of a wood. There are a number of cardboard bushes and trees. Flowers for the May Queen's bouquet are hidden in the bushes or behind them.*
At Rise: Wood Sprites *are hiding.* Boys *and* Girls *enter.*
1st Girl: Here we go on a May Day morning,
a May Day morning in May,
to see a world that is just a-borning,
all shiny and bright and gay.
1st Boy: We want some flowers
for a fine bouquet

to give Her Highness,
the Queen of May . . .

2ND GIRL (*Looking around*): But we've lost our way!

2ND BOY: We have lost our way!

ALL (*Looking around*): There isn't a single flower adorning this place where we chanced to stray.

SPRITES (*Softly, unseen*): On a rollicking, frolicking, lollicking, rollicking morning in May.

1ST GIRL: What shall we do?
Oh, what shall we do?

1ST BOY: There isn't a blossom, not one or two.

BOYS *and* GIRLS: There isn't a blossom that's old or new
to bring to the Queen of May.

SPRITES (*Louder*): Look around all over the ground.
You may discover that flowers abound
in this place where we like to play.

1ST GIRL (*Surprised*): Who's that?

1ST BOY: Yes, who?

2ND GIRL: Let's ask for a clue.

2ND BOY: Tell us, please . . . tell us, please . . . who are *you*?

SPRITES (*Dancing out*): We're the rollicking sprites of May,
the frolicking, jollicking,
merry, symbolicking,
lollicking sprites of May. (*They do the "Golliwog's Cake Walk," or some other amusing dance.*)

1ST GIRL: We're looking for flowers
for a spring bouquet
to bring to Her Highness,
the Queen of May.
But there *aren't* any flowers that we can see.

SPRITES (*Teasing*): No flowers? What a cat-cat-catastrophe!

1ST SPRITE: Speaking of *cats*,
  why don't you look
  in the nook by the crook
  of the May Day brook? (*Points*)
  There, by the willow tree.
2ND SPRITE: Count to three, and what do you see?
SPRITES: What do you, what do you, what do you see?
2ND BOY (*Going to look*): I see a cat!
  And he looks so lonely,
  all by himself, just one-and only.
  But there isn't a *flower* that I can see . . .
SPRITES (*Laughing*): Oh, what a cat-cat-catastrophe!
1ST SPRITE: How lonely the poor little cat must be.
2ND SPRITE: He'd blossom forth, as sure as he lives,
  if we gave him a couple of relatives.
SPRITES: And you'd have something for your bouquet
  to bring to the Queen of May!
2ND GIRL: What are you saying?
1ST BOY: They're only frolicking.
SPRITES (*Dancing around*): Rollicking, jollicking, and
  symbolicking some of the fun of May.
1ST SPRITE (*To children*): What are relatives?
  Rub your chin,
  scratch your head so your brains will spin.
2ND SPRITE: What are relatives?
  Come, you'll win
  if you think of a word that rhymes with *pin*.
BOYS *and* GIRLS: Kin!
SPRITES: Kin. You guessed it.
  The cat shall play
  with some of his *kin* this very day,
  and you'll have something for your bouquet
  this frolicking morning in May. (4TH SPRITE *goes out
  and returns with several toy cats while others dance.*)

Wave your hands and take a spin,
here's the way that flowers begin:
take a cat and add some kin (*They put toy cats near
tree*),
rollicky, jollicky . . . there, you see?
Catkin flowers on the willow tree!
BOYS *and* GIRLS (*Excited*): The prettiest flowers we've
seen today.
Catkin flowers for the Queen of May. (*They "pick"
some catkins that have been hidden in the tree.*)
SPRITES (*Teasing*): Not any flowers from floor to attic—
that's what you said. And so emphatic!
You surely looked *cowed* when you lost your way
and couldn't find flowers for the Queen's bouquet.
But you mustn't look *cowed* wherever you stray
on a lollicking morning in May.
2ND SPRITE: Speaking of *cows* . . .
You see that bush?
Give its branches a little push,
count to three and what do you see?
SPRITES: What do you, what do you, what do you see?
1ST BOY (*Going to look*): I see a cow . . .
a nice red and white one,
a very polite one,
a more-than-all-right one.
It may have a wonderful family tree,
but it isn't a *flower* that I can see.
SPRITES (*Dancing*): It may have a wonderful family
tree,
but it isn't a flower that he can see!
3RD SPRITE: A cow is a flower that cuts quite a caper,
if we slip it a slip of our magical paper.
2ND GIRL: What do you say?
1ST BOY: They're only frolicking.

SPRITES: Jollicking, rollicking, and symbolicking
  some of the fun of May.
3RD SPRITE: You shall have flowers for your bouquet
  to bring to the Queen of May. (*Skips out and returns
  waving a slip of paper. Joins others in wand dance.*)
SPRITES: Wave your wands as woodsprites should.
  Weave a spell that's understood,
  give a cow a magic slip
  and bring it to Her Ladyship.
BOYS and GIRLS: *Cowslip!*
SPRITES: You guessed it. (*Teasingly*)
  You just need some slyness
  combined with some spryness and rollicking wryness,
  and you'll get some posies to bring to Her Highness.
  (BOYS *and* GIRLS *"pick" cowslips hidden behind
  bush.*)
1ST GIRL: Cowslips and catkins
  so springlike and gay
  to put in a suitable, stylish bouquet.
OTHERS: This shiny bright morning in May.
SPRITES: Off you go on a May Day morning,
  a May Day morning in May,
  to see a world that is just a-borning,
  and foolishly lose your way,
  and say there isn't a flower adorning
  the place where you chance to stray!
1ST GIRL: There wasn't a blossom, not even a few,
1ST BOY: There wasn't a blossom, not one or two,
2ND GIRL: There wasn't a blossom, half-gone or new,
2ND BOY: There wasn't a blossom, till we met *you.*
BOYS *and* GIRLS: And now we have catkins and cowslips
    to lay
  at the feet of Her Highness, the Queen of May,
  this rollicking, lollicking day.

1ST SPRITE: We dance in the wildwood
   when winter is through
2ND SPRITE: We hear catkins purr
   and we hear cowslips moo.
3RD SPRITE: When anyone comes
   we can fade like a spark.
4TH SPRITE: That's why we find life
   such a wonderful lark!
SPRITES: A jollicking, frolicking lark.
1ST SPRITE: Speaking of *larks*, why don't you go
   tiptoe, and slow,
   where the boulders show
   and the grasses grow
   by the poplar tree,
   and count to three?
SPRITES: What do you, what do you, what do you see?
1ST GIRL: My word! A bird!
   With a flute-like note.
1ST BOY: And a yellow throat,
2ND GIRL: With a curved black mark.
2ND BOY: Feathers the color of mottled bark.
BOYS *and* GIRLS: It must be, it must be a meadowlark.
SPRITES (*Dancing*): Oh, what a lark to be a lark
   in the wood-sprites' park
   from dawn to dark!
2ND BOY: There's a lark, all right, by the poplar tree,
   but there isn't a *flower* that we can see.
1ST SPRITE: There isn't a flower, you say again.
2ND SPRITE: Your wits have got in the way again.
3RD SPRITE: It's time for us to display again
   some blossoms to fill your bouquet again.
4TH SPRITE (*To children*): Watch the lark so it doesn't
      stir.
   All we need is a magic spur
   To put on the feet of him (or her).
   (*Goes out*)

2ND BOY: What do they say?

1ST GIRL: They're only frolicking.

SPRITES: Jollicking! Rollicking! Just symbolicking some of the fun of May. (4TH SPRITE *comes back, bends over "lark" in grass.*)

SPRITES (*Dancing*): Wave your wands and twirl and spin,

that's the way the flowers begin.

Take a lark and add a spur,

watch the flowers begin to stir.

BOYS *and* GIRLS: Larkspur!

SPRITES: You guessed it.

Now pick some and test it. (*Children "pick" some larkspur previously hidden.*)

1ST GIRL: It's bright and gay

for our spring bouquet.

1ST BOY: Catkins, and cowslips, and larkspur—all three!

2ND GIRL: The essence of spring for Her Highness to see.

2ND BOY: And so *unexpected*—by you and by me.

SPRITES: When you go out on a May Day morning,

a May Day morning in May,

you must expect, with the world a–borning,

some magical kind of play.

You must expect, though you lose your way,

to gather a beautiful spring bouquet.

BOYS *and* GIRLS: When we go out on a frolicking,

jollicking,

rollicking

morning in May!

THE END

PRODUCTION NOTES
ALL ON A DAY IN MAY

Characters: 2 male; 2 female; Wood Sprites may be male and female. If desired there can be additional Boys, Girls and Wood Sprites, and the parts should be redistributed accordingly.

Playing Time: 10 minutes.

Costumes: Boys and Girls wear modern, everyday dress. Female Wood Sprites could wear long flowing light-green or light-brown costumes. Male Wood Sprites could wear green and brown elf costumes.

Properties: Artificial flowers for the May Queen's bouquet (catkins, cowslips and larkspur), several toy cats, slip of paper.

Setting: The edge of a wood. Cardboard bushes and trees are placed about the stage. Flowers for the May Queen's bouquet are hidden in the bushes or behind them.

Lighting: No special effects.

May Day Song

ALL: Who wants to dance a Maypole dance?
Today's the first of May!

GIRL: "We'd like to if we had a chance,"
the cherry blossoms say.

BOY: And so the wind begins to blow,
and up and down the blossoms go,
dancing with a dip and sway
upon the first of May.

ALL: Who wants to leave a May Day flower
at someone's door today?

GIRL: "We'd like to if we had the power,"
the cherry blossoms say.

BOY: And so the wind begins to blow
more blustery, and blossoms go
to scatter petals all the way

ALL: Along the streets of May!

155

Mother's Day
(2nd Sunday in May)

Time for Mom

Characters

KEVIN
PATSY
SAM
DEBBIE
MOLLY
JANIE
MOM
DAD
BOYS ⎱ *extras*
GIRLS ⎰

TIME: *Early May.*
SETTING: *A street. May be played before curtain.* KEVIN,
PATSY, SAM, DEBBIE, MOLLY, *and* BOYS *and* GIRLS
enter. Some have roller skates, others jump ropes,

balls, marbles, etc. They sing to tune of "My Bonnie Lies Over the Ocean":

ALL (*Singing*):

Oh, May is a wonderful season,

Of May we sing this little rhyme.

There's more than one jolly good reason

Why May is a jolly good time.

May brings spring things (*They jump rope, etc.*)

And school soon is over and through, and through,

May brings spring things

And May brings us Mother's Day, too.

KEVIN (*Stopping play*): It's almost Mother's Day! And I can't think of anything different to give my Mom. I've worn out my brains.

PATSY (*Teasing*): Which brains do you mean, Kevin? (*She giggles.*)

KEVIN: You can laugh if you want to, Patsy, but I can't think of a single good present to get with a dollar and fifteen cents.

PATSY (*Seriously*): Oh, that's different. What about Janie? Has she thought of anything?

KEVIN: No, but at least Janie has six cents more than I do. Last year we pooled our money and bought Mom a box of candy. But even if we put our money together this year, we couldn't get much of a box for only $2.36!

SAM: What about fish hooks? You can get plenty of those for $2.36, with a couple of sinkers thrown in.

KEVIN (*Exasperated*): Sam! My mother hates fishing! (*To* PATSY) Besides, Mom's on a diet, so candy probably isn't a good idea.

DEBBIE: My mother's always on a diet, but I'm giving her candy anyway—then I'll be able to eat it!

SAM: I have my eye on a model airplane kit for my mother.

MOLLY: You would, Sam! She'll love that about as much

as fish hooks. Why don't you think of something *she'd* like, for a change?

KEVIN: Do you have any good ideas for Mother's Day presents, Molly?

MOLLY: Well, I'm getting my mother flower seeds. You could get all kinds of them for $2.36, and your mother could have beautiful flowers all summer long.

KEVIN: But we live in an apartment, remember? We don't have a yard.

SAM: That's O.K. Get a flower box and stick it on the windowsill.

KEVIN: But we don't have enough money for seeds *and* a flower box.

DEBBIE (*Helpfully*): Well, then, how about handkerchiefs? Or perfume . . . or a memo pad for the telephone?

KEVIN: Those are all good gifts, Debbie, but we want to give Mom something different this year—something really special.

DEBBIE: You have awfully big ideas for such little money, Kevin. (*Turns to* PATSY) What are you giving your mother, Patsy?

PATSY: A scarf. A silk scarf with flowers and things on it. My Aunt Elizabeth helped me pick it out. She works at the store, so we got a discount. (*To other* GIRLS) Come on home with me and I'll show it to you. It's *beautiful!* (PATSY, DEBBIE, MOLLY *and* GIRLS *jump rope or skate out.*)

KEVIN (*Sighing*): Thinking's the hardest thing I do. And I don't seem to get anywhere.

SAM: Cheer up, Kevin. You'll think of something. . . . How about a couple of magazines from the supermarket?

KEVIN: My mother doesn't have much time to read, between working and taking care of our apartment and us kids.

SAM: Well, don't try to be so different, Kevin. (*Looks offstage*) Here comes your sister. Maybe she's thought of something. See you later. (*Exits, followed by* BOYS. *After a moment,* JANIE *enters.*)

KEVIN: Hi, Janie. Did you think of anything for Mom?

JANIE (*Excitedly*): I sure did. I've thought of something Mom would like more than anything else!

KEVIN: What is it?

JANIE: It's something we can't buy.

KEVIN (*Sarcastically*): That's a big help.

JANIE: But we can give it to her without buying it.

KEVIN: You mean we wouldn't have to spend $2.36?

JANIE: Right. We'll just have to spend some time and thought on it, that's all. And it'll go a long way, in small portions.

KEVIN (*Puzzled*): I still don't get it. What do you mean, small portions?

JANIE: Come on home, and I'll tell you all about it. (*They exit. Curtain*)

* * *

SCENE 2

TIME: *Mother's Day.*

SETTING: *Dining room. Table with four place settings and chairs is center. Baby's high chair may be added, if desired.*

AT RISE: *Noises—as if from kitchen—are heard offstage.* KEVIN *and* JANIE *tiptoe in carefully, look around, put small wrapped packages at one place at table.*

JANIE (*Calling off*): Need any help, Mom? (*Exits. After a moment,* DAD *enters with large package.*)

KEVIN: What did you get Mom for Mother's Day, Dad? You said you wanted to get her something different— something other than flowers.

DAD: And that I did, Kevin. (*Pats package*) I got her books. Art books.

KEVIN: Art books?

DAD: Your mother's always had a secret desire to draw and paint. I think she'd be quite artistic if she spent some time at it.

KEVIN: Does it take a lot of time?

DAD: Well, sure. You always have to work hard when you're trying to learn new things, and painting is no exception.

KEVIN: Gee, Mom's awfully busy, Dad. When she's not at the office she's taking care of the baby, or washing clothes, or cooking dinner, or baking cookies for us— stuff like that. I don't think she'll have any time to learn how to draw and paint.

DAD (*Musing*): You know, you're right, Kevin. I thought of something she'd like to do, but I didn't think of where she was going to find time to do it. (*After a pause*) That was pretty thoughtless of me. Maybe the books will just make her feel bad.

KEVIN: Don't worry, Dad. Cheer up! Wait till you see what Janie and I have for Mom. (MOM *and* JANIE *enter, with dishes.*)

JANIE, KEVIN *and* DAD (*Together*): Happy Mother's Day!

MOM (*Noticing gifts*): Is all this for *me?*

KEVIN: All for you, Mom. Dad's is the big one. You have to open that last.

JANIE: Ours are the little ones, and they're sort of alike. Open them, Mom!

MOM (*Picking up small package, reading tag*): To Mom, with love from Janie. (*Begins to open it*)

DAD: Looks like tickets of some sort.

MOM: What in the world? (*She holds up strips of cardboard with writing on them.*)

KEVIN: Read what it says, Mom.

MOM (*Reading*):
Dear Mom, this ticket you will see
Is worth two meals, to you from me.

(*Puzzled*) Two meals?

JANIE: Whenever you want time for something, Mom, I'll get dinner—from beginning to end. That includes doing dishes, and everything. You just tell me what to get.

MOM: How wonderful! (*Takes another ticket, reads*)
Dear Mom, you have some things, I trust,
That you would rather do than dust.
This ticket will entitle you
To seven dustings—good ones, too.

JANIE: See the numbers 1 to 7 along the bottom? Every time you want me to dust, I'll punch out a number, just like a conductor.

MOM (*Happily*): I can't think of anything I'd rather have than time to do a few things I never get around to. (*Looks at other tickets*) And here are tickets for babysitting . . . and washing dishes . . . and straightening up the living room . . . and setting the table. (*Looks up*) Thank you, Janie! How clever of you!

KEVIN: Open mine, Mom!

MOM (*Taking other small package*): Oh, I hope it's more tickets, Kevin! I hope it's a present of more time! How did you ever think of it?

KEVIN: We wanted to give you something different. And Janie figured out if you had some time to yourself, that would be different!

MOM (*Reading one of* KEVIN's *tickets*):
Dear Mom, this ticket means I'll run
Twenty errands, not just one.

KEVIN: See the twenty numbers around the edges to punch out?

MOM (*Reading another*):
Dear Mom, the grass could not be greener.
Go look . . . I'll run the vacuum cleaner.
(*Laughing*) Why, you're going to spoil me completely!

I'll have so much time on my hands I won't know what to do with it.

DAD (*Beaming*): Oh, yes you will! (*Points to large package*) Look and see.

MOM (*Opening package*): Now, what could this be? (*Holds up books; delighted*) Art books! How wonderful! How did you know I've always wanted to try to draw and paint? (*Hugs* DAD) Thank you!

DAD: Well, thanks to our ingenious children, now you'll have time to try your hand at it.

MOM: I can't tell you all how happy I am! Thank you!

KEVIN, JANE, *and* DAD (*Singing to the tune of "My Bonnie Lies Over The Ocean"*):

Oh, May is a wonderful season,
Of May we sing this little rhyme.
There's more than one jolly good reason
Why May is a jolly good time.
May brings spring things
And presents for people like you, like you. (*Nod at* MOM)
May brings spring things
And May brings us Mother's Day, too! (*Curtain*)

THE END

PRODUCTION NOTES
TIME FOR MOM

Characters: 3 male; 5 female; male and female extras.
Playing Time: 10 minutes.
Costumes: Modern everyday dress. Mom wears apron.
Properties: Jump ropes; roller skates; marbles; balls, etc.; 2 gift-wrapped packets of "tickets"; 2 or 3 large books, gift-wrapped; breakfast dishes.
Setting: Scene 1: a street. May be played before curtain. Scene 2: the dining room. A table with tablecloth and 4 place settings surrounded by 4 chairs stands near stage center. A baby's high chair may be added, if desired. There is an exit leading to kitchen.

That's the Way Mothers Are

GIRLS: What did she want for Mother's Day?,
we asked when we were tiny.
A pile of sand where it's fun to play,
and a bucket new and shiny!

ALL: That's the way mothers are.

BOYS: What did she want for Mother's Day?,
we asked when we were older.
A camping kit and a water bag
and a knapsack for her shoulder!

ALL: That's the way mothers are.

GIRLS: What did she want? Not anything
as frail as flowers or candy!
But a good strong rope (for a good strong swing),
or a bobsled would be handy!

ALL: That's the way mothers are.

GIRLS: Now that we've found her out, at last,
(after these years, who wouldn't?),
we're making up for her "sandpile" past . . .
though she always says we shouldn't!

ALL: That's the way mothers are.

For Mother's Day

1ST: What can we do
for Mother's Day?

2ND: Carry her breakfast
on a tray.

3RD: Wash the dishes
and shine the pots.

ALL: Give her a hug
and love her LOTS.

163

Better Than A Calendar

1ST BOY: Any errands? Mom, I'll run
as fast as I am able.

1ST GIRL: Let me water all the plants
and set the dinner table!

2ND BOY: I can clean the storage room,
eager as a beaver . . .

MOTHER: Children, is there something wrong?
Do you have a *fever*?

2ND GIRL: Where's the list? I'll tend to it
at the supermarket.

3RD BOY (*To* 2ND GIRL): You can use my bicycle.
Careful how you park it!

3RD GIRL: Do the spoons need polishing,
and the silver platter?

MOTHER: All this sudden thoughtfulness . . .
Goodness, what's the matter?

1ST BOY: There's the bell. I'll answer it . . .

2ND BOY: Any shoes for shining?

1ST GIRL: I'll sew Daddy's buttons on
and fix his jacket lining.

MOTHER: Children, you astonish me!
Such fervor sets me humming . . .
you're better than a calendar
to tell what day is coming!

ALL: MOTHER'S DAY!

Mother's Day

If we could trade places
I'll bet you a penny
you'd see that *my* mother
was better than any!

164

Memorial Day
(May 30)

Memorial Day Parade

Flags are out at the courthouse
and all along the street,
bands keep time with the shush, shush, shush
of scores of marching feet,

Ranks of old men, young men,
in khaki, blue, and gray,
shoulders straight and eyes ahead,
are marching past today.

Streets are lined with watchers
praying that wars will cease,
that all the countries in the world
will join to keep the peace.

Sing Out for Peace

ALL: Swing out, oh bells,
sing out, oh bells,
our prayer that strife be ended,
GIRLS: that guns be still
on plain and hill
BOYS: and all our discords mended.
GIRLS: Let weapons turn to plowshares now
and fighting planes be grounded
BOYS: as through the air of Everywhere
the words of peace are sounded.
ALL: Ring out, oh bells,
swing out, oh bells,
sing out from every steeple
GIRLS: the burning hope
the yearning hope
for peace by weary people.
BOYS: Let understanding be our aim,
the goal for which we're heading,
ALL: as through the earth a strong rebirth
of brotherhood starts spreading.

JUNE

Oh,—— say, can you see,——

Flag Day
(June 14)

Long May It Wave

Characters

JUDGE JOSEPH H. NICHOLSON
BECKY, *his wife*
DORCAS, *a maid*
FRANCIS SCOTT KEY
CHORUS, *any number of boys and girls*

TIME: *Morning of September 15, 1814.*
SETTING: *Breakfast room of* JUDGE NICHOLSON's *house in Baltimore.*
AT RISE: JUDGE *and* BECKY *are just finishing breakfast.*
BECKY: Oh, it's good to have you back safe and sound, Joseph! All Tuesday night I lay awake listening to that terrible bombardment from the British fleet, and wondering about you at the Fort.

168

JUDGE: All Tuesday night I not only listened to the bombardment, but I watched it from within the Fort . . . cannon flashes, rockets, bombs bursting in air. I wondered how good old Fort McHenry could take such a pounding and survive. But, thank God, it did survive! Becky, the night of September 13, 1814, will go down in history as the noisiest night in the War of 1812.

BECKY: It must have been dreadful there at the Fort.

JUDGE: We didn't know if we could keep the flag flying or not. (*Excited*) But we did! We did!

BECKY: Long may it wave, Joseph.

JUDGE: I'm glad I got there in time with my company of volunteers. We kept the guns hot, I can tell you. And I'm sure we did a great deal of damage to the British landing troops. (*Drains his coffee cup*) Any more coffee?

BECKY: Dorcas is keeping it hot. (*Rings bell.* DORCAS *appears at door.*) More coffee for the Judge, Dorcas. (DORCAS *exits, returns in a moment with coffeepot, pours coffee for Judge.*) Are you sure it's good and hot, Dorcas?

DORCAS: Yes'm. Piping hot.

JUDGE: Strong! I'm more interested in having it strong. I still haven't caught up on my sleep.

DORCAS (*Giggling*): Strong enough to swim across Chesapeake Bay, Judge Your Honor. And back again. (*Giggling, she goes out.*)

JUDGE: Did you hear from that brother-in-law of yours, Becky, while I was gone?

BECKY: Francis? No, I didn't, and I'm worried. The last I knew he was arranging for a vessel to take him out to the British fleet under a flag of truce. He was getting a Mr. Skinner to go along.

JUDGE (*Nodding*): Skinner is government agent for flags of truce and exchange of prisoners. Francis was sent from Washington to try to get his friend Dr. Beanes released as a prisoner of war.

BECKY: But that was days ago. I'm worried.

JUDGE (*Consolingly*): Francis is a gifted young lawyer. If anyone could get a prisoner released, he could. I trust he returned to Baltimore before the attack.

BECKY: But surely he would have been in touch with us, wouldn't he, Joseph? He'd know we'd be concerned. Do you think something might have happened to him?

JUDGE (*Doubtfully*): He was under a flag of truce. It's possible, of course, that the British detained him until the attack was over.

BECKY: My poor sister must be beside herself with worry. I wish Georgetown weren't so hard to get to. I'd go comfort her. (*Doorbell rings loudly.* DORCAS *passes through breakfast room to answer it.*) I wonder who it can be, so early in the morning.

JUDGE: A message from the Court, perhaps. I've been rather out of touch with things the last few days.

BECKY: I'm glad you were out of touch with some of those bombs bursting in air! (DORCAS *returns, walking center.*)

DORCAS: It's Mr. Francis Scott Key, wondering if it's too early to call.

BECKY: Francis! Have him come right in, Dorcas. (DORCAS *exits.*)

JUDGE: By all means. I'm relieved he's back. (DORCAS *returns in a moment, followed by* FRANCIS SCOTT KEY.)

BECKY: Francis, I'm so happy to see you!

JUDGE (*Shaking hands with* FRANCIS): Glad you're here, Francis.

FRANCIS: No happier than I am, Judge.

BECKY: Bring another cup of coffee, Dorcas. And some rolls.

FRANCIS: Just coffee, thank you. I had my breakfast at the hotel. (DORCAS *exits.*)

BECKY: When did you get back to Baltimore, Francis?

FRANCIS: I got back yesterday evening and went directly to the hotel. (*Hesitates*) I had something on my mind I wanted to finish . . .

JUDGE: I just got back last evening myself. From Fort McHenry.

FRANCIS (*Surprised*): Fort McHenry? As a judge, aren't you exempt from military service, Joseph?

JUDGE: When I heard the British fleet was planning to attack the Fort, I was glad to take command of a volunteer company of artillery. We were in the thick of the bombardment.

FRANCIS: And what a bombardment. I'll never forget it as long as I live.

JUDGE: Nor I. (DORCAS *enters, carrying tray with coffee, gives it to* FRANCIS, *and exits.*)

FRANCIS: I didn't sleep a wink all night. (BECKY *and* JUDGE *look at each other and smile.*) Mr. Skinner and I arranged for the release of my friend Dr. Beanes, all right, but by that time, it was too late to get back to shore. The British were ready to start their bombardment. Admiral Cochrane put our vessel under British guard and made us wait until the fight was over.

JUDGE: So you saw everything?

FRANCIS: From the British side. We were anchored so we could see the flag on Fort McHenry from the deck of our vessel. I watched every rocket, every bomb. How I strained my eyes into the dawn's early light to see if the flag was still there!

BECKY: You should have written a poem about it, Francis, with your knack of versifying.

FRANCIS (*Taken aback*): A poem . . . (*Humbly*) I've never taken my verse-making very seriously, you know. But . . . (*Takes paper from pocket*) . . . I *did*

171

write something. In fact, that's what brought me here so early this morning, to ask what you thought of it. It was written under the excitement of the bombardment.

BECKY: As you watched during the night?

FRANCIS: I kept putting down lines . . . phrases . . . words . . . on the back of an old envelope. Others I stored in the back of my head. Then yesterday afternoon when the British gave up the fight and prepared to sail away—and gave us permission to go back to Baltimore—I wrote a rough draft of the poem as we crossed the Bay. Last night at the hotel I finished it. I'm not sure how good it is, but I felt it pounding in my temples all night as I paced the deck, trying to get a glimpse of our flag that had been waving proudly in the last gleams of twilight. (*Hands the* JUDGE *the paper*)

BECKY: Read it aloud, Joseph.

JUDGE (*Reading*):

"Oh, say can you see, by the dawn's early light,
What so proudly we hailed at the twilight's last gleaming?
Whose broad stripes and bright stars, through the perilous fight,
O'er the ramparts we watched were so gallantly streaming!"

(*He looks up, exicted.*) Francis, it has a wonderful rhythm. Did you have a tune in mind when you wrote it?

FRANCIS: Not consciously. Though there did seem to be a melody running through my mind as I wrote it, like an undertone.

JUDGE (*Drumming on tablecloth as he repeats first few lines*): I think the words would fit beautifully to that tune that is so popular these days—"To Anacreon in Heaven." (*Drums and ta-dums some more*) Yes, I'm

172

sure they do. You probably had the tune in mind without realizing it, Francis.

FRANCIS: It's possible. But the words, Joseph. Do you see anything in the words? Do you, Becky?

BECKY (*Eagerly*): They're wonderful! (*Leans over, reads*) "And the rockets' red glare, the bombs bursting in air, Gave proof through the night that our flag was still there." Oh, and it *was* still there!

JUDGE (*Excited*): Yes. Yes. You've said just what I felt, too, Francis.

JUDGE AND BECKY (*Half-singing*):
"Oh, say, does that star-spangled banner yet wave
O'er the land of the free, and the home of the brave?"

JUDGE (*Jumping up*): Francis, this is the best thing you've ever written. It's stirring. It's splendid. The people of Baltimore must know about this. I'm going to take it right down to the *Baltimore American* and get them to run off some handbills.

BECKY: It will be all over town before noon. Everybody will be singing it!

FRANCIS: Don't put my name on it. Just say it was by a lawyer from Washington, written in honor of the gallant defense of Fort McHenry.

JUDGE (*On his way, turning at door*): Your name must go on, and the tune to which the words can be sung. The people of Baltimore, all the people in the United States must know about this! The star spangled banner . . . (JUDGE *hurries out. As curtain falls,* CHORUS *marches in, in front of it, singing.*)

BOYS:
"On the shore, dimly seen through the mists of the deep,
Where the foe's haughty host in dread silence reposes,
What is that which the breeze, o'er the towering steep,
As it fitfully blows, half conceals, half discloses?"

GIRLS:

"Now it catches the gleam of the morning's first beam,
In full glory reflected now shines on the stream;"

ALL:

" 'Tis the star-spangled banner; oh, long may it wave
O'er the land of the free and the home of the brave!"

BOYS:

"Oh, thus be it ever when freemen shall stand
Between their loved homes and the war's desolation!"

GIRLS:

"Blest with vict'ry and peace, may the heaven-rescued
   land
Praise the Pow'r that hath made and preserved us a
   nation."

ALL:

"Then conquer we must, when our cause it is just,
And this be our motto: 'IN GOD IS OUR TRUST!'
And the star-spangled banner in triumph shall wave
O'er the land of the free and the home of the brave."

THE END

PRODUCTION NOTES
LONG MAY IT WAVE

Characters: 2 male; 2 female; male and female extras for Chorus.
Playing Time: 10 minutes.
Costumes: All wear costumes typical of the period. Dorcas wears a white
   cap and apron. The Chorus may wear red, white and blue costumes.
Properties: Breakfast dishes, including cups and saucers; coffee pot; paper.
Setting: A breakfast room. The only necessary furnishings are a table and
   chairs. Other furnishings—a chest, candlesticks, etc.—may be added, if
   desired. The table should be set for breakfast with china, silver, linen
   napkins, etc.
Lighting: No special effects.

A Star for Old Glory

Characters

BETSY ROSS
SALLY
ANN } *children next door*
JANE
UNCLE GEORGE ROSS
TWO COMMITTEEMEN

TIME: *Afternoon of June 16, 1777.*

SETTING: *The Ross upholstery shop on Arch Street in Philadelphia. There are several old chairs around the room, with a sitting chair and table center right. Paper and scissors are on table. Door right leads to street. Door at rear leads to back.*

AT RISE: BETSY ROSS, *a vivacious young woman, is working on an easy chair.* SALLY, JANE *and* ANN *enter.*

SALLY: Are you busy, Mrs. Ross?

BETSY: Quite busy, Sally. I'm trying to fix this old easy chair for Uncle George Ross. And I must say this stuffing is very stubborn.

ANN: He's in the Continental Congress, isn't he? The uncle who signed the Declaration of Independence?

BETSY: Yes. My husband's famous Uncle George. I

175

promised him that the chair would be ready by Wednesday.

JANE: But it's only Monday, Mrs. Ross.

BETSY: I know, but I have other things to work on besides Uncle George's chair. Since my husband died, and I have to run the shop by myself, I never get caught up. . . . With the war on, and no more chairs coming from England, and prices so high and all, it seems everyone is having chairs reupholstered instead of buying new ones.

SALLY: That's why we want to make a doily.

ANN: For our mother's birthday.

JANE: And we haven't any money to buy one.

BETSY: What kind of doily were you thinking of?

SALLY: We can come back some other time, Mrs. Ross, when you aren't so busy.

BETSY (*Turning from her work on the chair*): Let's sit down and figure out what you want. I'm never too busy to talk to my neighbors. Really, I'm not. (*All sit.*)

JANE: You start to help us, and you'll forget all about the stuffing for the chair.

BETSY: I know. (*Laughs*) But it's so much more fun to make patterns for samplers and doll clothes—and doilies. What's that you have behind your back, Ann?

ANN (*Holding up pattern of large, very lopsided star*): Can you guess?

BETSY (*Cocking her head*): It has very long points. Or are they legs? Or both? Perhaps two ears, two legs, and a nose.

GIRLS (*Giggling*): It's a *star*, Mrs. Ross.

BETSY: You don't say. I didn't recognize it.

SALLY: It's the best we could do.

ANN: We thought a star would be a nice shape for a new doily on Mamma's round table. We'll embroider it with fancy stitches.

JANE: If we can make it look like a star.

BETSY: What a lovely idea! A star-shaped doily. (*Takes star*) Here, let me see what's wrong with your pattern.

SALLY: There must be some way to make a star so it doesn't look like a lopsided dog!

BETSY: I was very good at cutting out stars when I was young. But now I'm so old, I wonder if I can remember.

ANN: Are you so very old, Mrs. Ross?

BETSY: Oh, dear, yes. Twenty-five. Practically twenty-five and a half.

JANE (*Soberly*): That is old, isn't it? But maybe you can remember how to make them if you think very hard.

BETSY (*Picking up piece of paper and scissors from table*): Let's see. A star. Hm-m-m. There's a certain way to fold the paper, but I'm not sure just how. I used to cut two triangles, the same length on each side. (*Folds paper and cuts two triangles at same time*) There. You see, two equal-sided triangles. Now, put one over the other, like this, so the points stick out, and what do you have?

SALLY: Why, it's a six-pointed star.

JANE: And all the points are the same size.

ANN: You aren't too old, after all, Mrs. Ross—to remember all that. May we use the pattern for our doily?

BETSY: Of course.

JANE (*Hesitating*): But, there are only five of us in the family: Mamma, Papa, and the three of us. If it could be a five-pointed star, then one point would stand for each of us. A six-pointed star doesn't stand for anything.

BETSY (*Thoughtfully*): There's something to what you say, Jane.

SALLY: Do you know how to make a five-pointed star, Mrs. Ross? A nice even one like that?

BETSY: There's a special way to fold the paper. But I haven't needed to make stars in such a long time. . . . (*Takes paper and folds*)

ANN: I hope you can remember.

BETSY (*Trying various folds*): Let's see if I can figure out the folds. (*Girls watch intently.*) If we make a five-pointed star by a roundabout method first, then we'll know how to do it next time. Triangles won't do this time. We'll need arrowheads, as I remember. Two pointed heads with forked tails, like this (*Snips paper*). Now put them over each other so the tail-points overlap at one place.

GIRLS: Oh!

BETSY: You see, five points. (*Still experimenting*) Now I see how to fold the paper. Four times, and snip!

SALLY: A beautiful five-pointed star. It's much prettier than the six-pointed one, isn't it? Because the points aren't so squat.

JANE: May we use the pattern? It will make a lovely doily. (*Sound of hoof beats on the cobblestones outside.* SALLY *hurries to look out window.*)

SALLY: Oh, an elegant coach is stopping in front of the shop. Drawn by four dapple-gray horses.

BETSY: In front of the shop?

SALLY: Right in front.

BETSY: Heavens! (*Gets up hurriedly*) I wonder who it can be. (*Looks out window*) Why, it's Uncle George. (*Flustered*) And I'm not nearly finished with his chair.

ANN (*Looking*): And another gentleman is getting out, too.

JANE: And another!

BETSY: Dear me! Pick up all the scraps, girls—and hurry! Then slip out the back door. (*Handing pattern to* JANE) Here, here's your pattern. (*Nervously,* BETSY *fixes her hair, then turns to work on chair.*

Girls pick up scraps and all exit rear. After a moment, UNCLE GEORGE *and* TWO COMMITTEEMEN *enter through front.*)

UNCLE: Good afternoon, Elizabeth.

BETSY: Why, Uncle George, I'm glad to see you, but I'm sorry to say your chair isn't finished yet.

UNCLE: I haven't come about the chair, Elizabeth. (*Turns to men*) Gentlemen, this is my niece, Elizabeth Griscom Ross. Her father helped build the State House here in Philadelphia, where Congress has been meeting. (*Turns to* BETSY) Elizabeth, these men are members of a Congressional Committee.

BETSY: A Congressional Committee! Do be seated, gentlemen. (*Fussing*) Please excuse the looks of my workroom. When I have everything to tend to myself, I'm afraid . . .

UNCLE: As chairman of the Committee, it occurred to me that you might be a good person to consult, considering your years of experience with needle and thread.

BETSY: About what, Uncle George?

UNCLE (*Importantly*): Have you ever made a flag?

BETSY: No, I don't believe I ever have.

UNCLE: Do you think you could?

BETSY (*Thinking*): Make a flag? I don't see why not, Uncle George. It shouldn't be too difficult. Depending on the flag, of course.

UNCLE: Congress finally selected a design for a national flag two days ago, on the 14th.

1ST COMMITTEEMAN: It's about time. Long overdue!

UNCLE: We can't have every state flying a flag of its own, when we are all united to fight this war. We can't have Massachusetts hoisting a flag with a pine tree, and South Carolina one with a rattlesnake, and New York one with a beaver, and Rhode Island one with a blue anchor.

2ND COMMITTEEMAN: That would be ridiculous!

BETSY: But I thought there was a Continental Flag, one for all the states, Uncle George. Haven't I seen a flag with thirteen red and white stripes, and the British Union Jack in the corner, with the crosses of St. George and St. Andrew?

UNCLE: Yes, Elizabeth, we have been flying that flag since the beginning of 1776, and that flag makes me hot under the collar every time I see it. The Union Jack, indeed!

2ND COMMITTEEMAN: It was all right to include the British symbol when we were still colonies and felt loyalty to the Crown. But since our Declaration of Independence, that flag has been out of place, to say the least.

1ST COMMITTEEMAN: We need a flag of our own. A flag of independence.

UNCLE: Last Saturday, Congress adopted a flag resolution, Elizabeth. (*Takes slip of paper out of pocket, and reads*) "Resolved that the flag of the United States shall be thirteen stripes, alternate red and white, with a union of thirteen stars of white on a blue field, representing a new constellation."

BETSY: A new constellation—a group of stars standing for our new country! How wonderful!

1ST COMMITTEEMAN: One for each state.

UNCLE (*Handing paper to her*): Here, Elizabeth, is a rough design of the plan. (*Pointing*) You see the thirteen stripes, and here in the corner, thirteen stars on a blue field. It has been suggested that the stars be arranged in a circle.

BETSY: The design shows six-pointed stars.

UNCLE: Yes, they look a bit squat, don't they? But they said they'd be much easier to make.

BETSY (*Examining design*): A five-pointed star is much more interesting, gentlemen. With longer points . . .

1ST COMMITTEEMAN: But isn't it difficult to make five-pointed stars?

BETSY: It's not difficult at all. I used to make them when I was a child. (*Takes paper, folds it four times, snips and holds up five-pointed star, like the pattern she cut out for the girls. Note: Pattern can be all arranged beforehand, if desired.* UNCLE *takes star and holds it up.*)

UNCLE: Amazing! A perfect star. I was sure you'd be the one to consult, Elizabeth.

2ND COMMITTEEMAN: Marvelous! A perfect five-pointed star, and you did it so quickly, Mrs. Ross.

UNCLE: By all means make up the flag with five-pointed stars. (*Turns*) Don't you agree, gentlemen?

1ST COMMITTEEMAN: Yes, yes. They're so much more elegant.

UNCLE: Will you be able to make it soon? It's a disgrace to use the old Continental flag one day longer than necessary.

BETSY (*Doubtfully*): Well, Uncle, your chair . . .

UNCLE: There's no hurry about my chair, Elizabeth. No hurry at all.

BETSY: In that case, I can start the flag immediately.

UNCLE: Good!

2ND COMMITTEEMAN: Excellent. The sooner, the better.

UNCLE (*Smiling*): A flag of our own, with thirteen stars representing a new constellation—a brilliant new constellation. I am sure that is not too much to say of the United States of America. Well, Elizabeth, it's up to you.

BETSY: I shall let you know as soon as I finish the flag, Uncle George. (*To others*) Thank you, gentlemen. I can't tell you what a privilege this is to work on the new flag. What a wonderful change from—(*Looks at* UNCLE GEORGE's *unfinished chair*)—from stuffing a chair. Good day to you all.

COMMITTEEMEN (*Leaving*): Good day, Mrs. Ross.

UNCLE: Good day, Elizabeth. (*They exit.* BETSY *stands happily looking at the rough sketch.* SALLY *enters, followed by* ANN *and* JANE.)

SALLY: Are you busy, Mrs. Ross?

BETSY: I think I shall be busy for quite a while, Sally.

ANN: Will you be cutting out stars?

JANE: Five-pointed stars!

BETSY (*Laughing*): Have you been listening?

JANE (*Giggling*): We couldn't help it. We wanted to ask you something else—about a larger pattern.

SALLY: We heard all about the new flag and everything.

BETSY: Sit down, girls. Thanks to you, I recalled how to cut five-pointed stars. Snip! Snip! And the gentlemen were amazed.

GIRLS: Weren't they!

JANE: And you'll be making a brand new flag for the country!

BETSY: Yes, and I thank my *stars* that I have such helpful neighbors! (*Curtain*)

THE END

PRODUCTION NOTES
A STAR FOR OLD GLORY

Characters: 3 male; 4 female.

Playing Time: 15 minutes.

Costumes: All characters wear costumes typical of the Revolutionary period.

Properties: 3 star "patterns," as indicated in text; paper; scissors.

Setting: The Ross upholstery shop. The room is furnished in the colonial manner. There are several old chairs around the room, with a sitting chair and table center right. Sewing equipment—needles, bolts of material, stuffing, etc.—is placed around the room. Exit right leads to street. Exit down center leads to rear.

Lighting and Sound: No special effects.

The Red, White, and Blue

BOYS: What does it stand for—
       The Red, White, and Blue?
GIRLS: It stands for our country
       And what it went through
       To win us our freedom
       When freedom was new.

BOYS: What do they stand for—
       The stripes, red and white?
GIRLS: The states on the seaboard
       That braved England's might,
       Thirteen in number,
       United to fight.

BOYS: What do they stand for—
       The stars, one and all?
GIRLS: The States in the Union,
       The big states and small,
       Ready to answer
       America's call.

BOYS: What do they stand for—
       The colors we see?
GIRLS: Red stands for courage,
       And white—liberty,
       And blue for the staunch
       In this land of the free.

ALL: Hail to our banner
Still shining like new,
Symbol of faith
In the brave and the true,
Symbol of freedom . . .
The Red, White, and Blue!

 ## Old Glory

It's more than stripes of red and white
And stars upon a field of blue—
The flag that waves so high and bright
Is dreams come true:
  Daring dreams of liberty,
  With minds and tongues and actions free.
It's more than color in the sun,
It's one for all and all for one!

It's more than red and white and blue,
A star to represent each state—
The flag that waves the day-hours through
Is faith grown great:
  Faith in basic rights of man
  On a democratic plan.
It's more than stripes that rise and fall,
It's all for one and one for all!

Star-Spangled Banner

With thirteen stripes
of red and white
for thirteen colonies,

And fifty stars
for fifty states
(no stars more bright than these),

With blue for justice,
white for faith,
and crimson for the brave,

No wonder we
are filled with pride
to see our banner wave!

Bunker Hill Day

Bunker Hill

Up the hill the British came,
Their red coats flashing in the sun,
As flashing bright as freedom's flame
That fired our soldiers, every one.

Up the hill, three thousand strong,
The British marched to seize the height
Our men had strengthened all night long
In preparation for the fight.

Up the hill, our men's supply
Of powder was distressing small,
And then, at last, the battle cry!
Our volley struck the marching wall.

Redcoats fell and Redcoats ran.
Our farmer-soldiers watched them go,
And nodded grimly, man to man.
Confusion filled the field below.

A second charge! The British still
Outnumbered rebels two to one.
A second volley! Down the hill
The Redcoats ran as madmen run.

Behind the ramparts, powder gone,
Our soldiers waited, tense and true,
They had been fighting since the dawn,
They had been trenching all night through.

Would General Howe resume the fight?
The hill was soaked with British blood,
And then, the unexpected sight—
On came another British flood!

Our men had gunstocks, little more,
So Redcoats won the hill that day.
But, losing what they battled for,
Our soldiers won another way:

They won respect for standing firm,
They won recruits for liberty,
They won what patriots could term
A sort of splendid victory!

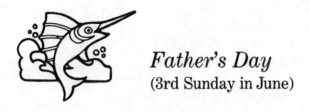

Father's Day
(3rd Sunday in June)

Long Live Father

Characters

TONY
LINDA, *his sister*
ANN, *her friend*
RADIO VOICE
DAD
MOM

SCENE 1

TIME: *A week before Father's Day.*
SETTING: *Combination living room/dining room. Near door right, which leads to kitchen, are table and chairs. Near door to front hall, left, is telephone table with book and newspaper on it. Other tables and chairs, a radio or stereo, and bookcases complete the scene.*

AT RISE: TONY *is on the telephone.*

TONY (*On phone*): Hello. May I speak to Eric, please? . . . Thanks. (*As he waits,* TONY *picks up newspaper and scans the ads, shaking his head dubiously.*) Hi, Eric. Tony. . . . Listen, you get the best marks in school. Maybe you can help me out. . . . No, it isn't math. It's Father's Day. Linda and I can't think of a thing to get my Dad that he doesn't already have. . . . Flies? What do you mean, flies? . . . Oh, fishing. Well, he isn't much of an outdoor man. He hasn't gone fishing in ages. . . . That goes for golf balls, too. . . . Well, thanks, anyway. (*Hangs up, sighs, looks around room and turns on radio*)

RADIO VOICE: . . . never be a chance like this again in a generation. Stock up now, folks, on gifts for the man of the house. (TONY *listens intently.*) Hartnagle's Fire Sale offers thousands of bargains at unheard-of prices. Neckties in all the new colors and designs . . . absolutely guaranteed not to show any effects of the fire. All half price! Take your pick! Socks in a gorgeous display of colors and patterns. Buy a dozen pairs and put them away for Christmas or your favorite guy's birthday. You can't go wrong! We also have handkerchiefs . . . (TONY *turns off radio, stands glaring at it.*)

TONY: Why can't you think of something *different!* (*He stomps out to kitchen.* LINDA *and* ANN *enter from front hall.*)

LINDA: What do you mean, you're giving your father a picnic?

ANN: The whole family's in on it. We're giving him a portable grill, a big picnic basket with plates, knives and forks, a bag of charcoal—the works! Everything you need for a picnic.

LINDA: That's a great idea, Ann. The trouble with my father is that he thinks resting is more of a picnic than

189

going on one. (*Sighs*) I wish Tony and I could think of something out of the ordinary like that, though, instead of socks, ties, cuff links, tie pins . . . year after year.

ANN: What about handkerchiefs? (*She giggles.*)

LINDA (*Chuckling*): What a novel idea, Ann! Something to give him a new lease on life! (TONY *appears at kitchen door.*)

TONY: A new lease on life! If there were only a gadget like that . . . something to make Dad live to be a hundred years old!

LINDA: Why stop at a hundred? Let's make it a hundred and ten.

ANN: The only trouble is, gadgets like that aren't for sale.

TONY: It's a good idea, though.

ANN (*Looking at her watch*): Well, I've got just ten minutes to get to my music lesson. Linda, where's that book you said I could borrow?

LINDA (*Going to bookcase for book*): Here it is, Ann. You'll love it, I'm sure.

ANN: Thanks. (*Takes book, then starts to exit*) You know, if your father thinks resting is such a picnic, why don't you give him a book? (*She exits.*)

LINDA (*Calling*): He only has about a thousand books already.

TONY (*Suddenly*): You know, Linda, a book's not a bad idea. It works right into the new lease on life.

LINDA: I don't get it.

TONY: We could buy him a book on how to live a long time. It would show him how much we love him.

LINDA: Where would we get a book like that?

TONY: At the bookstore, I suppose.

LINDA (*Suddenly*): I know the perfect gift for Dad, Tony.

TONY: What is it?

LINDA: In school we've been learning all about exercise, the importance of no fats, lots of vegetables, less salt, and vitamins. Right?

TONY: Right. (*Doubtfully*) So what's your idea?

LINDA: Well, we could write a book ourselves, just for Dad. We'd put in stuff about all the new discoveries on nutrition and food. He's way behind the times . . . otherwise he wouldn't spend so much time worrying. (*Sighs*) He doesn't realize what it's *doing* to him. I had to ask him a question three times yesterday before he even heard me.

TONY (*Enthusiastically*): Do you think we could do it? And would he read it?

LINDA: If we made it interesting enough.

TONY: Can we make whole-wheat bread and vitamins and exercise interesting?

LINDA: Sure! Why not?

TONY (*Hesitating*): Well . . . (*Brightens*) Hey! I've thought of the perfect title. *Long Live Father.*

LINDA: Tony, that's great! I know we can write it! And it's going to be a picnic.

BOTH (*Happily*): Long live Father! (*Curtain*)

* * *

SCENE 2

TIME: *The morning of Father's Day.*

SETTING: *The same. The table is set for breakfast. There's a flat package at one of the places.*

AT RISE: TONY *and* LINDA *sit at table.*

LINDA: Mom's dying of curiosity. (*Picks up package*) You haven't told her, have you?

TONY (*Shaking head*): Not a word. She's as much in the dark as Dad.

191

LINDA: I never thought so hard in my life, did you?

TONY: My brains are worn to a frazzle.

LINDA: Do you think Dad even remembers it's Father's Day?

TONY: I doubt it. (MOM *enters from kitchen with dishes. She sets them down on table, then picks up package.*)

MOM: Aren't you going to tell me what this great surprise is? I can't stand the suspense much longer.

TONY: You can guess if you want, Mom. We'll tell you when you get hot.

MOM (*Feeling package*): It's a strange shape. (*Shakes it*) Might be a big box of handkerchiefs.

TONY: Wrong!

LINDA: Nothing as *ordinary* as handkerchiefs. This is a life-long present, Mom.

MOM: Life-long! I didn't know anything would last that long.

TONY: Well, you might say this is a new slant on life.

LINDA (*Looking slyly at* TONY): Yes. On life with Dad!

MOM (*Impatiently*): I wish he'd hurry. (DAD *enters with newspaper, nods pleasantly but absent-mindedly at family. He sits at his place and begins to scan headlines.*)

DAD (*Automatically*): Good morning, everyone.

OTHERS (*Ad lib*): Good morning, Dad. How are you? (*Etc.*)

DAD: Nice day.

MOM: It's a wonderful day.

TONY: Very special.

LINDA: It's your day, Dad. (DAD *looks up from newspaper.*)

DAD: My day? What do you mean, Linda?

LINDA: It's Father's Day! The third Sunday in June.

LINDA, TONY *and* MOM (*Together*): Happy Father's Day!

DAD (*Surprised*): Why, thank you. I forgot all about it. (*Notices package*) What's this?

MOM: It's a present from Tony and Linda.

TONY: This is something special for you, to be sure you live to be a hundred, Dad.

DAD: What? A hundred!

MOM: Please open it, dear. I can't wait to see what it is.

DAD: All right. Hm-m . . . what could it be? (*Picking up package, reading card*) "From your loving son and daughter, Tony and Linda, who are concerned about your future." (*Looks up*) What's wrong with my future?

TONY: We just want to be sure there'll be a lot of it.

DAD (*Unwrapping package, pulling out book*): What's this? A book!

MOM: It looks like a very special edition.

TONY: Privately printed!

DAD (*Slowly reading title*): Long . . . Live . . . Father! Well! "Subtitle: You Can't Live Too Long to Suit Us. Sub-subtitle: A Few Rules for a Long Life and a Healthy One." (DAD *looks up, surprised.*) Well, nobody ever took my future so . . . so seriously before. I'm touched. I really am. Thank you very much.

MOM (*To* TONY *and* LINDA): So *that's* what you meant by life-long present.

DAD (*Thumbing through book*): You mean to say you went to all this work just for me?

TONY (*Eagerly*): We divided it in several parts, Dad. There's a section on safety . . . with lots of facts on safe driving habits.

MOM: That's wonderful!

LINDA: And there's a section on exercise, with information on how many calories you burn off while doing certain activities.

TONY: We also covered things like vitamins, cholesterol,

salt intake—all the really important facts we thought you should know.

LINDA: We've been learning all about it in school, Dad.

DAD (*Reading*): "If you sit around and worry
Like a one-horse cart or surrey,
You'll age like sixty in a hurry."
(*Horrified*) Like sixty! Is that a fact?

TONY: Absolutely. There's nothing like worry to make you show your age.

DAD (*Reading again*):
"Throw your chest out. Breathe down deep.
A youthful figure you will keep."
(*Looks up*) You two are real poets! This is great! (*Reads again*)
"To keep your teeth both white and real,
Brush them after every meal."
(*Looks up*) After every meal? That's a lot of exercise.

TONY: It's the recommended procedure, Dad.

LINDA: Turn to the eating part, Dad. You haven't been drinking enough milk, and you put too much salt on everything.

DAD: You mean at my age I should still be drinking milk?

LINDA: Of course. (*To* MOM) And you too, Mom. You need it even more than Dad.

MOM: Why, you children are so knowledgeable about health and fitness!

DAD: I really am deeply touched. (*Reads*)
"Good fresh air is dynamite
For blasting worries out of sight
And giving you an appetite."

MOM: Your appetite hasn't been very good lately, Phil.

DAD: That's true, it hasn't. (*Reads again*)
"A change of thought and change of scene
Is worth the ransom of a queen."

TONY: Linda thought of that. The only rhyme I could

194

think of was *submarine,* and it didn't make much sense.

DAD: I don't know about that. You could have worded it this way:

"Unless you change your thought and scene
You're sunk—just like a submarine."

LINDA: Daddy, you're wonderful! (*Hugs him*)

DAD (*Modestly*): Oh, I don't know about that. After all, I can't help being affected by a masterpiece like this. (*Reads again*)

"You'll stretch your legs if you are wise
And give yourself some exercise."

(*He jumps up, begins to walk around room.*) I feel better already. (*Sticks head out window and takes deep breaths*) Better and better. In fact, I'm getting a new lease on life. (TONY *and* LINDA *smile broadly.*)

DAD: There's no holding a man down (*He gives a little jump.*) . . . when he finds out (*Another jump*) . . . for the first time (*Jump*) that his two favorite and only children . . . (*Jump*) want him to live to be a hundred.

TONY *and* LINDA: A hundred and ten!

DAD: It gives one pause. (*He stops his antics, comes back solemnly to table.*) Change of scene . . . fresh air . . . exercise . . . appetite . . . as far as I can see this all adds up to one word.

TONY *and* LINDA: One word?

MOM: What do you mean, Phil?

DAD: One little six-letter word. (*Others are completely mystified.*) Now that you're learning all these new-fangled things about how to live to a ripe old age, don't they teach you how to *spell* anymore?

TONY: Sure, Dad, but I don't know what you mean.

LINDA (*Musing*): A six-letter word . . .

DAD: Why, change of scene, fresh air, exercise and appetite mean only one thing to me—PICNIC!

195

OTHERS (*Ad lib*): Picnic! Great idea! A Father's Day picnic! (*Etc.*)

DAD: What about it? Barbecued chicken at Perch Lake? (MOM *raises her coffee cup,* TONY *and* LINDA *their juice glasses, as they stand and toast* DAD.)

MOM, TONY and LINDA (*Together*): Long live Father!

THE END

PRODUCTION NOTES
LONG LIVE FATHER

Characters: 2 male; 3 female; 1 male or female for Radio Voice.
Playing Time: 15 minutes.
Costumes: Everyday, modern dress. Ann wears watch.
Properties: Dishes.
Setting: Combination living/dining room. Near door right, leading to kitchen, are table and chairs. Near door to front hall, left, is telephone table with book and newspaper on it. Other tables and chairs, a radio or stereo, and bookcases complete the scene. In Scene 2, dining room table is set; at one place setting is a flat, wrapped package.
Lighting and Sound: No special effects.

When Father Comes Home

(To the tune of "Home on the Range")

Oh, give me a home
With an elf or a gnome
Or a sprite that will put things away,
So playthings and toys
Of my girls and my boys
Won't be scattered on carpets all day!

Home, home, how I wish
When I walk up the steps through the door,
I never need slip on some marbles or trip
On the playthings around on the floor.

JULY–AUGUST

Independence Day
(July 4)

Our Great Declaration

A round-the-table reading play

Characters

NARRATOR
JEFFERSON
BOY
GIRL
CHORUS
WASHINGTON
FRANKLIN
PRIME MINISTER
AGENTS
MEN
WOMEN
PATRICK HENRY
WILLIAM PITT
TOWN CRIER

MARTHA
STEPHEN
JOHN ADAMS
READER
JOHN DICKINSON
JOHN DUNLAP
HELPER
ABIGAIL ADAMS
JOHN QUINCY ADAMS, *age nine*
SONS OF LIBERTY
MRS. JACKSON
HUGH JACKSON
ANDREW JACKSON, *age nine*
LINCOLN

198

NARRATOR: This is the story of the noblest document in the history of our country—the Declaration of Independence. It is not a long document. You can read it aloud in fifteen minutes, including the names of the fifty-six signers. Leaving out the recital of grievances, you can read it in less than five minutes . . . words that are as stirring and full of meaning now as when they were first penned in that hot Philadelphia summer of 1776! Think of Thomas Jefferson, a young lawyer of thirty-three, sitting in a stuffy lodging-house room, writing those noble words. . . .

JEFFERSON: How can I write this down so it will carry conviction? What I want to say is that governments are established to secure the liberty and happiness of the people, all people—not just a favored few. When a government shows a determination to rob the people of their rights, it is their duty to overthrow that government and establish another that assures them liberty and safety. "When in the course of human events . . ."

NARRATOR: Jefferson finished the first draft in two days. Only two days to compose a document that stands as one of the greatest in the history of the English-speaking world! The parchment, once so fresh and bright with new ink upon it, is faded now. But the ringing challenge is still there . . . even as the message of liberty still speaks from the long-silent Liberty Bell that pealed out during the celebration of the adoption of the Declaration. (*Sound of bell*)

LOUDSPEAKER: "Proclaim liberty throughout all the land and unto all the inhabitants thereof." (*Sound of bell*)

NARRATOR: Liberty! The keyword of the great Declaration.

JEFFERSON: "We hold these truths to be self-evident,

199

that all men are created equal, that they are endowed by their Creator with certain unalienable Rights, that among these are Life, Liberty, and the pursuit of Happiness."

NARRATOR: Twice the Declaration was whisked out of harm's way during the Revolutionary War. Twice it was almost burned. It was almost captured by the British in the War of 1812. But now the historic document is safe. Any time you go to Washington, D.C., you can see it in its shrine in the National Archives Building sealed in a bronze and glass case and ready to be lowered at a moment's notice into one of the strongest safes in the world.

BOY (*Eagerly*): There it is standing up in the case! "The Unanimous Declaration of the thirteen United States of America." It's funny handwriting, isn't it? Not the kind we learn in school.

GIRL: I think it's beautiful writing.

BOY: But hard to read. Some of the words are so dim I can scarcely make them out. And look at those signatures.

GIRL: They're blurred because that's where the parchment was rolled and unrolled so often.

BOY: Say, look at that first *s* in *necessary*. Just like an *f*. "When in the course of human events it becomes nec-ef-sary . . ." If I didn't know the words, I'd have a hard time making them out.

GIRL: Look at John Hancock's signature. Big as life right in the middle, at the top. Nobody could miss it.

BOY: He wrote it big on purpose . . . so King George could read it without spectacles and know that the richest man in the colonies was for independence!

GIRL (*Thoughtfully*): I wonder what it was like then, way back when there were thirteen colonies standing together for independence.

NARRATOR: You wonder what it was like then? Well, you have to go back a long way in time—back to the days when we weren't singing "My Country 'Tis of Thee," but "God Save the King"—King George, the Third.

CHORUS:

> "God save our gracious King,
> Long live our noble King,
> God save the King!
> Send him victorious,
> Happy and glorious,
> Long to reign over us,
> God save the King!"

NARRATOR: We can't imagine, of course, how it felt to have a king reign over us. But in the middle of the eighteenth century the King meant a great deal to the colonists. All through the troubles that led to the war with England, the colonists kept hoping that Parliament would give in and remedy their grievances. Even as late as 1774 George Washington said . . .

WASHINGTON: I am well satisfied that no such thing as independence is desired by any thinking man in all North America. I abhor the idea of separation.

NARRATOR: And about the same time Benjamin Franklin said . . .

FRANKLIN: Whatever else the Americans might desire, they do not want independence.

NARRATOR: Before the Revolution, most of the colonists had a feeling of pride in being part of the great British empire. They did not want the tie broken. They merely wanted to have their rights as Englishmen respected. If this had been done, who knows, we might still be singing "God Save the King" instead of "America." (CHORUS sings first stanza of "America.")

CHORUS:

> "My country 'tis of thee," (Etc.)

201

NARRATOR: Trouble started brewing after the end of the French and Indian War in 1763. Up to that time, the colonists had been fairly well satisfied with English rule. True, Parliament had tried to control colonial trade by levying taxes on imports. But England was too busy fighting long wars to enforce the tax laws. It was only after England emerged victorious that she could turn her full attention to the colonies. In the winter of 1763–4, the Prime Minister of England called together the agents of the colonies:

PRIME MINISTER: Gentlemen, the time has come when we should be getting substantial revenue from America. Our long-drawn-out wars with the French and Indians have been costly. I propose that a specific sum be levied on the colonies, to be paid yearly.

AGENT: May I interrupt, Mr. Prime Minister. I am certain that levying a specific demand on the colonies for revenue will lead to the direst consequences. The Americans will not stand for it, sir.

OTHER AGENTS: Hear! Hear!

PRIME MINISTER: Perhaps a stamp tax, then. We must have revenue, gentlemen. I shall propose at the coming session of Parliament that a stamp duty be levied on the colonies. Or if not a stamp tax at first, then some other tax, on imports, say.

NARRATOR: In 1764, Parliament passed the Sugar Act, levying a tax on certain colonial imports including sugar. Up and down the Atlantic seaboard outraged colonists objected and petitioned for repeal. But Parliament stood firm. Early the next year, it passed the Stamp Act. In all, fifty-five articles were taxed. Opposition raged like a prairie fire throughout the colonies.

1ST MAN: Dig down in our pockets and pay for stamps to be pasted on legal papers and the like? Not on your life.

2ND MAN: Six pounds for a license from the governor to do business!

3RD MAN: Four pence for a bill of lading!

WOMAN: A shilling for a pack of cards. Ridiculous.

YOUNG MAN: We can't even go to college without paying tribute. Two pounds for a college diploma!

2ND WOMAN: A penny for a sheet of newspaper. A shilling for a pamphlet. Two shillings for an advertisement. It will drive us to ruin.

NARRATOR: Riots broke out from New Hampshire to South Carolina when the colonists learned the names of the stamp distributors. Mobs threatened them and forced them to resign. In Virginia, Patrick Henry made his famous speech in the House of Burgesses . . .

PATRICK HENRY: "Caesar had his Brutus, Charles the First his Cromwell, and George the Third . . ."

VOICES: Treason!

PATRICK HENRY: "George the Third may profit by their example. If *this* be treason, make the most of it."

NARRATOR: Soon the rallying cry of "No taxation without representation" was spreading through the colonies—from lawyer to merchant to mechanic, laborer, farmer, housewife.

MAN: To submit to tyranny is slavery.

WOMAN: England is driving us to war.

MAN: Taxation without representation is unjust.

VOICES: Tyranny! Tyranny!

NARRATOR: The Sons of Liberty were organized to prevent the sale of the tax stamps. Public gatherings and town meetings protested that there would be an end to liberty if the Stamp Act were enforced. The colonists began to boycott British goods. Finally the Stamp Act Congress, meeting in New York, protested vigorously and petitioned for repeal of the Act. The hubbub in the colonies brought on a bitter debate in the English Parliament. The great William Pitt eloquently urged the House of Commons to repeal the Act . . .

WILLIAM PITT: I rejoice that America has resisted. Three million people so dead to all feelings of liberty as voluntarily to submit to be slaves, would have been fit instruments to make slaves of all the rest. . . . The Americans have been wronged. They have been driven to madness by injustice. Will you punish them for the madness you have occasioned?

NARRATOR: British merchants and businessmen urged repeal because of the falling off in trade due to the boycott. At last Parliament yielded and repealed the Stamp Act. News of repeal was the signal for rejoicing in England as well as in the American colonies. But the rejoicing proved premature. Parliament refused to give up its right to tax the colonies. In 1767 news of another tax came.

MARTHA: Whatever is the matter, Stephen? Did something go wrong at the office today?

STEPHEN: Bad news, Martha.

MARTHA: Have you lost a case?

STEPHEN: Not I. We! We Americans have lost a case. Not long ago we celebrated when Parliament repealed the Stamp Act. Now we hear that England has not given up the right to levy taxes upon us. News comes that Parliament has passed a new revenue act to make us pay duties on glass, paper, tea . . .

MARTHA: A tax on tea! Why, that is preposterous, Stephen.

NARRATOR: A tax on tea—the drink loved by all colonists of English ancestry! Indignation against the tax led to the Boston Tea Party in December, 1773, when citizens of Boston, disguised as Indians, dumped chests of tea from three British vessels into the harbor. Parliament retaliated immediately.

TOWN CRIER: Hear ye, hear ye, hear ye—as a result of the Boston Tea Party, Parliament has enacted new laws to punish the colonists. The port of Boston is closed to all trade by sea! Town meetings are subject to the control of the English governor! British troops are to be quartered in Massachusetts towns! Hear ye, hear ye, hear ye!

NARRATOR: Indignation at the treatment of Boston swept from one end of the colonies to the other. Paul Revere rode the three hundred and fifty miles to Philadelphia on horseback to spread the news. Soon help began coming in from all quarters—rice from South Carolina, money and flour from Virginia, flocks of sheep from Connecticut. In the Virginia Convention of July, 1774, George Washington stood up and made a startling proposal . . .

WASHINGTON: I will raise one thousand men, subsist them at my own expense, and march myself at their head for the relief of Boston.

NARRATOR: A few rash patriots even began to talk of independence, of separation from England.

1ST MAN: Instead of fighting for the restoration of our privileges, let us fight for freedom and independence.

2ND MAN: Independence? Who wants independence? All we want is justice and an end to tyranny.

NARRATOR: Colonists were eager to show their sympathy with Boston, so they were glad when Virginia called for a Congress of all the colonies. The first Continental Congress met at Philadelphia. It drew up a Declaration of Rights and Grievances, and to put teeth into it, declared a boycott on British goods. John Adams, a delegate to the Congress from Massachusetts, wrote to his wife Abigail:

JOHN ADAMS: "September 17, 1774. This is one of the happiest days of my life. In Congress we had generous, noble sentiments, and manly eloquence. This day convinced me that America will support Massachusetts or perish with her."

NARRATOR: Relations between England and America grew worse with the boycott in effect. In the colonies, lines were drawn between those who upheld the boycott and those who continued to buy British goods. A man was either a patriot, true to the spirit of America; or he was a Tory, loyal to England. There was no middle ground. And then in April, 1775, a shot was fired that was heard 'round the world. Blood was shed at Lexington and Concord!

VOICE: Disperse, you rebels—damn you, throw down your arms and disperse. (*Sound of shot*)

NARRATOR: Which side fired that first shot is still a mystery. But the die was cast. The Revolutionary War was on. Within a month after Lexington, the Second Continental Congress met in Philadelphia and drew up a fervid statement of the grievances of the colonists . . .

READER: Journals of Congress, Philadelphia. In brief, we are reduced to the alternative of choosing an unconditional Submission to the tyranny of irritated Ministers, or resistance by Force. The latter is our choice. We have counted the cost of this contest, and find nothing so dreadful as voluntary Slavery. Honour, Justice, and Humanity forbid us tamely to surrender that freedom which we receive from our gallant Ancestors, and which our innocent Posterity have a right to receive from us.

NARRATOR: The Congress humbly petitioned the King for a redress of wrongs. But its petitions were met with scorn and contempt. Parliament proceeded to raise a great army, including hired Hessian soldiers from Germany, to put down rebellion in the colonies.

Shortly, Thomas Paine, who emigrated to America in the midst of the excitement of the year before, wrote a pamphlet called "Common Sense." Over 100,000 copies were distributed in three months and men and women talked about it up and down the Atlantic seaboard.

WOMAN: Thomas Paine doesn't mince words. He calls anything but independence an outrage to common sense.

2ND WOMAN: Isn't that part exciting where he says, "O! ye that love mankind! Ye that dare oppose, not only tyranny, but the tyrant, stand forth! We have it in our power to begin the world over again."

MAN: I wasn't sure before, but Tom Paine makes me see that independence is our only way out.

NARRATOR: John Adams sent a copy of "Common Sense" to his wife Abigail, who greeted it with enthusiasm. General Washington called Paine's arguments unanswerable. He agreed that "an open and determined declaration for independence" was the only solution for America. Thousands of colonists, heretofore wavering, came over to the patriot side, stirred by Paine's ringing words:

READER:
"From the east to the west, blow the trumpet to arms,
Thro' the land let the sound of it flee,
Let the far and the near—all unite with a cheer,
In defence of our Liberty tree."

NARRATOR: In June of 1776 a delegate to Congress from Virginia offered a resolution that "These United States are, and of right ought to be free and independent states." John Adams seconded the resolution. A committee was appointed to draw up a formal declaration of independence, and the actual writing fell to Thomas Jefferson. On the 4th day of July, Congress adopted the momentous Declaration!

READER: "When in the course of human events it becomes necessary for one people to dissolve the political bands which have connected them with another . . . decent respect to the opinions of mankind requires that they should declare the causes which impel them to the separation . . ."

NARRATOR: There followed the deathless preamble and a long list of grievances against the King. And then the resolution . . .

READER: "We, therefore, the Representatives of the United States of America . . . solemnly publish and declare, That these United Colonies are and of Right ought to be *Free and Independent States.*"

NARRATOR: Not all the delegates to the Second Continental Congress were willing to vote for independence. Some felt that the Declaration was premature. After the adjournment of Congress on that memorable day, Benjamin Franklin and John Dickinson stand talking on one side of the room. Both are delegates from Pennsylvania.

FRANKLIN: I hoped until the last, Mr. Dickinson, that you might change your mind and vote with the majority in our delegation.

DICKINSON: I could not vote against my conscience, sir. I believe the declaration of our independence should have been delayed a while longer.

FRANKLIN: How long, Mr. Dickinson? The King and Parliament will never give in!

DICKINSON: But, Mr. Franklin, we have no army worthy of the name, no way of financing a war against the strongest power in the world.

FRANKLIN: We must depend on help from abroad, and independence is a necessary step in getting it. Now we can obtain a treaty with France . . .

DICKINSON: How can we expect France to unite with us

when we have not united with each other? No! Union should come first and then the declaration. I feel we have made ourselves ridiculous in the eyes of foreign powers.

FRANKLIN: Nonsense. But it is a comfort to know that we live in a country where thinking men can differ about the best means to achieve the end we all seek.

NARRATOR: At the very time when Congress was passing the Declaration of Independence, General Washington, in New York, was issuing an order to his troops:

WASHINGTON: The time is now near which must determine whether Americans are to be Freemen or Slaves . . . whether their houses and farms are to be pillaged and destroyed. The fate of unknown millions will now depend, under God, on the courage and conduct of this Army. We have, therefore, to resolve to conquer or die.

NARRATOR: Right at this time the British fleet was sighted off the New Jersey coast. Washington sent word of it to Congress, the messenger arriving in the midst of the debate.

And how was the Declaration of Independence received by Americans of 1776? The very night it was adopted, John Dunlap, owner of a print shop in Philadelphia, stayed up all night trying to get the stirring words into print by morning. He speaks to his helper as they pick out letters from the type-cases.

DUNLAP: "All men are created equal." Mark what I say . . . there will be volumes spoken and written about those five words.

HELPER: What does it mean? Created equal! You and me equal, Mr. Dunlap? I wouldn't be one to say it myself.

DUNLAP: Equal in the eyes of the Creator, that's what it means. And so all men should be *treated* equal. That's it. Treated alike, and have the same chance.

HELPER: I can say Amen to a thought like that, sir.

DUNLAP: It's what we're going to stand for even more from now on. And the minute we forget, that minute we'll see our liberty beginning to slip through our fingers.

NARRATOR: Dunlap's handbills were on the streets of Philadelphia soon after sun-up. Avidly the citizens of Penn's city read the words. Some men and women were jubilant, some doubtful, some downright angry. But few realized that here, on a page of print, were historic words that would take their place beside the Magna Carta, that first great document to define the rights of man.

In her home near Boston, Abigail Adams received an enthusiastic letter from her delegate-husband. Their 9-year-old son, John Quincy Adams, listens eagerly as she reads the letter aloud:

ABIGAIL: "This will be the most memorable epoch in the history of America. I believe it will be celebrated by succeeding generations as the great anniversary Festival. . . . It ought to be solemnized with Pomp and Parade . . ."

JOHN: Do you think there will be a parade, Mother? In Boston?

ABIGAIL: In all the cities of America, I should think, Johnny. Now listen to the rest of what your father has to say. "It ought to be solemnized with Pomp and Parade, with Shows, Sports, Guns, Bells, Bonfires and Illuminations . . ."

JOHN: Oh, Mother! Bonfires and Illuminations!

ABIGAIL: ". . . from one end of this Continent to the other, from this time forward, forevermore."

JOHN: Every year? An independence celebration every year?

ABIGAIL: That's what your father thinks, and rightly so,

210

for such a tremendous thing as freedom, Johnny. Let's see, there's more. (*Reading*) "I am well aware of the Toil and Blood and Treasure it will cost us to maintain this Declaration, and support and defend these states. Yet, through the gloom I can see the rays of light and glory."

JOHN: Do you think a *hundred* years from now, they will still be celebrating, Mother?

ABIGAIL: A hundred years, yes. And two hundred years. And longer. Maybe you can help some time, Johnny, to keep those rays of light and glory shining bright.

NARRATOR: The first big public Fourth of July celebration took place in Philadelphia on July 8th, in that momentous year of 1776. Bells rang all day and most of the night, the Liberty Bell among them, clanging away in the tower of the State House where the Declaration was adopted. Cheering and more cheering resounded through the city. Battalions of soldiers paraded on the Common and fired their guns with unrestrained joy. Even the scarcity of gunpowder did not stand in the way. (*Sound of voices, cheering*)

VOICES: Three cheers for the United States of America!

OTHER VOICES: Hurrah! Hurrah! Hurrah!

VOICE: Three cheers for freedom and independence!

NARRATOR: It was not until the next day, July 9th, that New York had its big celebration. The Continental army was in camp there, and General Washington had the troops drawn up on parade, to listen to a reading of the Declaration. The soldiers listened in silence to the Preamble and to the long list of abuses charged against the King. Then came the solemn pledge at the end:

READER: "And for the support of this Declaration, with a firm reliance on the protection of Divine Providence, we mutually pledge to each other our Lives, our Fortunes and our sacred Honour."

SOLDIERS (*Voices up*): . . . "we mutually pledge to each other our Lives, our Fortunes and our sacred Honour." (*Great cheers and hurrahs*)

NARRATOR: Other patriots were celebrating on Bowling Green in New York City, where a statue of King George the Third had held the place of honor for six years. The King, robed like a Roman emperor, was seated on a horse. Horse and rider, larger than life, had been cast in lead and covered with gold leaf. The high ironwork fence around the statue could not keep out some of the Sons of Liberty who were bent on destroying the statue of the King.

2ND: Topple him over. Here, throw me that rope.

3RD: We'd do better without these fifteen feet of pedestal! Sling a rope around him.

1ST: Four thousand pounds—that's what they say the King and his horse weigh. Good British lead. We'll melt it down for bullets.

2ND: Bullets! Thousands of bullets. Tens of thousands. Heave, boys, heave!

3RD: Look out! Here it comes! (*Great crash and cheering*)

NARRATOR: Great bonfires burned in many other cities. Soldiers fired thirteen volleys for the thirteen states, and in the taverns men drank thirteen toasts to the United States of America. In a few days express riders had carried handbills to the newspapers up and down the coast. But news did not reach some of the outlying corners of the States until August, even September.

In the Waxhaw Indian country of South Carolina, a group of patriots gathered to hear the first reading of the Declaration in August, 1776. The reader was a 9-

year-old boy named Andrew Jackson, who later became the seventh President of the United States. As the meeting breaks up, Andrew's mother and older brother congratulate him.

MRS. JACKSON: You read it very well, Andy. Good and loud so we didn't miss a word.

HUGH: Didn't even stumble over the big words. "Unalienable rights!" You know what it means?

ANDREW: I asked the preacher. It means rights that can't be given away or taken away. Rights that are ours for keeps.

MRS. JACKSON: I only wish your father could have lived to see this day. It would have been a great day for him, listening to his son reading out the Declaration of Independence.

ANDREW: Pa was always for liberty, wasn't he?

MRS. JACKSON: That he was. 'Twould have delighted his heart, Andy, to hear those words about government being for the safety and happiness of the people, and getting its powers from the people.

HUGH: People like us. Ma, I've decided I'm going to join up and fight. That's something worth fighting for.

MRS. JACKSON: I'd fight for a government of the people myself, if they'd let me.

ANDREW: So would I, if nine years old weren't too young. But I'll fight for freedom *some* day, somehow.

NARRATOR: Well, there it is . . . the story of the noblest document in our whole history, the Declaration of Independence.

The idea of liberty is now ingrained in every American. We take it for granted, just as we take the free union of our fifty great states for granted. How many of us ever stop to ask what it is that has held our union together for so many years? How many of us ever try

213

to answer that question? Abraham Lincoln did, a hundred years ago . . .

LINCOLN: "It was not the mere matter of separation of the colonies from the motherland, but that sentiment in the Declaration of Independence which gave liberty, not alone to the people of this country, but hope to the world, for all future time. It was that which gave promise that in due time the weight would be lifted from the shoulders of all men and that all should have an equal chance."

NARRATOR: That is the secret of the nobility of the Declaration—the promise in it, the promise of liberty not only for the thirteen states along the Atlantic seaboard, but in due time for all men everywhere. Our forefathers lived for that promise and died for it. We owe our liberty to them and are grateful for their sacrifice. But now the challenge that faces us demands a rededication to the great cause of freedom. In the spirit of '76 we must be willing to live and die that the hope of liberty may be kept alive for all men everywhere.

VOICES: And for the support of this Declaration, we mutually pledge to each other our Lives, our Fortunes and our sacred Honour!

THE END

Ask Mr. Jefferson

Characters

PHIL
SHERRY
CLARK
DONNA
THOMAS JEFFERSON

BEFORE RISE: PHIL, SHERRY, CLARK *and* DONNA, *with notebooks and pencils, enter. They seem perplexed.*

PHIL: Interview him in the library, Miss Whitney said.
SHERRY: I guess that's about the only place we *could* interview him in this day and age. He'll come alive for us there.
PHIL: I'll bet he's an old fogy. Out of date. Stuffy.
DONNA: I don't know about that, Phil. Abraham Lincoln said that Jefferson's principles are the definitions of a free society.
CLARK: What's a free society?
DONNA: A democracy. The United States of America!
PHIL: Well, we're going to have to change the name of the report, that's for sure, or no one in class will listen. JEFFERSON'S IDEAS OF DEMOCRACY AS APPLIED TO MODERN AMERICA. Can you imagine holding anyone's attention with that?

215

SHERRY: We'd better all keep the problem of a title in mind during the interview. We need something snappy. Something catchy. There's only one rule Miss Whitney laid down, remember. She doesn't want us to make anything up. She wants us to quote Jefferson word for word.

PHIL: O.K. Let's get it over with. (*They exit.*)

* * *

SETTING: *A library.*

AT RISE: THOMAS JEFFERSON *is seated at one of the tables, with books, manuscripts, letters around him. He is looking through some papers when* SHERRY, PHIL, CLARK *and* DONNA *enter.*

SHERRY (*To* PHIL): Miss Whitney was right. There he is!

PHIL: How do you know?

SHERRY: I've seen pictures. So have you, Phil.

CLARK: How do we go about it? Where do we start?

DONNA: Why don't we just lay the facts on the table— tell him why we're here, and begin to ask him some questions about rights and freedom?

PHIL: You start, Donna. You've been to the library before! (*They approach* MR. JEFFERSON.)

DONNA (*Sweetly*): Pardon me, Mr. Jefferson. Would you be so kind as to answer a few questions? You see, we have to give a report to the class about your ideas of democracy and . . .

PHIL: Frankly, we're not too sure of our ground.

DONNA: We want to quote you *directly*, so there won't be any doubt about what you believe. Clark, you ask Mr.

216

Jefferson the first question. You're good at asking questions.

CLARK (*Hesitating*): Well . . . well, do you believe in liberty, sir?

JEFFERSON (*Slowly, in measured tones*): "The God who gave us life, gave us liberty at the same time."

CLARK (*Surprised, to* DONNA): What do you know! He had the answer on the tip of his tongue. (*Interviewers take notes throughout.* JEFFERSON *speaks slowly and impressively.*)

DONNA: Let's ask him about rights. That's one of the big things in a democracy. (*To* JEFFERSON) You believe that men are born with certain rights that can't be taken away from them, don't you?

JEFFERSON: "Certain unalienable rights."

DONNA: Just what rights do you mean, Mr. Jefferson?

JEFFERSON: "Among these are life, liberty, and the pursuit of happiness. . . . To secure these rights governments are instituted among men."

PHIL: You mean it's up to a *government* to see that everyone has freedom and happiness?

JEFFERSON: "The freedom and happiness of man . . . are the sole objects of all legitimate government."

PHIL (*Taking notes*): Gosh, that's good. That's where dictators go wrong, see? They want freedom for themselves, but they want the people to take orders. We're really lucky in the United States. Say, Mr. Jefferson, do you believe our idea of freedom and happiness for everyone is going to spread . . . around the world, maybe?

JEFFERSON: "This ball of liberty, I believe most piously, is now so well in motion that it will roll round the globe, at least the enlightened part of it, for light and liberty go together."

CLARK: Not so fast, sir. Would you mind repeating the end of that again?

JEFFERSON: . . . "light and liberty go together."

PHIL: This is great stuff.

DONNA (*To* PHIL): Coming from an old fogy! (*To* JEFFERSON) You believe in equality, don't you, Mr. Jefferson?

JEFFERSON: "All men are created equal."

SHERRY: Equal in rights and opportunity. And that means the government should be in the hands of all men, not just the rich . . . isn't that true, sir?

JEFFERSON: "I am not among those who fear the people. They, and not the rich, are our dependence for continued freedom."

DONNA: But how can people, just *any* kind of people, be trusted with running the government, Mr. Jefferson? They at least have to have an education, don't they?

CLARK: Of course, they do. That's taken for granted.

JEFFERSON: "No one more sincerely wishes the spread of information among mankind than I do, and none has greater confidence in its effect toward supporting free and good government."

PHIL: Say, Mr. Jefferson, you're right up to date!

SHERRY: You mean, when voters keep up with what's happening, and know what they're voting for, there's nothing to worry about. Is that it, Mr. Jefferson?

JEFFERSON: "Whenever the people are well-informed, they can be trusted with their own government: whenever things get so far wrong as to attract their notice, they may be relied on to set them to rights."

CLARK (*Looking up from notebook*): Sometimes it takes people an awfully long time to wake up to what is wrong, though.

PHIL: But trusting the common sense of the people is a surer way to freedom and happiness than trusting a dictator. Isn't that right, Mr. Jefferson?

218

JEFFERSON: "The way to have a good and safe government is not to trust it all to one, but to divide it among the many. . . . I would rather be exposed to the inconveniences attending too much liberty, than those attending too small a degree of it."

PHIL: Me, too. And nobody's ever going to brainwash me out of it. (*Suddenly*) Say, let's ask Mr. Jefferson what he thinks of brainwashing.

CLARK: He never even heard of it.

DONNA: Put it in terms of the Bill of Rights, Phil, and he'll know what you're talking about. You know, ask him about freedom of speech and all that.

PHIL: What do you think about our right to say what we want, and worship the way we please, and think our own thoughts, sir?

JEFFERSON: "There are rights which it is useless to surrender to the government, and which governments have yet always been found to invade. These are the rights of thinking, and publishing our thoughts by speaking or writing. . . . I have sworn upon the altar of God hostility against every form of tyranny over the mind of man."

PHIL (*Excited*): Wait a minute! That sounds like the lead sentence in our report. Mr. Jefferson, you've got all the answers! Would you mind repeating that last sentence again, sir?

JEFFERSON: "I have sworn upon the altar of God hostility against every form of tyranny over the mind of man."

SHERRY (*Looking up from her notes*): Say, I've thought of the perfect, catchy title for our report. Phil, you gave me the idea just now.

PHIL: Me?

SHERRY: You said Mr. Jefferson had all the answers. And it's true. He's got the answers for our day as well

219

as his. All we have to do is ask him. The way we've been doing.

PHIL: So what?

SHERRY: So let's call our report, "Ask Mr. Jefferson."

CLARK: That'll catch attention, all right. What do you think, Mr. Jefferson?

JEFFERSON (*Smiling roguishly*): "I tolerate with the utmost latitude the right of others to differ from me in opinion."

SHERRY (*Laughing*): You see, he's got all the answers— on the tip of his tongue.

DONNA (*Showing paper*): Look, I've written a little verse. Maybe we could start our report with it and go on from there. (*Reads*)

> He spoke for freedom years ago—
> His vision still is clear today,
> His words still guide us as we go
> Along the democratic way . . .

OTHERS: Ask Mr. Jefferson!

THE END

PRODUCTION NOTES
ASK MR. JEFFERSON

Characters: 3 male; 2 female.

Playing Time: 10 minutes.

Costumes: Modern, everyday dress for the students. Jefferson wears the typical dark suit and ruffled shirt of the period.

Properties: Notebooks, pencils for the students.

Setting: Scene 1 may be played before the curtain; no furnishings are necessary. Scene 2 is a library. There are several tables and chairs in the center of the room; bookcases filled with books line the walls. One table is covered with books, manuscripts and letters.

Lighting: No special effects.

My Bet on the Declaration

I have a brother in college. He's studying law, and I mean studying, putting in long hours and all that. According to him I waste too much time on sports and TV when I ought to read history. The other night I was watching a football game on TV and he broke in and made a five-dollar bet with me. I took him up on it before he had a chance to change his mind. It was something about the Declaration of Independence—the men who signed it, I mean. He wanted me to imagine myself back there in 1776 and pick out one signer of the Declaration I would rather have been than any other. My brother bet he could guess the signer I'd pick—and if he didn't guess right, he'd pay me five dollars. Of course, I couldn't pick out one whose only claim to fame was that he signed the Declaration. There had to be some other reason behind my choice. Leave it to a law student to talk about logic!

The first name I thought of was George Washington. Maybe because I knew most about him, the courage he had, and the way he kept on fighting when he had next to nothing to fight with. Then I looked up the signers, and I discovered that George Washington didn't sign the Declaration of Independence at all. If I'd used my head I'd have known that, because he wasn't in Congress in 1776 but off in camp, training the army to fight.

What about Benjamin Franklin, I thought? I always liked him, the way he kept experimenting and inventing things. Besides, he was on the Committee appointed by Congress to draw up the Declaration. Not only that, but he was sent to England to protest in Parliament there against the tyranny and injustice that made the colonies want to be independent. Then I figured out that Franklin was seventy years old in 1776. Too old for me to want to be Franklin, I decided, so I passed him by.

Next I thought about Thomas Jefferson. He was only thirty-three at the time, and I wouldn't mind looking like him—over six feet tall and with a shock of red hair. The four other men on the Committee had him draw up the Declaration, and he worked so hard at it that he had a first draft written in two days. "All men are created equal," he wrote. By that he didn't mean that we're all alike. What he meant was that we all ought to be treated alike. He believed in fair play, and so do I. So I'm for him and for what he wrote about everybody having a right to "life, liberty, and the pursuit of happiness." And I'm for government by the people and not by dictators. Everybody ought to be for that when they see how the modern dictators rule through fear. I had just about decided to pick Jefferson, when I realized that I wouldn't know how to act if I were as brainy as he was. I wouldn't feel like myself at all!

That was the trouble with Samuel Adams and with John Adams, too. They liked studying too much. They went to Harvard and practiced law. And I couldn't imagine myself doing that. So I looked at the signers again. There was Robert Morris. I remembered hearing my brother call him a financial wizard one time. Morris saved our young republic from bankruptcy, I guess. But I'm no financier—I always have trouble trying to make my allowance last—so I decided Robert Morris wasn't for me. Then I came to the name of Caesar Rodney, and I remembered something I'd read about him—something about a horse—a horse! That was my man. He could ride like the wind, and I imagined I could, too, if I had a horse! So I looked him up at the library. What happened was this. Caesar Rodney should have been in Philadelphia, in his seat as a delegate to the Continental Congress from Delaware. But instead he was back home in the thick of things, leading his band of militiamen to southern Delaware to put down a Tory uprising there. He didn't have any use for Tories because they sided with the British. And this time he was angrier with them than usual, because he knew he was missing out on the hot argument in Congress for Independence.

Then an express rider dashed up with a message from Congress. Rodney tore it open and discovered that his vote was needed to swing Delaware into line for Independence. Otherwise Delaware would be the one colony standing out against the break with England, and that would never do. There had to be a united front for freedom or the cause of Independence would suffer.

I'd give a lot to have been in Rodney's boots at that minute. Not that I'd care to look like him. He was an odd-looking man, according to John Adams—tall and thin (I wouldn't mind that), with a face no bigger than an apple. But there was sense and fire and humor in it, and he needed all three in this crisis. The Declaration would be adopted anyway, even if one colony dissented, but Rodney felt it was up to him to have Delaware counted on the side of freedom. So he decided to ride eighty miles to Philadelphia, hoping to get there in time to cast his vote. He galloped all night, drenched by thunder storms, stopping only long enough to change horses. Digging his spurs into each fresh horse, on he went with only one thought in mind: to get there in time. And he did. Spattered with mud from head to foot, he dashed up to the State House in Philadelphia in the nick of time to cast the vote that made Delaware go down in history on the side of Independence.

Rodney was the man who made it possible for the Declaration to be adopted without a single colony dissenting. And then later, when it came to the actual signing of the parchment copy of the Declaration, the one now in the National Archives, Caesar Rodney signed his name with a flourish. He knew it would mean a traitor's death if England won the war, but he was proud to take that chance.

Yes, there was no doubt of it, Caesar Rodney was my man. And there was no doubt that I'd have to do something to throw my brother off the track. If he happened to remember that mad ride of Rodney's, I'd never win that bet. So I began to ask him a lot of questions about some of the other signers, and particularly about John Adams, his special favorite. And what did he do but toss me a life of Adams and tell me to read it! Every time he was around, I'd open it and pretend to be interested. And the ruse worked. He guessed that Adams was my man! I won the five dollars. My brother may turn out to be a good lawyer, but he'd make a bad detective, not to guess that I'd gallop through the night to win that bet.

Summer

Jack Straw

Characters

MR. BARN
JACK STRAW
MRS. SWALLOW

TIME: *An afternoon in late summer.*
SETTING: *A barnyard.*
AT RISE: MR. BARN *is standing in the center of the*
  stage. JACK STRAW *is on one side of him,* MRS. SWAL-
  LOW *is on the other.*
MR. BARN:
  The breath of fall is in the air,
  It whispers up the valley.
JACK (*Jumping up*):
  I feel it in my yellow hair.
  Horray! I must not dally:
  I'll ride the wind, I'll ride the breeze,
  I'll ride them both together,
  While *you* sit here and sneeze and sneeze
  Throughout the winter weather.

MR. BARN:

Some can go, but some must stay.
The days are getting hazy.
My loft is full of needed hay . . .

JACK:

I think you just are lazy!
Not me—I'm off to see the sights,
All dressed in shiny yellow.
I'll travel days, I'll travel nights.
Oh, I'm a dandy fellow!

MRS. SWALLOW (*Softly*):

Pride goes before a fall, you know.

JACK:

What's that? Oh, Mrs. Swallow.
I bet I'll beat you south. Ho, ho!
I'll lead and you can follow.

MRS. SWALLOW:

You try to sound so fine and big
With all your foolish bragging,
You'd think you were a little pig
That had two tails a-wagging.

JACK (*Strutting around proudly*):

To tell the truth, I'm quite a chap.
I'm off to see the city.
Well, Mr. Barn, enjoy your nap.
I'll think of you with pity.

MR. BARN:

Some must stay, but some can go.

JACK:

And I, for one, am going.

MR. BARN:

I shield the cattle from the snow
And from the north wind blowing.

JACK:

You sit and never see a thing.
A life could not be dumber.

MR. BARN:

    I see the orchard bloom in spring,
    The meadow bloom in summer,
    The trees turn red and gold in fall;
    And winter brings a beauty
    No other time can touch at all.
    Besides, I do my duty.

JACK:

    Of course, you're pretty old and fat,
    Not full of vim and vigor. (*He jumps around to show
    how fit he is.*)

MRS. SWALLOW:

    He serves a use. It's certain that
    His part in life is bigger
    Than if he flitted east and west
    And acted very badly!
    Come, Jack. Next spring I'll build a nest,
    And I could use you gladly.

JACK:

    Who, me? I've better things to do.
    I'm much too good for sitting.
    Why, I'm a dandy, through and through.

MRS. SWALLOW:

    I've thought of something fitting,
    I heard it one time from an elf . . .

MR. BARN:

    Come, tell us, Mrs. Swallow.

MRS. SWALLOW:

    "A person full of just himself
    Is apt to be quite hollow!"

MR. BARN (*Chuckling*):

    I think that isn't far from wrong.

JACK:

    This barnyard is so stuffy,
    I wonder why I've stayed so long.

MRS. SWALLOW:

You sound a little huffy.

JACK:

Ah, there's a breeze for me to ride!

I'll leave this place forever.

MRS. SWALLOW:

A peacock never had more pride.

JACK:

I'm off. Ho. Ho. I'm clever.

I'll see the world from east to west,

Oh, I'm a dandy fellow,

Now folks can see how well I'm dressed

In all my shiny yellow. (*He hurries out.*)

MRS. SWALLOW:

I'm going to follow just for fun.

That lad will get in trouble . . .

It doesn't do for anyone

To blow up like a bubble. (*She goes out after* JACK.)

MR. BARN (*Slowly*):

Winter . . . summer . . . spring . . . and fall . . .

Here I sit and watch them all.

Summer . . . winter . . . fall . . . and spring . . .

All are nice as anything!

MRS. SWALLOW (*Rushing back in*):

The wind, my friend, has let him down.

MR. BARN: What! Let him down already?

MRS. SWALLOW:

He didn't even get to town.

He looks a bit unsteady . . .

He landed in a *bramble* bush.

MR. BARN:

My, that was quite a tumble.

MRS. SWALLOW:

He begged me for a little push.

He really seemed quite humble.

His shirt was torn, his yellow cap,
His jacket and his britches,
And he confessed—the little chap—
That he was full of itches!
(JACK *comes limping in.*)

JACK:

Hello. (*He looks around.*) Oh, what a lovely view!
You people are in clover:
You both have useful things to do . . .
I've thought my travels over . . .
My goodness, how those brambles sting!
I guess my head *was* hollow.

MRS. SWALLOW:

I'd like to use you, Jack, in spring.

JACK (*Happily*):

Oh, thank you, Mrs. Swallow.
I think this place is rather nice.

MR. BARN:

You've finished with your rambles?

JACK:

I do not have to tumble twice.
My pride is in the brambles.

MR. BARN (*Smiling at* JACK):

Winter . . . summer . . . spring . . . and fall . . .
We'll be here to watch them all.

THE END

PRODUCTION NOTES
JACK STRAW

Characters: 2 male; 1 female.
Playing Time: 10 minutes.
Costumes: Mr. Barn is dressed in red. Jack Straw has a yellow costume
    with bits of hay or straw pinned on it. Mrs. Swallow wears a gray dress.
Properties: None required.
Setting: A barnyard. A mound of dried grass may be placed upstage center,
    a wheel barrow at right, farm implements at left.
Lighting: No special effects.

229

In the Good Old Summertime

Characters

MOTHER
NEIGHBOR
BOY
GIRL

MOTHER: I rather dread it in a way—
this summer-long vacation.
NEIGHBOR: No school, no plan for every day,
no settled occupation!
Whatever will the children do
to pass the time, I wonder?
MOTHER: That's something I've been wondering, too.
Vacations are a blunder.

(BOY *and* GIRL *come running in, excited.*)

BOTH: Mother, may we have a rope?
BOY: I want to do some stalking
of cowboy horses . . .
GIRL: And I hope
to do some tight-rope walking.
BOTH: We're going to give a circus, see?
You each must buy a ticket.
GIRL: We'll have a zoo. It's up to me
to find a bright, black cricket.
Mother, may I have a box?
BOY: We just saw Ann and Freddy . . .
They caught a toad behind some rocks
and have a mouse already.
GIRL: We'll make some lemonade that's pink.
We'll need a lot of glasses . . .
I'm sure that we can sell a drink
to everyone who passes.
BOY: We'll have a sideshow and parade
and entertain the neighbors,

	and buy a treat with what we've made
	from all our circus labors.
GIRL:	And *then* we'll have a barbecue
	at Johnny's house, and after,
	we'll all have funny stunts to do
	and split our sides with laughter.
BOY:	And *next* week we'll put on a play.
GIRL:	I'll be a fairy in it.
BOY:	I'll be an aviator . . . say,
	there's Johnny! (*Calls*) Wait a minute!

(BOY *and* GIRL *rush out.*)

MOTHER: Goodness, what a lot of schemes!
NEIGHBOR: What plans, what pep, what hurry!
MOTHER: Vacation dull? My dear, it seems that
we were dull—to worry.

Apple Trees

How do apple trees
know how
to hang the apples
on a bough?

They haven't hands
to glue them on
or nail them on
or screw them on
or pin them on
or sew them on.
Who holds them
while they *grow* them on?

I never thought
of it till now . . .
I wonder
did the apple bough?

231

SEPTEMBER

School Again!

BOY:
Part of me's sad,
and part of me's glad,
and part of me's in-between:
the weather is clear
as crystal this year
and maple trees still are green,
but . . .

ALL:
         It's pencil and pen
and counting by ten
and reading and writing at—school
again!

GIRL:
Part of me's gay
and part of me's gray
and part of me's sort of blue:
the summer was free
as wind in a tree,
but summer is mostly through,
so . . .

ALL:	It's paper and pen and spelling, and then arithmetic problems at—school again!
BOY *and* GIRL:	Part of me blinks, and part of me winks as mischievous as an elf: for where'd be the fun now school has begun to stay at home *by myself!* So . . .
GIRLS:	It's Nancy!
BOYS:	And Glenn!
GIRLS:	And Kathy!
BOYS:	And Ken!
ALL:	Hello there, hello there—it's school again!

Back to School

Characters

MOTHER
BOY
GIRL

MOTHER:	What's the matter? You're looking so glum.
BOY:	I don't want the end of vacation to come. I don't want to add or subtract or divide or go to a schoolhouse with lessons inside.
MOTHER:	And what are you thinking of doing instead?

BOY: I'll hide in a barrel
and cover my head.
I'll sit in a tree
or behind a big stone
and keep my vacation . . .

MOTHER: You will? All alone?

GIRL (*Running in, excited*): I'm getting so eager.
Tomorrow I'll see Myrtle,
and Susan, and Cathy!

BOY (*Grumpily*): *I'll* talk to my turtle.

GIRL: The Allens are back.
I saw your friend Les.
He says he will show you
some tricks at recess.
And Johnny says he
has a present for you,
and Ken knows some jokes
that are screamingly new,
and Tom has a football . . .

BOY: He has!

MOTHER: I presume
he'll get up a team
from the boys in your room.
Too bad you'll be hiding
from everyone, son. . . .

GIRL: Hiding? You mean
after school has begun?

MOTHER: He won't let vacation
be over and done.

GIRL: Really?

BOY: Well, maybe . . .
my friends may feel sad
and miss me. . . . and maybe
school isn't so bad!

Future Unlimited

Characters

Mr. Future
Nurse
Doctor
Mr. X
Johnny
Liz, *Johnny's sister*
Beanie
Boys and Girls

SETTING: *Mr. Future's study. It is furnished with couch, some chairs, a desk and some bookshelves. Newspapers are on desk. Doors are right, left, and at the back.*

AT RISE: MR. FUTURE, *in bathrobe, lies on couch. He is ill.* NURSE *bends over him, putting cold towel on his head.*

FUTURE: Everything is such a *headache* these days. My nerves are all on edge. . . . I feel as if the world's on the brink of disaster.

NURSE: You do seem distraught and unhappy about something—everything.

237

FUTURE: It's people. Take the Americans, now. I've been counting on them to straighten out some of the threats to my happiness and well being, but I'm afraid they're going to let me down.

NURSE: See if you can get some sleep. Just close your eyes and relax.

FUTURE: Closing my eyes to what's going on in the world is no solution to the problems that are giving me these headaches. What I want is some assurance that my condition isn't going to be permanent.

NURSE: The doctor has been doing his best. But he hasn't found the right prescription yet. Give him time.

FUTURE: There's no time to spare. (*Looks around nervously*) Where's my attorney?

NURSE: Mr. X? He left some time ago.

FUTURE: Did he say where he was going?

NURSE: No, he didn't. But I noticed he was walking very fast, as if he had something very important on his mind. Perhaps he was pursuing one of his ideas, Mr. Future.

FUTURE: Well, I hope it's a good one . . . with my life in such a precarious state. (NURSE *removes pad from* MR. FUTURE's *head, feels his brow, shakes her head.*)

NURSE: You're still running a temperature. You worry too much, Mr. Future. The Doctor thinks that your troubles are all in your mind.

FUTURE: All in my mind! (*Agitated*) Hand me those newspapers on my desk, Nurse. All in my mind, indeed! (NURSE *hands him papers. He scans headlines.*) Listen to this. Is it any wonder I have the jitters? (*Reading*) LESS THAN FIFTY PER CENT OF VOTERS TURN OUT IN RECENT ELECTION . . . DISCRIMINATION IN HOUSING PROJECTS IS DISCLOSED . . . JUVENILE CRIME ON THE INCREASE . . . (*As* MR. FUTURE *reads, he gets more and more upset.*)

NURSE (*Running to door; calling*): Doctor! Doctor!

FUTURE (*Still reading*): AMERICAN BUSINESSMEN TOO BUSY TO SERVE ON JURY . . . RACIAL DISCRIMINATION IN JOBS AT NEW PLANT . . . FREEDOM OF SPEECH ON TRIAL . . .

DOCTOR (*Rushing in*): What is it?

NURSE: I'm afraid he's going to get himself into a worse state than he's in.

DOCTOR (*Grabbing papers*): Take these papers away, Nurse. It's obvious they set Mr. Future's nerves on edge. If he must read, give him a dictionary, or the telephone book!

NURSE: Yes, sir. (NURSE *takes papers away from* MR. FUTURE, *exits.*)

FUTURE: Those headlines! No wonder I'm a wreck.

DOCTOR: But what you read in the papers isn't the whole picture, Mr. Future. They always play up the sensational events. There's another side to it.

FUTURE: I'd like to know what it is! I never hear about the good side. (*Very depressed*) I had been counting a lot on America, Doctor.

DOCTOR: I understand.

FUTURE: Such a wonderful experiment . . . in freedom . . . in democracy. Ever since 1776 I have been looking to America. . . . Such promises. Such hope. "All men are created equal. Life, liberty, and the pursuit of happiness."

DOCTOR: Brave words.

FUTURE: Wonderful words! For years they inspired me. And the United States Constitution! Never was a country founded on such ideals of justice, welfare, and the blessings of liberty. And look what happens!

DOCTOR: What happens?

FUTURE: Restricted residential areas, where certain American citizens aren't wanted. Discrimination in jobs. A small turnout at the polls.

DOCTOR: You mean you're afraid Americans aren't living up to the ideals of democracy?

FUTURE: Mortally afraid, Doctor. It's my biggest headache.

DOCTOR (*Pacing*): If only we could find some prescription for reassurance! There must be one somewhere.

FUTURE: If you could convince me, Doctor, that things aren't as bad as they sound in the headlines . . . if you could convince me that there is hope, that democracy is strong, I'd recover without any medicine.

DOCTOR: If only . . . (MR. X *suddenly bursts into the room with* JOHNNY.)

MR. X: Excuse me, Doctor. Excuse me, Mr. Future. But I have an idea. (*To* DOCTOR) How's the patient?

DOCTOR: No better, I am afraid.

MR. X: I would like to try an experiment, if you don't mind.

DOCTOR: I'm ready to try anything . . . anything.

MR. X: Gentlemen, I have here an average American boy. His name is Johnny. I met him on the street as he was going to play baseball.

DOCTOR: I don't see what this has to do with anything, Mr. X.

JOHNNY (*Timidly*): I don't either, sir. How can I help?

MR. X: It occurs to me, Doctor, that Johnny may be very helpful. By questioning him, we may be able to discover just how much basis there is for Mr. Future's troubles. (*To* JOHNNY) Johnny, would you mind answering a few questions?

JOHNNY (*Doubtfully*): I don't mind, but I'm no genius.

MR. X: Johnny, do you believe that everybody in the United States ought to have an equal chance?

JOHNNY: You mean to go to school . . . to get on the baseball team if he's good enough . . . to live where he wants . . . that sort of thing?

240

MR. X: Yes, exactly that sort of thing.

JOHNNY: Sure. Everybody ought to have an equal chance. That's what America stands for.

FUTURE (*Perking up*): And who *is* on your baseball team, Johnny?

JOHNNY (*Enthusiastically*): We have some great new players. Jose Alvarez is our pitcher. He just moved here from Puerto Rico with his family. And are we lucky to have him on our team! Billy Derby is our new shortstop. He came here from Alabama, just a few months ago.

FUTURE: You mean you have boys on your team who just moved to town, and some who just came to the United States?

JOHNNY: Sure, Mr. Future. Why not? They're good players, and that's what matters.

FUTURE (*Sitting up*): Where do you live, Johnny?

JOHNNY: In a new housing development. My dad bought a house; he got a loan.

FUTURE: What kind of people live in this new housing development?

JOHNNY: All kinds.

FUTURE: *All* kinds?

JOHNNY: Sure, why not? There's a Japanese family next to us, and they have the best garden in the development. We even elected Mr. Yamawaka head of the Beautification Committee for the project. I mean, our parents elected him.

FUTURE: Well! (*He has obviously forgotten his headache.*)

MR. X: Speaking of elections, Johnny, do you think it's important to vote?

JOHNNY: I sure do. On election days my sister Liz and I go around the neighborhood and babysit, to let the grownups go to the polls. We know voting is one of the

241

most important rights in a democracy—that's what we learned in school. And we have elections in school, too.

FUTURE (*Jumping to his feet*): I haven't felt so good in a long time. Johnny, have you any ideas about why it is so important to vote?

JOHNNY: Of course. How else are we going to have a say on who runs things? You have to find out all about the candidates ahead of time. You don't just vote for somebody because he looks good on TV. He has to stand for something worthwhile. He has to be honest, care about the people who elect him, so he can represent them. And he has to be courageous.

FUTURE: Why?

JOHNNY: So he'll stand up for our freedoms, and for what's right, no matter what others say.

FUTURE (*Happily*): What freedoms do you mean?

JOHNNY: Why, freedom of speech, and the press, and religion, the right to associate with anyone you like, to hold meetings. We don't want to lose those rights—or any other rights, either. Like the right to a fair trial, if we get in trouble. When I'm old enough to vote, you can bet I'm not going to miss a single election.

FUTURE: Great! (*He jumps up and does a little jig.* DOCTOR *hurries over to him.*)

DOCTOR: You're not overdoing it, are you Mr. Future?

FUTURE: Overdoing it? Why, I feel like turning handsprings. I haven't felt this well in a long time. What Johnny said is just the tonic I need. (*To* MR. X) It was a brainstorm, Mr. X, to find a typical American boy like Johnny. After all those headlines in the paper . . . (*To* DOCTOR) You know, you're right, Doctor, those scary headlines are only part of the picture. (*To* JOHNNY) Johnny, you've given me new hope. From now on my good health is up to you and all the other young citizens who feel the way you do.

JOHNNY (*Uncertainly*): I'm not sure I know what you mean.

MR. X: Mr. Future has put you on the spot, young man. Johnny . . . on the spot.

FUTURE: It's up to you and all good citizens to see that democracy keeps its ideals. You have to see that everyone gets a fair chance. You have to choose straight-thinking, honest, courageous men and women to run this country.

JOHNNY: There's only one of me, and . . .

FUTURE (*Waxing eloquent*): You have to keep working to make sure those freedoms apply to everyone.

JOHNNY (*Really alarmed*): Me! (*Sinks into chair*) I feel sort of weak—nervous, too. I'm not sure I'm up to what you expect.

DOCTOR (*Hurrying to* JOHNNY): I hope you aren't coming down with something, my boy. Stick out your tongue. (DOCTOR *shakes head.*) Let me feel your head. Does it ache?

JOHNNY: It sure does!

DOCTOR (*To* FUTURE): He seems to have caught all your symptoms, Mr. Future!

JOHNNY (*Moaning*): See that democracy keeps climbing ahead . . . that everyone gets a fair chance . . . that voters elect the right people! Phew! I can't stand up under a load like that. (*Slumps in chair*)

DOCTOR (*To* Mr. X): You are a man of ideas, sir. Have you any suggestions?

MR. X: You heard what he said, Doctor. He can't stand up under the load. The remedy is obvious. Johnny needs some good big shots of vitamins A, B, C, D, E, F, G, and maybe X, Y, Z. He needs something to bolster him up . . . to help him carry the burden that Mr. Future has put on his shoulders.

JOHNNY (*Smiling*): That's right. I need some help. But

there's something a whole lot better than vitamins! (*He whistles shrilly.* LIZ, BEANIE, BOYS, *and* GIRLS *burst in from all doors.*)

BEANIE: We've been listening to everything. (*To* MR. X) After all, we couldn't let you run off with our first baseman. (*To* JOHNNY) We've come to your rescue, Johnny. You can count on us to help.

LIZ (*To* MR. X *and* FUTURE): Johnny's my brother, and you've put him on the spot. (*Turns to* JOHNNY) But you don't have to be on the spot all by yourself, Johnny. We're all ready to pitch in and help do the things Mr. Future wants because we believe in them, too.

BEANIE: You bet! You won't have anything to worry about, Mr. Future, with all of us in there pitching.

MR. X (*Smiling*): You make it sound like a ball game, Beanie.

JOHNNY (*Cheerfully*): Maybe it is, in a way. With all of us teamed up together and our eyes on the ball, Mr. Future won't get sick again. We'll keep scoring on the side of democracy and freedom. What do you say, Liz? Beanie? Everyone?

ALL: Three cheers for democracy! Three cheers for the future! (*Curtain*)

THE END

PRODUCTION NOTES
FUTURE UNLIMITED

Characters: 5 male; 2 female; as many as desired for Boys and Girls.
Playing Time: 15 minutes.
Costumes: Modern, everyday dress. Mr. Future wears a bathrobe. Nurse wears a white uniform, and Doctor may wear a white coat.
Properties: Baseball and mitt for Johnny, pad or compress for Nurse.
Setting: Mr. Future's study. It is furnished with a couch, some chairs, a desk and some bookshelves. There are some newspapers on desk. There is a door at either side, and also one at the back.
Lighting: No special effects.

Thank You, America

1ST BOY: Thank you, America,
for our beautiful and spacious land,
our millions of acres of fields and wooded
    hills,
our forests and grasslands,
our mountains and treeless plains.

1ST GIRL: Thank you for our rivers and lakes,
and for the pattern of brooks flowing to the
    sea;
for two great oceans—on the east and west,
and two peaceful borders on the north and
    south.

BOTH: Thank you, America, for all the beauty of
    this land.

2ND BOY: And thank you, America, for abundance:
for the trees in our forests—hardwoods, soft-
    woods,
that give us lumber for building houses and
    stores,
factories and furniture.

2ND GIRL: And thank you for the wild life in our forests,
and the fish in our streams;
and above all for the fertility of our soil
that enables us to produce so large a share
of the world's meat and cotton and corn and
    wheat.

ALL: And thank you for the riches under the
    earth—
silver and copper, gold and lead and zinc,
oil and coal, iron and uranium . . .
Thank you, America, for all this bounty we
    are blessed with.

3RD BOY: Thank you, America, for opportunity—
the open door, the rungs on the waiting ladder.

3RD GIRL: Thank you for the chance to live where we please,
to work where we want,
to own property, and manage our own affairs,
and to succeed or fail according to the way we develop our abilities.

ALL: Thank you, America,
for our heritage of freedom and independence,
for ringing words that come out of the past
as strong as the day they were spoken:

BOYS: "Give me liberty or give me death."

GIRLS: "Liberty and justice for all."

BOYS: "Life, liberty, and the pursuit of happiness."

GIRLS: "From every mountain side let freedom ring."

ALL: Thank you, America,
for your faith in us and in the future.
May we be given the foresight to care for the bounty
which you have entrusted to us
so that Americans who follow
will know the same plenty we are grateful for today.
Thank you, America,
for the past,
and the present,
and the future,
and help us be worthy of our heritage.

OCTOBER

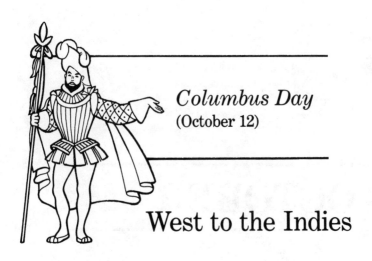

Columbus Day
(October 12)

West to the Indies

Characters

SENHORA PERESTRELLO
FELIPA PERESTRELLO
CAPTAIN DE ANDRADA
BARTHOLOMEW COLUMBUS
SENHOR VINCENTE
CHRISTOPHER COLUMBUS
MARIA

TIME: *1477, an evening that might have been.*
SETTING: *A parlor in the home of Senhora Perestrello. Fireplace is up center, with chair beside it. Other chairs, small tables, etc., are placed about the stage. Candles are on tables. Doors are right and left.*
AT RISE: SENHORA PERESTRELLO *is embroidering handkerchief.* FELIPA *is hemstitching a smaller square of linen.*

SENHORA: Linen such as this is a delight to the touch, my daughter.

FELIPA (*Stroking her square*): So soft and fine, it feels like silk. Linen from the Indies, so far away. The very thought weaves a spell of romance, and I dream of a wedding dress.

SENHORA: A wedding dress?

FELIPA: Yes, Mother, of linen from the Indies. If only father had lived to see me in my wedding dress.

SENHORA: My daughter, as yet no man has asked me for your hand. Is there someone that you have not told me about?

FELIPA (*Sighing*): No one seeks to marry me.

SENHORA: It is well, my dear, for you are young.

FELIPA (*Impulsively*): Christopher Columbus . . . you like him, Mother, do you not?

SENHORA: It is true I like him, but . . .

FELIPA: But what, Mother?

SENHORA: Perhaps young Christopher Columbus comes to us too often.

FELIPA: Yet all he does when he comes is pore over father's old charts and log books.

SENHORA: He is welcome to your father's records, but that is all. He would not be a suitable husband for you, Felipa.

FELIPA: Please, Mother, do not say anything against Christopher.

SENHORA: For marriage, Felipa, you must think of more than good character, though that is important. You must think of social standing. You must not forget that both your father and I come of Portuguese families highly respected in Lisbon.

FELIPA: And Christopher's family, is it not respected in Genoa?

SENHORA (*With a shrug*): His father works with his hands. He is a weaver.

FELIPA: A master weaver, Mother. He has his own looms and hires journeymen weavers to work for him.

SENHORA: True, but I have been told that he is not a good businessman. He has not provided well for his family.

FELIPA: He has been a good father. When Christopher and Bartholomew were little he would always shut up shop on a fine day to take them fishing.

SENHORA: A lovable father, no doubt, but I fear he has not set his boys a good example.

FELIPA: He wanted Christopher to become a good sailor. When Christopher was only ten years old, his father let him sail with a neighbor to Portofino.

SENHORA: You must turn your thoughts away from this young man. You must not forget that your father was the first governor of Porto Santo and a hereditary captain.

FELIPA: If Father had lived, I'm sure he would like Christopher. They would have the love of the sea and the spirit of adventure in common. Father would see a great future for him. But now there is only my Uncle-Captain. Oh, if only Christopher will find favor in his eyes.

SENHORA: Tonight we shall see.

FELIPA: I am so nervous about their meeting, Mother. Since Father died, Uncle-Captain is not so playful. Now he gives advice and talks about family traditions.

SENHORA: As your father's closest friend, he feels a sense of responsibility for your future and your happiness, Felipa.

CAPTAIN (*Offstage*): Thank you, Maria. (SENHORA *raises her finger for silence.* CAPTAIN *enters.*)

SENHORA (*Warmly*): Welcome, Captain. It is good to see you.

FELIPA (*Running to him*): I am glad you are here, Uncle-Captain.

CAPTAIN: I am happy to see you both.

SENHORA: I have asked the Columbus brothers to meet you this evening. They are map makers from Genoa.

CAPTAIN: And already well-known here. Even in the few days I have been back I have heard of them several times.

FELIPA (*Slipping her arm through his*): Uncle-Captain, I am going to ask a very big favor of you.

CAPTAIN: What is it I can do for you, little one?

FELIPA: Please—speak kindly to Christopher. It is so easy to hurt the feelings of someone so sensitive.

CAPTAIN: So I am a gruff old bear, am I? (*Laughs*)

FELIPA: Oh, no, Uncle-Captain. But Christopher is so sensitive, so proud.

CAPTAIN: For your sake, I shall try to remember.

FELIPA: Thank you, Uncle-Captain!

CAPTAIN: And where is Senhor Vincente this evening? Has he become too feeble to walk about?

SENHORA: He will be coming before long, Captain. Senhor Vincente knows he is welcome to sit here by the chimney without talking.

CAPTAIN: I would feel more comfortable if he would join in the talk. When he turns his hollow eyes on me, I feel he can read my thoughts.

FELIPA: I do hope he won't mention the future. At least not Bartholomew's or . . . or Christopher's.

CAPTAIN: Senhor Vincente might say something bad about my future, too, you know.

SENHORA: All your concern is for nothing, I assure you. The poor old man will say nothing at all, nothing. (*Door knocker sounds.* SENHORA *opens door.* BARTHOLOMEW *enters.*)

BARTHOLOMEW (*Bowing*): Good evening, Senhora.

SENHORA: Good evening, Bartholomew.

BARTHOLOMEW (*Bowing to* FELIPA): Good evening, Dona Felipa. (FELIPA *smiles and inclines her head.*)

SENHORA (*Gesturing*): I have the honor to present you to Captain Pedro Aranha de Andrada, a great navigator, as you know. Captain, allow me to present the younger Columbus brother, Bartholomew.

BARTHOLOMEW: I have long known you by reputation, Senhor.

CAPTAIN: And I have been hearing good things about the Columbus brothers, especially about the charts and maps you are making. I understand you have opened a shop of your own.

BARTHOLOMEW: We started our own charting business soon after Christopher joined me here in Lisbon.

CAPTAIN: Has it turned out well?

BARTHOLOMEW: Better than we had a right to expect, Senhor. And best of all, it keeps us in close touch with the masters and pilots in the merchant service. It is almost as good as a life at sea.

FELIPA: Bartholomew, is Christopher not coming?

BARTHOLOMEW: He will be here without doubt. Christopher stayed to finish a chart he wants to show you, Captain. (SENHOR VINCENTE *enters left, muffled in a scarf. Leaning on his cane, he shuffles across room, speaking to no one, and sits by chimney.* FELIPA *unwinds his scarf and lays it on chair with his cane. She returns to* CAPTAIN.)

CAPTAIN (*With good humor*): Felipa, it seems that I am to see a sample of the work of a good chartmaker this evening.

FELIPA: Father used to say that a good chartmaker is a navigator's best friend.

BARTHOLOMEW: And I say that a good navigator is a chartmaker's best friend. We would be at a loss indeed without the rough sketches navigators bring back from their voyages. (*Door knocker sounds.*)

SENHORA: Felipa, will you see about the tea and cakes?

(FELIPA *exits left.* SENHORA *opens door.* CHRISTOPHER *enters, carrying a rolled chart.*)

CHRISTOPHER (*Bowing*): Good evening, Senhora.

SENHORA: Good evening, Christopher. And now it is my pleasure to present you to a navigator as great as my husband was. Captain Pedro Aranha de Andrada, Senhor Christopher Columbus.

CHRISTOPHER: I had hoped to meet the distinguished captain long before this. But, Senhor, when you were home from a voyage, it seems that I was away on one.

CAPTAIN: Before I sailed for the Gulf of Guinea in the spring, I heard about the voyage you were about to make to the north. The master of the vessel, my good friend, had ambitious plans about exploring to the north of Iceland.

CHRISTOPHER: What a voyage it was! We sailed on and on into the north, to the very edge of the ice. But I want to hear what happened on your last voyage, Captain, to delay your return so long.

CAPTAIN: We ran into monstrous seas. I would not be here at all if our fleet had not been specially designed for the African trade. (FELIPA *returns left, followed by* MARIA, *carrying tea service which she sets on a low table beside* SENHORA. MARIA *exits.*)

CHRISTOPHER (*Eagerly*): Good evening, Dona Felipa.

FELIPA: Good evening. May I not relieve you of your chart?

CHRISTOPHER: Bartholomew may need to add a line or two. (*He hands chart to* BARTHOLOMEW, *who opens and studies it.* SENHORA *pours tea and* FELIPA *serves, then sits and resumes sewing. She listens intently.*)

CAPTAIN: Senhor Columbus, for a young man well under thirty, I should say you have done very well. Is it your intention to continue as a chartmaker?

CHRISTOPHER: Not permanently, Captain. The sea has always called me.

CAPTAIN: Then the Portuguese merchant service—the fastest and farthest-ranging in the world—ought to interest you.

CHRISTOPHER: The merchant service would be more adventurous than life on land. There is danger and daring in it, but it follows the known routes of trade. I am eager to explore unknown waters.

CAPTAIN: Unknown waters! And what do you hope to find?

CHRISTOPHER: The desire of my life is to find a water route to the Indies, to the fabulous lands in the Far East that Marco Polo tells about.

CAPTAIN: I confess to having the same ambition. The unknown waters off the coast of Africa beyond the Gulf of Guinea draw me like a magnet. Even at my age I yearn to sail around Africa to India.

CHRISTOPHER: And I hope that you will be the first man to sail around Africa. I intend to reach the Indies by quite a different route—by sailing west, into the setting sun, across the Ocean Sea.

CAPTAIN: Senhor, surely you speak in jest.

CHRISTOPHER: No. I speak in deadly earnest.

CAPTAIN (*Shaking his head*): Pardon, Senhor, but your venture is bound to strike a seasoned navigator as . . . well, shall I say, as highly impractical.

BARTHOLOMEW: Captain, may I ask if you consider it impossible to reach the East by sailing west?

CAPTAIN: Impossible? Of course not. The earth is round without a doubt. Men have known that since the days of the Greeks.

CHRISTOPHER: Men have talked of sailing west to reach the East, Captain, since the days of the Roman Empire.

CAPTAIN: True enough, but what have they done about it? Nothing. To circle the globe is not impossible in theory, but it is impossible in practice.

CHRISTOPHER: I shall never be at peace until I have made the attempt.

CAPTAIN: You will risk a mutiny if you man vessels for this venture. What can you expect of superstitious sailors? Three weeks out of sight of land, and they will believe you are mad to keep on sailing into nothingness, perhaps to fall off the edge of the earth and be heard of no more. Believe me, they will throw you overboard and turn back home.

CHRISTOPHER: Bartholomew, if you please, sketch in the point where we expect to break the voyage . . . the point where we hope to find the legendary Island of Antilia. (BARTHOLOMEW *busies himself with chart.*)

CAPTAIN: What if the island proves to be only a legend and there is no break in your voyage, week after week, month after month?

CHRISTOPHER: We will sail on.

CAPTAIN: Why, Senhor Columbus, it would take the greatest seaman of all time.

FELIPA: Who knows? The greatest seaman of all time may be Christopher Columbus. (CHRISTOPHER *smiles in acknowledgment.*)

CAPTAIN: Everyone knows the Ocean Sea is one and indivisible. But no one knows how broad it is.

CHRISTOPHER: It cannot be so very broad, to my way of thinking.

CAPTAIN: Who knows how much space both land and water cover? Who knows the circumference of the globe?

CHRISTOPHER: I have figured it. Others have, too. I am sure enough of the distance to risk my life on it. (CAPTAIN *shrugs.*)

255

SENHORA: Christopher, you sound like my dear husband.

FELIPA: Once Father made up his mind, nothing could shake his faith.

BARTHOLOMEW: At first I thought Christopher had figured the ocean too narrow. But now I am certain he is right.

CAPTAIN: It is all speculation, I tell you. Some say one thing, some another. What is your guess, Senhor?

CHRISTOPHER: You may think me presumptuous to disagree with Ptolemy, but my estimate is less than his. Forty-five nautical miles instead of his fifty.

CAPTAIN (*Taking a notebook from pocket and figuring*): Then the distance around your globe of 360 degrees is only a little more than 16,000 miles. Ptolemy figures it almost 2,000 miles more. A miscalculation of that size could mean the failure of your expedition. And what if your underestimate should turn out to be 5,000 miles, or even more? Don't you see how impossible the whole thing is? How could you take enough food on board for a journey that might last one year, two years, three years?

CHRISTOPHER: That could not be, Captain. For the distance by water is all that need concern me. And I figure that no more than 67 degrees of the earth's surface is covered by water.

CAPTAIN: And what is your authority for such a calculation?

CHRISTOPHER: Marinus of Tyre, Senhor, and Marco Polo.

CAPTAIN: Marco Polo? That weaver of fantastic tales!

FELIPA: Uncle-Captain, do you not believe Marco Polo?

CAPTAIN: Such tales. Houses roofed with gold. All the people dressed in silks and their hair braided with precious stones. Bah!

256

CHRISTOPHER: Marco Polo may have embroidered the facts, Captain, but gold and gems and silks and spices are there in abundance.

BARTHOLOMEW: The Moslems of Aleppo and Alexandria wax richer every year dealing in the luxuries of India and Cathay, do they not?

CAPTAIN: All too true. We are at the mercy of the Moslems who control the overland routes to the Far East. We must outwit them by discovering a water route, a feasible one. That can only mean a route around Africa.

CHRISTOPHER: By all means find a route around Africa, but will not two water routes be better than one? Before either is discovered, who can say which will prove the shorter or better? Bartholomew, please point out to the Captain on the map how far we figure the Indies extend into the Ocean Sea. (BARTHOLOMEW *holds map open for* CAPTAIN *to study.*)

BARTHOLOMEW: Here, Captain, this line is where land ends.

CAPTAIN: I see. So you figure Europe and Asia together cover about 283 degrees. A mere guess, and again you differ from Ptolemy. He figured the land covered no more than 180 degrees.

BARTHOLOMEW: In that we believe Ptolemy was mistaken.

CHRISTOPHER: I am not one to let such fears deter me. All that stands in my way is money for ships, cargo, and men.

CAPTAIN: A fortune is what you ask, a fortune only a royal treasury could yield. And what King would drain the royal treasury for so reckless a venture? Do you think King John of Portugal would consider it?

CHRISTOPHER: It is to King John I shall appeal first. Everyone knows of his eagerness to find a water route to the East. So far he has been interested only in a route around Africa, but I expect my plan to appeal to his spirit of adventure.

BARTHOLOMEW: As well as to his hope of gain.

CAPTAIN: If King John and his hardheaded advisers refuse you, then where will you turn?

CHRISTOPHER: Perhaps to the Court of Spain, Senhor.

CAPTAIN: Spain must continue to spend its energies trying to drive out the Moors. You can expect no help from that quarter. (SENHOR VINCENTE *rises slowly and steadies himself on his chair.*)

SENHOR VINCENTE: Christopher Columbus will sail for the Indies. (*Sinks into his chair*)

BARTHOLOMEW: There, Captain, you see! Somehow, somewhere, Christopher will get ships and provisions and men.

CHRISTOPHER: And that means that I will reach the Indies! For once I embark on my voyage across the Sea of Darkness, I cannot fail.

CAPTAIN: Your faith begins to impress even me. If nothing will deter you, let me ask where you propose to take leave of land . . . at the Azores, I suppose?

CHRISTOPHER: No, Captain. I know too much of the Azores to risk the westerly winds that have turned back vessel after vessel. What I want is the benefit of steady easterly trade winds and by heading south to the Canaries I shall find them.

CAPTAIN: To go so far out of your way is ill-advised, Senhor. No one will approve the waste of time and money.

SENHOR VINCENTE (*Rising unsteadily*): I see yet more. Christopher Columbus, you will never reach the Indies. And yet it is strange, very strange. For you will die believing you *have* reached the Indies. (*Sinks down*)

CHRISTOPHER: Some say that I am already a little mad. (*Taps his forehead and smiles*) But you, Senhor, would have me stark mad. Not to reach the Indies and yet to believe that I reach them!

BARTHOLOMEW: Do not think of the bad omen, but only that you will make the voyage.

CHRISTOPHER: I may not reach the Indies, but nothing can keep me from trying.

SENHORA: May nothing daunt your proud spirit, Christopher. (SENHOR VINCENTE *rises and shuffles over to* SENHORA)

SENHOR VINCENTE: You will excuse me now, Senhora?

SENHORA: Certainly, Senhor. Good night. (*He moves forward and stops.*)

SENHOR VINCENTE: I hear voices shouting and cheering. . . . Admiral of the Ocean Sea. Admiral of the Ocean Sea. (*Moves toward door, right*)

BARTHOLOMEW: Senhor Vincente, permit me to see you safely home this dark night. (*They exit.*)

CAPTAIN: Senhor Columbus, I want you to know that I wish you well in your venture.

CHRISTOPHER: You are very kind, Captain.

CAPTAIN: I must confess, were I King John of Portugal, I should refuse to back so impossible an undertaking, and who would blame me? Not even Felipa here.

FELIPA: In that you are mistaken, my Uncle-Captain.

CAPTAIN (*Surprised*): What?

FELIPA: Were I King John, I should be proud to back a man who dreams great dreams and has the courage to make his dreams come true. (CHRISTOPHER *bends low over* FELIPA's *hand. Curtain*)

THE END

(Historical note: Within a year or two Christopher and Felipa were married. They had one child, Diego. Before Columbus secured support for his first voyage he was forty-one years old and his hair had turned white.)

Characters: 4 male; 3 female.

Playing Time: 15 minutes.

Costumes: Portuguese clothing of the 15th century. Men wear hose and long-sleeved doublets. Captain wears a sea captain's uniform. Senhor Vincente wears scarf and leans on a cane. Women wear long-sleeved dresses with long bodices and full skirts. Maria wears black dress and white apron.

Properties: Handkerchief and embroidery; linen square; folded chart; tea service; notebook and pen.

Setting: Home of Senhora Perestrello, in Lisbon. Fireplace is up center, with chair beside it. Other chairs, small tables, etc., are placed about the stage. There are candles on tables.

Lighting: No special effects.

The Dreamer

1ST: *Some* boys played with marbles

2ND: Some boys whittled chips.

3RD: *One* boy chose the harbor
and watched the sailing ships.

4TH: Some boys scoffed at dreamers
and thought themselves profound
to chide a lad who ventured
to say the world was round.

1ST: Some boys were unfriendly—
What jeers and taunts they hurled!

2ND: *One* boy named Columbus
opened up a world.

Light in the Darkness

(October 11, 1492)

BOYS: "I saw a light," Columbus said,
        straining his anxious eyes.
        "There in the darkness, straight ahead,
        seeming to fall and rise.
        The waxen gleam of a candle beam,
        seeming to fall and rise!"

GIRLS: Was it a light from far away?
        Was it a wind-blown star?
        Twelve leagues ahead the islands lay!
        Nothing could show so far.

BOYS: "I saw a light," Columbus cried,
        tense as a tightened wire.
        "There on the wave it seemed to ride,
        flashing its waxen fire.
        Yellow-bright as a taper's light,
        flashing its waxen fire!"

GIRLS: Was it a light the Captain saw?
        Was it but fancy's wraith?
        The only light that could show so far,
        bright as the brightest guiding star,
        was the light of the Captain's faith.

ALL: The light of the Captain's faith!

Halloween
(October 31)

Halloween Concert

BOYS: "It's cold," said the cricket,
"my fingers are numb.
I scarcely can fiddle,
I scarcely can strum.
And oh, I'm sleepy,
now summer has gone."

ALL: He dropped his fiddle
to stifle a yawn.

GIRLS: "Don't," said the field mouse, "act so sober.
You can't stop *yet*, when it's still October."

BOYS: "I've played," said the cricket,
"for weeks and weeks.
My fiddle needs fixing—
it's full of squeaks.
My fingers need resting . . ."
He yawned. "Ho, hum,
I'm quite . . . (*Yawn*) . . . ready
for winter to come.
I've found me the coziest,
doziest house . . ."

262

GIRLS: "You can't stop *now*," said his friend the mouse.
BOYS: "No?" yawned the cricket,
and closed his eyes.
"I've played so much
for a chap my size.
It's time (*He yawns*)
for my winter snooze:
I hear the creak
of November's shoes."
GIRLS: "You *can't* . . ." said the mouse in a voice of
sorrow,
"you can't desert us until tomorrow.
Tune up your fiddle for one last scene . . .
don't you remember it's HALLOWEEN?"
BOYS: "What!" cried the cricket.
He yawned no more.
"You should have mentioned
the fact before!
Is everyone ready?
And where's the score?
What in the world
are we waiting for?"
ALL: The cricket fiddled,
the field mouse squeaked,
the dry weeds twiddled,
the bare twigs tweaked,
the hoot-owl hooted,
the cornstalks strummed,
the west wind tooted,
the fence wires hummed:
Oh, what a concert all night long!
The fiddle was shrill, and the wind was strong.
"Halloween, Halloween, crick, crack, creak.
Halloween, Halloween, scritch, scratch, squeak."

The Night of Halloween

Characters

READER
DEBBIE
PETER
JOHN

READER (*In costume*): Debbie was a witch
all black and with a switch.
(DEBBIE *rides in on her broom.*)
Peter was a ghost
more quavery than most.
(PETER *enters, moaning and groaning.*)
John wore a pirate suit,
a dagger in his boot.
(*Swashbuckling* JOHN *enters.*)
We said it was a lark,
but, oh, the night was dark.
(*Horrible Halloween noises.*
READER *joins the others.*)
And when we scared some elves,
we really scared *ourselves.*
(*They collapse on the floor.*)

An October Night

NINE CHILDREN *in Halloween costume enter one by one and stand in line, showing large cardboard letters when they speak.*

> 1ST: H for hoot and witch's hat
> and haunted house and hark! (*Puts
> hand to ear*) What's that? (*Offstage
> noise is heard.*)
> 2ND: A for apples, all afloat,
> each a-bobbing like a boat.
> 3RD: L for jack-o'-lantern's light
> and leering looks to give you fright.
> 4TH: L for lark, for having fun
> looking, laughing on the run.
> 5TH: O for oddities that howl
> and spooky ogres on the prowl.
> 6TH: W for windy weather,
> witches whisking off together.
> 7TH: E for eager eyes that see
> eerie shapes behind each tree.
> 8TH: E for eating treats galore,
> with stops at each and every door.
> 9TH: N for noises without number
> when no ghosts or goblins slumber.
> ALL (*Holding up letters*): That spells an
> October night
> when scary figures glide in sight
> and pumpkin faces round and bright
> fill us all with giggly fright:
>
> HALLOWEEN!

Jack-o'-Lantern

Jack-o'-lantern, Jack-o'-lantern,
orange-front-and-back-o'-lantern,
sitting-on-the-sill-o'-lantern,
where's your sister Jill-o'-lantern?

What Is It?

It isn't two, it's only one,
and yet we use it twice.

It's round and fat and full of fun
which makes it doubly nice.

In fall it has a special place,
and here's the reason why:

Its outside makes a smiling face,
its inside makes a pie.

Starting from Scratch

(*To the tune of* "Billy Boy")

Oh, you cannot blame a match, Billy Boy, Billy Boy,
When you give the head a scratch, master Billy,
It is pretty sure to light
And to catch things left and right;
And a fire may be very hard to smother.

When you have a match to strike, Billy Boy, Billy Boy,
For a campfire on a hike, master Billy,
Just be sure the flame can't spread
Left or right or overhead,
For a fire may be very hard to smother.

Did you ever see a fire, Billy Boy, Billy Boy,
Sweeping grass and weed and briar, master Billy?
It's a fearful sight to see,
And I'm sure you will agree
That a fire may be very hard to smother.

So treat a match with care, Billy Boy, Billy Boy,
When you strike one anywhere, master Billy,
For you cannot blame the *match*
If you start a fire from scratch,
And a fire may be very hard to smother.

NOVEMBER

Election Day
(November)

Voting Against the Odds

Characters

DOUG
RALPH
COLEMAN
PEGGY
NORMA
CELIA

TIME: *After school.*
SETTING: *A living room.*
AT RISE: RALPH *is thumbing through some comic books.*
   DOUG *enters, carrying two huge sandwiches, hands*
   one to RALPH.
DOUG: Here. Peanut butter and honey.
RALPH: Thanks!
DOUG: There's more where this came from. (*Looks at*
   comic books) Well, what do you think of my comics,
   Ralph? I'll trade you mine for yours.

RALPH: Maybe. (*He eats as he continues to look at books, and pulls one out*) Say, what kind of comic book is this?

DOUG: Oh, that. (*Laughs*) My mother brought it home from the P.T.A. rummage sale, but when she read it, she was furious. The funny thing is, it made me mad, too.

RALPH (*Reading title*): "What's the Matter With the U.S.A.?" (*Looks up*) What made you mad?

DOUG: Turn the page.

RALPH (*Turning page, skimming it*): It's about voting. That's an odd subject for a comic book. (*Reads aloud*) "In an average election only about half our qualified voters take the trouble to vote." Is that what upset your mother?

DOUG: Partly. The worst is yet to come. Go on!

RALPH (*Reading on*): "America is supposed to be the champion of democracy. Yet every one of the following countries has a better voting record than ours: Sweden, Norway, Italy, Holland, Great Britain, France, Finland, Denmark and Canada." (*Looking at* DOUG) Well, what do you know!

DOUG: My mother says it's a disgrace. The P.T.A. is trying to do something about it. "Get Out the Vote" is their slogan this year.

RALPH: You'd think that, as a democracy, the United States would have the best voting record of all.

DOUG (*Somewhat pompously*): You can't keep the government of the people, by the people, and for the people unless the people vote to make it work. (*Chuckles*) That's a quote from my mother!

RALPH: It seems to me there's a lot of talk about voting lately.

DOUG: I guess you could call that a good sign.

RALPH: Well, anyway, our homeroom didn't have any

trouble electing a member to the Student Council. Not the way some classes have.

DOUG: Yes, my sister told me about that. Her class is still trying to cut down its list of candidates to only two before the final vote tomorrow.

RALPH: Peggy's on the list of candidates, isn't she?

DOUG: Uh-huh. She was one of six on the ballot in to-day's run-off. I wonder how she made out?

RALPH: Peggy's popular. She should do fine. Who's running against her?

DOUG: Coleman Winter and a couple of others.

RALPH: Coleman! She'd have to be some vote-getter to beat Coleman. He's the best football player and basketball player in school. To say nothing of winning practically every award in track. If it comes to a choice between Coleman and Peggy . . . I don't know, Doug, I sort of feel sorry for Peggy.

DOUG: The funny thing is, Peggy likes Coleman. She'd probably vote for him instead of for herself. I think she's crazy. He doesn't care about anything but sports.

RALPH: There's nothing wrong with sports.

DOUG: No, but Peggy has a lot of other ideas. Good ones that would improve things at the school—not just for athletes, but for everyone. She'd be good on the Student Council . . . even if she *is* my sister. (*Pauses*) How about another sandwich?

RALPH: Sure.

DOUG: O.K. I'll get it while you make up your mind about the comic books. (*Picks up book*) This one on voting's the only one that isn't a comic. (*Exits.* RALPH *looks through more comics. There is a tap on door.* COLEMAN *enters.*)

COLEMAN (*Walking center*): Hi, Ralph. Is Peggy home?

RALPH: Hi, Coleman. No, she's not here.

COLEMAN: Do you have any idea when she's due home?

RALPH: I don't, but Doug may know. (*Calls off*) Hey, Doug! When's your sister coming home? (DOUG *enters.*)

DOUG: Oh, hi, Coleman. Sorry, I don't have any idea. Want to leave a message?

COLEMAN: Well, yes. (*Hesitating*) Will you just tell her I'd appreciate her help in the election? As long as she won't be running against me in the finals.

DOUG (*Surprised*): You mean Peggy lost?

COLEMAN: Celia Upton squeezed her out by one vote. It's Coleman Winter against Celia Upton in the finals tomorrow.

DOUG: Who's Celia Upton?

COLEMAN: Oh, she's been around all year. She doesn't make much noise, but she's a real brain. Gets terrific grades. She hasn't got Peggy's class, though. The election ought to be a cinch.

RALPH (*Mischievously*): For Celia?

COLEMAN (*Snickering*): What do *you* think? (*To* DOUG) Tell Peggy I came around to console her, will you? And tell her I'd appreciate her support. The more votes, the merrier. If she could make a pennant or something . . . with my name on it . . . well, you know, whatever she can think of.

DOUG: Coleman, how do you think the money in the Student Council treasury should be used?

COLEMAN: I don't know anything about it.

DOUG: It's what the Student Council is going to decide about first.

COLEMAN: It's never hard to spend money. It's one of the easiest things I do. (*Moves toward exit*) You'll tell Peggy about the pennant, huh? If everyone knows she's for me, I'm as good as in right this minute. See you later! (*Exits*)

DOUG (*Shaking his head*): He may be a good football

player, but. . . . Just a minute, I'll get those sand-wiches. (*Exits;* RALPH *looks at comic books. In a moment, there is another rap at the door. It opens, and* NORMA *enters, carrying books.*)

NORMA (*Calling*): Peggy!

RALPH: She's not home from school yet.

NORMA (*Crossing to table*): Well, then, I'll wait. Aren't you Shirley Harper's brother? (*Puts books down.* RALPH *nods.*)

RALPH: Yes, I'm Ralph.

NORMA: Where's Doug?

DOUG (*Entering with sandwiches*): Hi, Norma. Want a snack?

NORMA: No, thanks. When do you think Peggy will be home?

DOUG: Search me. Everybody's looking for her.

NORMA: Everybody?

DOUG (*Sarcastically*): Even Coleman the Great was here.

NORMA: He was? What did he want?

DOUG: He wants Peggy to support him in the election tomorrow.

NORMA: As if he couldn't win against Celia Upton without lifting a finger!

RALPH: Maybe he wants to make it unanimous.

DOUG: What I want to know is how Celia got more votes than Peggy.

NORMA: Only *one* more. And you know how modest Peggy is. She didn't push herself forward at all . . . even though she's done a lot of thinking about how to use the Student Council money. I don't know Celia very well, but she's smart—and lots of kids look up to her.

RALPH: Who's getting your vote, Norma? (PEGGY *enters, stands at door unobserved.*)

NORMA: Nobody! I'm not going to vote. I've made up my mind.

PEGGY (*Entering*): Norma, you have to! Everybody should vote in an election.

OTHERS (*Ad lib; surprised*): Peggy! Hi! When did you get here? (*Etc.*)

DOUG: Peggy, I'm really sorry you didn't make the finals.

RALPH: Yes, that's really too bad.

PEGGY: Well, it's a democratic process, and I lost, that's all. I guess I didn't try hard enough to get votes. . . . But Norma, you absolutely have to vote!

NORMA: No I don't. You were my candidate, Peggy, and if I can't vote for you, I won't vote.

PEGGY: What's the matter with Coleman? He's the most popular boy in school.

NORMA: The most popular *athlete*, Peggy. But he's a yes-man, haven't you noticed? Not that it makes much difference in football . . . but I wouldn't want him deciding how to spend our Student Council money— not after all the work we put into raising it.

PEGGY: I don't know why you think he's a yes-man. He's always been awfully nice . . .

NORMA: Being nice has nothing to do with it, Peggy. A candidate has to *stand* for something. What did Coleman say in his speech this morning? It boiled down to absolutely nothing.

PEGGY: What about Celia? What did she say? I was so nervous thinking about my own speech, I didn't really listen.

NORMA: Celia had some pretty good ideas, but she talked so softly, I could hardly hear. It doesn't matter, though, Peggy. If I can't vote for you, I'm not going to vote. I should have done some campaigning for you, but I was sure you were going to win.

PEGGY: Oh, well . . .

DOUG: Coleman was here a little while ago, Peggy. He wants your support. He said something about making a pennant with his name on it.

NORMA: He would! (*Sulks*) I don't know why I didn't think of putting your name on a pennant, Peggy.

PEGGY: A pennant. Of course, I'll do it . . . for Coleman. We've got some scraps of felt here somewhere. I'll be right back. (PEGGY *exits.*)

RALPH (*To* NORMA): You *are* going to vote, aren't you? This book says you're a poor patriot if you don't.

NORMA (*Dejectedly*): I suppose so.

DOUG: In our class it wouldn't *occur* to anyone not to vote. (*Turning to* RALPH) What about the comic books, Ralph?

RALPH: I'll trade you.

DOUG: Great! I'll help you carry them over to your house. (*They gather up books.* RALPH *hands* NORMA *voting booklet as they start to exit.*) Here's one you ought to read cover to cover. (*They exit. In a moment,* PEGGY *re-enters, carrying piece of felt, scissors, etc.*)

PEGGY: I had a hard time finding the right stuff for a pennant. (*Puts things down*) Let's see. (*Counts on fingers*) C-o-l-e-m-a-n. Seven letters. I have just enough scraps here. Want to help, Norma?

NORMA: No, thanks. I'll watch. I just can't support a yes-man, Peggy.

PEGGY: Oh, I think you're exaggerating. (*Begins to cut letters*) Anyone who can play football like that . . . and look like that . . .

NORMA: You know what? I'll bet if I called Coleman up and asked him if he thought it would be a good idea to buy footballs with Student Council money, he'd say yes.

PEGGY (*Laughing*): Not when the library needs books

276

so badly. That's ridiculous. (*Goes on cutting*) But go ahead, call him. See what he says. (NORMA *goes to phone, dials, waits.*)

NORMA: Nobody seems to be home . . . (*Into phone*) Oh, is that you, Coleman? . . . This is Norma. I'm so glad you were home. . . . Well, I'm *glad* you had to mow the lawn, or you'd be out practicing something or other. Look, Coleman, when you get elected to the Student Council, don't you think it would be a good idea to invest all the money in the treasury—you know, the money we raised all year—in footballs and basketballs and sports equipment? . . . I *knew* you'd say that. See you tomorrow. (*She hangs up, turns.*) He agreed with everything I said. Now you call him, Peggy . . . hurry . . . before he gets out in the yard again. Ask him about library books.

PEGGY (*Going to phone, dialing; into phone*): Coleman? Peggy. Doug says you stopped by to see me. Sorry I missed you. . . . Well, of course, it's hard when you lose by one vote, but I probably couldn't have won against *you*, anyway. Look, Coleman, one thing I had in my platform was more books for the library. And that international relief program to send books and science equipment to schools abroad. You agree, don't you? . . . Will you? . . . Can I count on it? . . . Will I support you? What a question! Of course. . . . O.K., Coleman. Be seeing you. (*Hangs up phone*)

NORMA: He agreed with everything you said, didn't he?

PEGGY: Yes, he did. (*Half-heartedly she goes back to work on the pennant.*)

NORMA: And it doesn't take a master mind to figure out that you can't spend money for *all* those things he agrees to.

PEGGY (*Putting down scissors*): What are we going to do? I've got most of the letters cut out. . . .

NORMA: We don't have to vote. Nobody's going to *make* us.

PEGGY: But that never solves anything.

NORMA (*Sighing*): Life is so full of problems. (*Doorbell rings.* PEGGY *goes to door, opens it.*)

PEGGY: Why, Celia! (*Hesitates*) Won't . . . won't you come in? Norma Jackson is here. (CELIA *enters.*)

CELIA: Thanks, Peggy. Hi, Norma.

NORMA (*Trying to be pleasant*): Hello, Celia.

CELIA: I suppose you think I've come to ask you to vote for me tomorrow, but I haven't. I've come to say I'd vote for you, Peggy.

PEGGY (*Amazed*): But I lost. I'm out of the running. Completely.

CELIA: If I withdrew you wouldn't be! You were next in line. Only one vote less.

NORMA (*Suspiciously*): But why would you want to withdraw, Celia? You wanted to win, didn't you?

CELIA: Yes, I suppose everyone does. But I realize now that I can't beat Coleman. Not without the support of you and your friends, and I don't have that. We don't even know each other very well.

NORMA: You're scared you'll lose to Coleman, so you'd rather not be in the finals. Is that it?

CELIA (*Embarrassed*): No. It sounds crazy, maybe. But I'm more scared of Coleman's winning than I am of my losing. I mean, it's important for someone to beat him.

PEGGY (*Puzzled*): Why do you say that?

CELIA: Because he's not the kind of person we need on the Student Council. Oh, he's a great athlete, and everybody likes him, but he's always making promises and not keeping them. And whenever he does a good turn, he wants to get something out of it for himself.

NORMA (*Excitedly*): See, Peggy, it's not only that he's a yes-man.

CELIA (*With growing confidence*): We need someone on the Council with ideas about how to help the whole school, and even schools in other countries. You had good ideas in your talk, Peggy. And with my group on your side, you could beat Coleman!

PEGGY: Would you give up your place to me . . . for a few ideas?

CELIA: That library book program, for instance—it's important for everyone in the school.

PEGGY: I didn't even know you thought about it.

NORMA: Too bad you spoke so softly, Celia.

CELIA: I was nervous, too. You see, being here only a year and a half still makes me sort of an outsider.

NORMA: You got more votes than Peggy.

CELIA: Only one. And I worked for it. And with the vote split six ways, that's not so surprising. But there's no way I can win against Coleman. Peggy, you're the only one who can.

NORMA (*To* PEGGY; *enthusiastically*): Why don't you do it, Peggy? I think Celia has a good idea. With her group and ours behind you, you can beat the mighty Coleman.

CELIA (*To* PEGGY): I feel the way you do about the library, and sending science equipment to poor schools abroad. But Coleman isn't a bit interested in things like that. There is a place where he belongs—but it's not on the Student Council.

PEGGY (*Slowly, nodding*): You're right, Celia.

CELIA (*Eagerly*): Then you'll run if I withdraw?

NORMA: Of course you will, won't you, Peggy? You *have* to!

PEGGY: Celia, you won fair and square, against much greater odds than I had. You deserve to keep your place, and I won't take it. But I will support you. Norma and I will tell our friends how we feel, won't we, Norma?

279

NORMA (*Enthusiastically*): You bet we will, Celia. I wasn't going to vote because Peggy lost. But I've changed my mind—and I'm *not* voting for Coleman.

CELIA (*Uncertainly*): Well, I don't know what to say. I would have been glad to withdraw. All I can say is that I'll do my best, if I win.

PEGGY: *When* you win. No if's about it! (NORMA, *at the table, is placing letters on pennant.*)

NORMA: What do you know!

PEGGY: What, Norma? (PEGGY *and* CELIA *move to table.*)

NORMA (*Picking up letters*): We can use the letters you cut out for our candidate. C. . .E . . .L . . .A. All we need is an I.

PEGGY (*Picking up scissors and letter M*): Here, I have it. (*As she works*) All we need to do is cut the straight piece from the M. Voilà—an I. (*Arranges letters on pennant*) There. Look, Celia! C-E-L-I-A. That's the pennant we'll be waving tomorrow for the winning side. (*Quick curtain*)

THE END

PRODUCTION NOTES
VOTING AGAINST THE ODDS

Characters: 3 male; 3 female.

Playing Time: 20 minutes.

Costumes: Everyday, modern dress.

Properties: Comic books (including one booklet on voting); four large sandwiches; scissors; scraps of felt (letters and pennant may be pre-cut).

Setting: Living room. At one side is a large table holding telephone and pile of comic books. Several chairs are near table. The other furnishings may include easy chairs, lamps, etc. Exits are right and left, one leading to kitchen, the other to front door.

Lighting: No special effects.

Sound: Doorbell, as indicated in text.

Voting Day

*A group of boys and girls are looking at a large sign
(tacked to a screen or desk) which says* VOTING DAY.
*Behind the screen hide three girls and three boys, each
holding a placard with a letter of the word* VOTING.

1ST GIRL (*Looking at sign*):
　　　　　　　Today, they say, is Voting Day,
　　　　　　　with posters everywhere.
　　　　　　　But all the fuss is not for *us*—
　　　　　　　we're much too young to care.

1ST BOY:　　　We cannot vote, it's sad to note,
　　　　　　　until we're twenty-one,
　　　　　　　so why should we care one-two-three
　　　　　　　what voting-things are done?

2ND GIRL:　　Today, they say, is Voting Day—
　　　　　　　for grownups. Some are keen,
　　　　　　　but some stay home and sigh and groan:
　　　　　　　"Huh, what does voting mean?"

2ND BOY:　　　The posters shout, "Turn out, turn out
　　　　　　　and vote! It's up to you
　　　　　　　what laws get passed." But, first and
　　　　　　　last,
　　　　　　　I wonder if that's true.

ALL: Today, today, is Voting Day.
                      Before the day is spent,
                      we wish we'd hear, as clear as clear,
                      exactly what is meant!

(Boys and girls behind the sign run out in order, so the letters they hold spell VOTING.*)*

ALL SIX: You wish to know what's thus and so
                      in VOTING? Listen well,
                      and we will try to clarify
                      just what our letters spell.

BOY WITH V: V for vision of the kind
                      of life that's worth foreseeing.
                      Voting is the way to bring
                      that vision into being.

GIRL WITH O: O for obligation
                      on the part of you, and me,
                      to keep Old Glory waving
                      in a land of liberty.

BOY WITH T: T for thought and teamwork
                      in choosing right from wrong.
                      And no one is too young or old
                      to help that cause along!

GIRL WITH I: I for international—
                      applied to point of view,
                      for insight into others' needs,
                      ideas of what to do.

BOY WITH N: N for nation that we love;
                      and need of serving, giving.
                      If we cannot vote, we still
                      can serve by friendly living.

GIRL WITH G: G for government in gear
                      to serve the greatest good,
                      government not based on force,
                      but faith and brotherhood.

ALL SIX: That spells VOTING. You'll agree
                that a simple word can be
                mighty big, although it's small—
                full of meaning for us all.
*(Boys and girls of first group summarize the meaning
of VOTING, as each member of the letter-group steps
forward in turn and holds his letter high.)*
1ST GIRL: *V*ision!
1ST BOY: *O*bligation
                to keep our country free.
2ND GIRL: *T*eamwork!
2ND BOY: *I*nsight!
1ST GIRL: *N*ation
                in need of you and me.
1ST BOY: *G*overnment in gear to serve
                the greatest good . . .
ALL: It's clear
                all of us have parts to play,
                today . . . and all the year!

Book Week
(November)

The Magic Card

GIRL:	I have a card that lets me go
	to any country that I choose—
	to Sweden, Spain, or Mexico—
	and doesn't cost a cent to use.
1ST BOY:	A card? You're talking through your hat!
	Where could you get a card like that?
GIRL:	It is a magic kind of pass
	that opens up a hundred doors,
	like stepping through a looking-glass
	to realms of queens and emperors.
2ND BOY:	A card? I'm curious as a cat.
	Where could *I* get a card like that?
GIRL:	To guess the secret isn't hard . . .
BOYS:	Don't keep us both on tenterhooks!
GIRL:	What simple little magic card
	will open up the world of *books*?
BOYS:	A library card!

Open Sesame!

BOY: You needn't buy a ticket
           on a bus-line or a train,

GIRL: You needn't ride a rocket
           or a steamer or a plane,

BOY: To go to famous highlands
           and peninsulas and islands
           and to jungle-lands and drylands
           or a cannibal's domain.

GIRL: You needn't pay a penny
           for a long and careful look,

GROUP: You only need,
         you only need,
           you only need A BOOK.

GIRL: You needn't own a panda
           and you needn't buy a gnu,

BOY: Or an elephant or monkey
           or a jumping kangaroo,

GIRL: To learn about a creature—
           every tooth and claw and feature
           and the tricks that you can teach her
           (or can teach *him*) how to do.

BOY: You needn't peek from bushes
           for a scientific look,

GROUP: You only need,
         you only need,
           you only need A BOOK.

BOY: And so it is with wonders
in a test-tube and a vat,
GIRL: And astonishing adventures
of a cowboy or a cat,
BOY: And the customs and the rations
of the folks of other nations,
and their games and occupations,
and their thoughts, and such as that.
GROUP: You needn't spend a lifetime
trying to peer in every nook,
you only need,
    you only need,
        you only need a BOOK!

Adventure Ahead

1ST: A book is a boat that takes you sailing
far and away . . . you grip the railing
and shade your eyes, and see strange places
with unexpected sights and faces.
2ND: A book is a road that takes you ranging
far and away . . . where scenes keep changing,
now through cities with streets and alleys,
now through countries with hills and valleys.
3RD: A book is a key that opens gateways
far and away . . . through curved and straight
ways.
ALL: A book is a boat, a road, a key . . .
adventure ahead! Just read and see.

Thanksgiving
(4th Thursday in November)

Thanksgiving Feast

Characters

MRS. COOPER
MRS. BREWSTER
GOVERNOR BRADFORD
MR. WHITE
WILLIAM
SAMUEL
HUMILITY

TIME: *Morning of a fall day in 1621.*
SETTING: *The outskirts of the little town of Plymouth.*
AT RISE: MRS. COOPER, *carrying something in her apron, enters from one side of the stage as* MRS. BREWSTER, *with a kettle in each hand, comes in from the other.*
MRS. COOPER (*As she approaches*):
Is it not fine, this autumn day?
The sting in the wind has died away.
Sister Brewster, look you here:
(*Opens her apron, which is full of late autumn leaves, cones, and sprigs of evergreen*)

Some token of the fading year
To deck the tables for the feast!

MRS. BREWSTER (*Looking into the apron*):
Well, it seems that you, at least,
Think of more than pots and kettles.
Cones, and leaves like scarlet petals!
They will deck the feast, indeed.
But the men have not agreed
How many tables we shall need.
How many turkeys shall we fix?
How many batters shall we mix?
How many guests—a score, or six?
We asked the Indians; will they come?

MRS. COOPER:
Tomorrow we'll know.

MRS. BREWSTER:
              'Tis troublesome
Not to be sure.

MRS. COOPER:
           Now, don't go fearing.
The crops we gathered from our clearing,
The fish in the sea, the clams on the shore,
And game in the woods to go hunting for—
There will be plenty, don't you worry!

MRS. BREWSTER:
Can we be sure? Well, I must hurry
And help with the baking and the stewing.

MRS. COOPER:
And I have my tasks I must be doing—
So many plans as there are brewing!
(*The women hurry out in opposite directions. After a
moment* GOVERNOR BRADFORD *and* MR. WHITE *en-
ter, talking. They slowly cross the stage.*)

GOV. BRADFORD:
Squanto thinks the chiefs at least
Will join in our Thanksgiving feast:

Massasoit and several more . . .
At the most, perhaps a score.
MR. WHITE:
I should say it's better thus.
With only fifty-five of us,
Scores of Indians would be frightening.
GOV. BRADFORD:
Brother White, we have been tightening
Bonds of friendship all the year.
Surely there is naught to fear.
Think how Squanto helped us here—
Taught us how to plant and till
And put two fish in every hill!
MR. WHITE:
I know, but can we trust the others?
GOV. BRADFORD:
If we look on them as brothers.
We shall have a real Thanksgiving
In this land where we are living
If the Indians come to add
Their thanks to ours—for gifts we've had
Of sun and rain and peace and plenty.
MR. WHITE:
Governor, if more than twenty
Should arrive, are we prepared?
GOV. BRADFORD:
All provisions will be shared,
And we'll give our thanks together.
MR. WHITE:
Aye, and hope for more good weather.
The air today is like a feather!
(*They begin to exit.*)
When do you expect our friends?
GOV. BRADFORD:
Perhaps before this evening ends.
Perhaps tomorrow—I wish we knew.

There still are many things to do
And when they come, we must be through.
(*After a pause,* WILLIAM *and* SAMUEL, *two Pilgrim boys, come in furtively, walking carefully as if they are trying to elude someone. They look back over their shoulders as they move along.*)

WILLIAM:
No one saw us! Can it be
We even fooled Humility?

SAMUEL:
Your sister sticks to you like glue.
She watches everything you do.

WILLIAM:
We fooled her . . . and the others, too.

SAMUEL:
But just the same we'd best take care—
With all that work to do back there.
Wood to carry from the hill,
Fish to clean, and pails to fill.

WILLIAM:
Well, we'll soon be out of sight.
Samuel, are we doing right?

SAMUEL:
*Some*one ought to do some scouting.
I heard several people doubting
Just how many would arrive.

WILLIAM:
Father looks for four or five.
There should be a few, at least,
Coming to our harvest feast.

SAMUEL:
No one thinks they'll be here soon,
Not till late this afternoon
Or tomorrow—who can say?
Some may come from far away,

But we'd feel a lot of shame
Not being ready when they came!
WILLIAM (*Pointing*):
If we climb that highest tree
Atop the hill, we ought to see . . .
(*Suddenly* HUMILITY, WILLIAM's *sister, rushes up behind the boys.* WILLIAM *and* SAMUEL *are startled and disgusted.*)
HUMILITY: William!
SAMUEL: Aw, Humility . . .
WILLIAM: Can't you ever let me be?
HUMILITY:
Tell me what you plan to do—
Running off from work, you two.
WILLIAM:
Never mind, and do not bother!
HUMILITY:
Then I'll tell on you, to Father.
Boys are lazy, always shirking
When they know they should be working.
With so much that must be done,
You can only think of fun!
WILLIAM:
We were thinking that we should
Sight the Indians . . . if we could.
SAMUEL:
Watch the trails, or hear their drumming,
So we'd know if they were coming.
HUMILITY:
But it's much too early yet!
Why, the tables are not set,
And our elders are not dressed
To receive a single guest!
Shame on you, with chores to do,
Running off like this, you two.

WILLIAM (*Pointing*):
　　See that tree? The highest one?
　　We could reach it on a run.
　　It stands high above the ground—
　　We could climb and look around.
　　We could see the trails that sally
　　Through the woods and down the valley.
SAMUEL:
　　You come too, Humility!
　　All of us can climb the tree.
HUMILITY (*Hesitating, tempted*):
　　Well . . . perhaps . . . if we can hurry . . .
　　No one in the town will worry.
　　(*The three children run out. In a few seconds, they
　　hurry across the stage again. Then again. HUMILITY
　　lags farther behind each time. Finally she sinks to the
　　ground, panting.*)
　　All the breath is out of me.
WILLIAM *and* SAMUEL (*Calling back over their shoulders*):
　　We will tell you what we see.
　　(*HUMILITY gradually recovers her breath. She makes
　　herself comfortable against the stone. After a few min-
　　utes she begins to hum a simple little tune. Then she
　　puts words to the music.*)
HUMILITY:
　　Boys! Boys! Boys!
　　They make a lot of noise,
　　And every time there's work to do,
　　Like pails to fill or wood to hew,
　　They never are around, it's true.
　　Boys! Boys! Boys!
　　(WILLIAM *and* SAMUEL *call excitedly from offstage.*)
WILLIAM: Humility!

SAMUEL: Humility!
HUMILITY (*Jumping up*):
  Is there anything to see?
WILLIAM (*Running in*):
  They're coming . . . several dozen strong!
SAMUEL (*Running in*):
  We saw them as they walked along
  Across the swamp, some miles away,
  In single file, as big as day!
  But . . . several dozen, did you say?
  It looked to me like several *score:*
  Sixty . . . eighty . . . maybe more!
HUMILITY:
  Are you sure there are so many?
  Father looked for hardly any.
  And who'd think they'd come so
  soon—
  Long before the afternoon!
WILLIAM:
  You should see them.
SAMUEL: What a sight.
  We are getting guests all right!
HUMILITY:
  Hurry . . . hurry . . . we must run
  And tell our elders what we've done.
  They must be all dressed and ready,
  Not surprised . . .
WILLIAM: And not unsteady.
HUMILITY:
  They must put more food to boiling,
  Fix more venison for broiling,
  Clean more fish, and bake more
      bread . . .
  Boys, forget those things I said:

That you seemed to like to shirk.
You have done a big day's work!
WILLIAM (*Running out*): Hurry!
SAMUEL (*Running out*): Hurry!
HUMILITY (*Following after*):
                Did you say
Several score were on the way?
SAMUEL (*Offstage*):
    Sixty . . . seventy . . . at least.
HUMILITY:
    What a big Thanksgiving feast!
    (*The children run back and forth across the stage several times, with* HUMILITY *lagging more and more. Finally, out of breath, she sinks down to rest. After a few minutes she remembers her little song . . . but this time the words are different.*)
Boys! Boys! Boys!
They make a lot of noise,
But they are handy in a way
For sometimes, I am glad to say,
They try a plan that saves the day.
Boys! Boys! Boys!

THE END

PRODUCTION NOTES
THANKSGIVING FEAST

Characters: 4 male; 3 female.
Playing Time: 10 minutes.
Costumes: All of the characters wear typical Puritan costumes. Mrs. Cooper has an apron.
Properties: Kettles, autumn leaves, cones, sprigs of evergreen.
Setting: The outskirts of the little town of Plymouth. Bushes, shrubs and vines may be placed around the stage, and a backdrop of trees may be used. Downstage center is a large stone or stump.
Lighting: No special effects.

# First Thanksgiving

FOUR BOYS *and* FOUR GIRLS *enter and line up across stage.*

1ST BOY: The harvest has been gathered now,
  it's time that we took stock.

1ST GIRL: Just half of us are living now who came to
  Plymouth Rock.

1ST GIRL *and* BOY (*Together*): Fifty graves are on the
  hill . . .
  yet we praise this freedom still
  and face our hardships with a will.

2ND BOY: The first long months are over now,
  our colony takes form:

2ND GIRL: Eleven buildings have been built,
  secure against the storm:

2ND GIRL *and* BOY (*Together*): Seven dwellings, plus the
  four
  for common use and common store
  where there was wilderness before.

3RD BOY: The months of fear are ended now,
  and no one will forget
  how Squanto came . . .

3RD GIRL: And Massasoit and friendly Samoset.

3RD GIRL *and* BOY (*Together*): They gave our frightened
  hearts release
  and made our dread of Indians cease.
  We live together here in peace.

4TH BOY: The first lean year is ended now,
　we've had good land to till:
4TH GIRL: Twenty acres sowed to corn, three herrings in
　each hill.
4TH GIRL *and* BOY (*Together*): Our barley patch was not
　too bad,
　and there were green-things to be had.
　Our harvest makes us humbly glad.
GIRLS: To signify our gratitude,
　we'll hold a feast of thanks.
BOYS: Let Squanto tell our Indian friends to come and
　join our ranks!
ALL: We'll share the feast and dine in state.
　Raise the cup and fill the plate!
　In thankfulness we'll celebrate.

Thanksgiving Spelldown

Turkey sizzling,
Happy hearts,
Apple stuffing,
Nuts and tarts,
Kitchen smells
So nice and sniffy,
Guests arriving
In a jiffy,
Voices raised
In festive mood—
Not forgetting
Gratitude. . . .

Just as sure
as you are living,
that's the way
to spell THANKSGIVING.

Thanksgiving Day in the Morning

GIRL: What is the place you like the best
Thanksgiving Day in the morning?
BOY: The kitchen! with so many things to test,
and help to measure, and stir with zest,
and sniff, and sample, and all the rest—
BOTH: Thanksgiving Day in the morning.
BOY: What are the colors you like the most
Thanksgiving Day in the morning?
GIRL: The color of cranberries uppermost,
the pumpkin-yellow the pie tops boast,
the crispy brown of a turkey roast—
ALL: Thanksgiving Day in the morning.
GIRL: What are the sounds you think are gay
Thanksgiving Day in the morning?
BOY: The sizzly sounds on the roaster-tray,
the gravy gurgling itself away,
the company sounds at the door . . . hooray!
ALL: Thanksgiving Day in the morning.

On Thanksgiving Day

For tasks that are finished,
and tasks to be done,
for fears we have conquered
and challenges won,
for trials that are over
and pleasures that stay,
we lift up our voices
on Thanksgiving Day.

What Makes Thanksgiving?

Characters

BOY
GIRL
TWELVE BOYS AND GIRLS

AT RISE: BOY *and* GIRL *are on stage.*
BOY: What makes Thanksgiving,
        I wonder, I wonder?
        What on the surface,
        And what things down under?
GIRL: Feast things, and fun things,
        And good things in living—
        Twelve things together
        Will spell out Thanksgiving.
  (TWELVE BOYS AND GIRLS *enter in turn, holding letters that spell* THANKSGIVING.)
1ST: T . . . for the turkey
          that weighs down the
          table.
2ND: H . . . for a house
          full of joy to the gable.
3RD: A . . . for abundance
          of things that count most.
4TH: N . . . for our neighbors—
          let's give them a toast!
5TH: K . . . for the kitchen
          so cram-full of flavors,
6TH: S . . . for the season
          of sizzles and savors.
7TH: G . . . for the giving
          of thanks—and to spare.

8TH: I . . . for inviting
our cousins to share.
9TH: V . . . for vacation
with fun in full measure.
10TH: I . . . . for each item
of good cheer and pleasure.
11TH: N . . . for November—
who cares if it blows?
12TH: G . . . for the gratitude
everyone knows.
GIRL: *That* spells Thanksgiving.
BOY: No wonder, no wonder.
It shines on the surface
And shines way down under.
ALL: Feast things, and fun things
And good things in living.
Twelve things together
Will spell out Thanksgiving!

The Animals' Thanksgiving

GIRL: Are you thankful, robin, wren,
bluebird, mallard, swallow,
that you've found the sun again
in each southland hollow?
BOY: Are you grateful, chickadee,
in your frosty-windowed tree,
that you need not follow?
GIRL: Are you thankful, squirrel, mouse
in your cozy burrow,
that in stocking up your house
you were brisk and thorough,
BOY: Bringing nuts and grain and seeds
for your simple winter needs
from each field and furrow?

GIRL: Are you thankful, rabbit, deer,
　　　at your wildwood table,
　　　that you nibble through the year
　　　free of fence and stable?
BOY: Oh, I think, like me, you'd say,
　　　"Yes, I'm full of thanks today". . . .
　　　if you just were able!

Harvest Feast

BOYS: Fetch the wood and feed the fires,
　　　keep the kettles steaming:
　　　such a feast as this requires
　　　more than wishful dreaming.
GIRLS: Stir the batter, Pilgrim daughter!
　　　Son, another pail of water!
　　　Pile the clams beneath the coals,
　　　make the meat-spit stable.
BOYS: Bring the planks and set the poles
　　　for the harvest table.
GIRLS: Pilgrim son, more wood, more water!
　　　Help to pluck the turkeys, daughter!
BOYS: Roast the ears of yellow maize,
　　　pile the nuts and berries
　　　next to grapes on pewter trays
　　　near the sun-dried cherries.
GIRLS: Guests are coming, son and daughter,
　　　over hills and running water!
BOYS: Rake the coals and pile them up,
　　　praise the harvest weather,
GIRLS: Set the table, cup by cup,
　　　guest and host, together.
ALL: Draw the ties of friendship tauter
　　　with thanksgiving, son and daughter!

DECEMBER

The Smiling Angel

Characters

TWO BOYS
TWO GIRLS
TWO WORKMEN
THREE WOMEN
MAN
SINGERS, *8 or more*
TOWN CRIER
TOWNSPEOPLE
BROTHER
SISTER

TIME: *The day before Christmas.*
SETTING: *The town square. At the back is a conspicuous stone wall. A section of the wall may be made on painted cardboard boxes, so that it can be torn down. On either side of wall toward wings are low steps. At front, above audience, stands statue of an angel.*

AT RISE: TWO BOYS *enter.*

1ST BOY: I'm almost afraid to look.

2ND BOY: So am I. (*As they near center stage, they slowly lift their eyes to statue.*)

1ST BOY: She isn't smiling yet!

2ND BOY (*Sadly*): No. And if our angel doesn't smile by midnight, something terrible will happen.

1ST BOY (*Shaking his fist in the direction of the wall*): It's our enemies' fault—behind the wall! They're always plotting against us. They've done something to make our angel stop smiling.

2ND BOY: You'd think someone could win the reward the Mayor offered to anyone who makes the angel smile again. The Stonecutter chiseled on a new smile last week, but next morning the angel was sad again.

1ST BOY: The mason made a cement smile, but it wouldn't stay, either.

2ND BOY: And the potter thought he could make a new smile for the statue, but it only crumbled and fell off. No one has won the reward. And it's almost Christmas Eve!

1ST BOY: My father is sure our enemies have invented a secret weapon and trained it on our statue.

2ND BOY: My father thinks they've developed a deadly cosmic ray that can turn smiles to frowns.

1ST BOY (*Suddenly*): Maybe we should build our wall higher, high enough to protect the angel and hide her from the enemy.

2ND BOY (*Excited*): Maybe that's the idea that will win the award . . . and make the angel smile again. Let's wait for the Town Crier, and tell him to rush our plan to the Mayor. Why didn't anyone think of it before? It's a great idea! (TWO BOYS *go over to wall, examine it, then sit on steps.* TWO GIRLS *enter, hurry to center, and look up at statue.*)

1ST GIRL (*Disappointed*): She's not smiling. She looks very sad.

2ND GIRL: What could we do to make her happy? (*Turns to angel*)

What makes our smiling angel grieve?

1ST GIRL: Our enemies, my folks believe,

Have fearful vengeance to achieve.

2ND GIRL: And, now, tonight comes Christmas Eve.

1ST GIRL: My mother says the grocer told her.

He is sure our foes get bolder.

Every minute it gets colder.

And *he* wouldn't be surprised

If their bombs are super-sized.

2ND GIRL (*Looking at wall*): Why don't we make our wall of brick

So bombs could not break through so quick?

1ST GIRL: You're right. That plan may do the trick.

Let's tell the Crier—he'll come soon—

To tell the Mayor this very noon.

(GIRLS *examine wall, then sit on steps.* TWO WORKMEN *enter, carrying various tools. They hurry to center of stage and look up at statue.*)

1ST WORKMAN (*Shaking his head*): No smile yet. I tried! I worked!

2ND WORKMAN: I never shirked.

The smile I made

Was all inlaid

With hammered gold.

It wouldn't hold!

1ST WORKMAN: I volunteered

To make a smile

Of powdered brick.

It wouldn't stick!

(WORKMEN *turn angrily toward wall.*)

304

2ND WORKMAN: Our enemies pollute the air.
  We must beware
  Where poisons lurk
  That spoil our work!
1ST WORKMAN: They break the law!
  And then guffaw.
  Come, time is short . . .
  Let's tell the Court
  To build a roof
  That's poison-proof.
  (WORKMEN *go toward wall, look at it, then sit on steps.*)
2ND WORKMAN: Our scheme is great.
  We'll save the state!
  (TWO WOMEN, *carrying market baskets, enter, hurry over to angel, sigh in disappointment.*)
1ST WOMAN: Not smiling yet.
2ND WOMAN: Bewitched, she is, by our enemies on the other side of the wall. Here it is the day before Christmas, and she's still so sad.
1ST WOMAN: And not smiling.
2ND WOMAN: Did you hear that Patrick O'Brien, the glassblower, tried blowing her a smile of glass? But our enemies sent over a whirlwind, and the glass smile shattered in his hand.
1ST WOMAN: If we could take her somewhere safe, she'd be smiling again.
2ND WOMAN: But where could we be safe, Maggie?
1ST WOMAN: In a tunnel under the ground. Not so pleasant to be living like moles, but we could come up at night for a breath of fresh air.
2ND WOMAN (*Enthusiastically*): That's a good idea. It's a wonder nobody thought of it before. I'm for passing it on to the mayor. Isn't it about time for the Crier to be coming to take a message?

1ST WOMAN (*Looking at angel*): Heaven help us if she's not smiling by midnight. (*They sit on steps.* MAN *and* 3RD WOMAN *enter and look at statue.*)

3RD WOMAN: No sign of a smile. And the time's getting shorter and shorter.

MAN: Why wasn't some ordinance passed? They could have done *something,* I think.

3RD WOMAN: They tried, but nothing would work.

MAN: So I heard.

3RD WOMAN (*Sighing*): At least we are safe till tonight.

MAN (*Impatiently*): I am tired of this waiting.
　Why not attack our foes?
　We know they are plotting and hating.
　"Strike first" is my motto. "Be bold."
　(*Looks around*) *This* method is . . . irritating.

3RD WOMAN (*Horrified*): That's war!

MAN: But we can't let those scoundrels outdo us.
　If they think we're afraid, unprepared,
　They'll soon do their best to subdue us.

3RD WOMAN: No wonder the angel won't smile.

MAN: My anger grows stronger and stronger.
　We should not delay any longer.
　(MAN *and* WOMAN *sit on steps.* SINGERS *enter. They look eagerly at angel, then look disappointed.*)

1ST SINGER: She isn't smiling.

2ND SINGER: She's still sad.

3RD SINGER: Maybe our song will cheer her up.

4TH SINGER: We can try. (*They start to sing lively Christmas carol. After a few stanzas, they stop suddenly and look at statue.*)

5TH SINGER (*Shaking her head*): She didn't smile.

6TH SINGER: Maybe if we try a different song . . .

7TH SINGER (*Sighing*): It's not that. It's our enemies behind the wall. It's their fault! Somebody told my father that they've discovered a way of scrambling sound waves so that everything we say sounds terrible to the angel.

8TH SINGER: No wonder she won't smile.

1ST SINGER: But she *has* to smile by tonight . . . or else. (*More cheerfully*) Maybe if we practice carols it will help. (SINGERS *go to back of stage and begin to hum a Christmas carol. Others join in. They are interrupted by offstage clanging of* TOWN CRIER's *bell.* TOWN CRIER *enters, followed by as many* TOWNSPEOPLE *as desired. He approaches angel, then unrolls a scroll and reads from proclamation.*)

CRIER: Hear ye, hear ye: By order of the Mayor it is hereby proclaimed that any citizen, or citizens, who can make our angel smile by midnight tonight, Christmas Eve, shall receive a double reward equal to one-half the gold in the vaults of the entire town. (BROTHER *and* SISTER *enter slowly from the wings, listen intently. They are not noticed.*)

CROWD (*Ad lib*): By midnight tonight? Double reward? (*Etc.*)

CRIER: All citizens, young and old, are urged to present their plans immediately. The time is short. The need is pressing. Be it further proclaimed that if the angel does not smile by midnight, Christmas Eve, the Mayor and his councilors do hereby disclaim responsibility for any disaster that may befall the town.

CROWD (*With murmur of fear*): Disaster!

CRIER (*Rolling up proclamation*): Now, my friends, who has a suggestion to send to the mayor?

1ST BOY (*Stepping up*): We think the wall should be built higher—high enough to protect the angel from our enemies. (CROWD *murmurs approval.*)

CRIER (*Writing down suggestion*): Wall should be built higher!

SISTER (*Quietly*): That won't make the angel smile. You

can't build a wall to the top of the sky. (*Everyone looks curiously at* BROTHER *and* SISTER.)

1ST GIRL: We think the wall should be made of brick
So bombs could not get through so quick.
(CRIER *makes note of suggestion; some in crowd nod approvingly.*)

BROTHER: That won't make the angel smile. You can't build a wall as wide as the earth.

1ST WORKMAN: We need a roof
That's poison-proof
To keep the town
From crumbling down.

BROTHER: That won't make the angel smile. You can't cover the world with a roof.

1ST WOMAN: We could burrow under the ground like moles, and that should make the angel smile, to see us safe. (*Crowd murmurs.* CRIER *makes note of the suggestion.*)

SISTER: The angel wouldn't smile for that. You can't burrow to the core of the earth. (MAN *comes forward, impatiently, followed by* 3RD WOMAN.)

MAN: Why not get the jump on our foes?
It's foolish to hide in a grotto!
Come, everyone, get on your toes:
Let "Strike the First Blow" be our motto!

CROWD (*Ad lib*): Yes! No! (*Etc.*)

CRIER (*Making note*): Strike the first blow.

BROTHER: Then the angel would *never* smile again. She would be destroyed, like all of us. (CRIER, *angry, but baffled, walks over to* BROTHER *and* SISTER. *Others follow curiously.*)

CRIER: And who are you anyway, may I ask? What is your authority for what you say? How do *you* know?

BROTHER: We live in the last house on the last street, near the turn in the wall. All year we wondered how to make the angel smile.

SISTER: One day we saw a little crack in the wall where it curves around the hill. We thought if we could make the crack bigger, we might be able to slip through the wall to the other side and see what our enemies did to make *their* angel smile.

CROWD (*Startled; ad lib*): Weren't you afraid? That's enemy country! (*Etc.*)

BROTHER: And so we worked at the crack for days and days, and at last it was big enough to squeeze through.

CRIER (*Taking notes*): Very dangerous. But I am sure the Mayor and his councilors will be interested in this. Proceed. And what did you find on the other side of the wall?

SISTER: We found that people have streets and houses very much like ours. We found that they eat and sleep and work and go to school and play and read books, and watch TV, just the way we do. And some of them wear overalls, and some of them wear glasses, and some of them have freckles, and some of them sing, and some of them just twiddle their thumbs.

2ND BOY: They're like us?

BROTHER: And the people on the other side of the wall have an angel, too, in their town square.

CRIER: Ah! And did you find out how they get her to smile?

SISTER: She never smiles any more. She hasn't smiled for almost a year.

CRIER (*Excited*): This is news indeed!

BROTHER: The people on the other side of the wall are frightened and worried. They don't know what to do. They are sure we have invented a secret weapon and trained it on their statue.

CROWD (*To each other; baffled*): A secret weapon! (*Etc.*)

SISTER: They are afraid we have developed a deadly cosmic ray that can vaporize stone, and turn smiles to frowns. They think our bombs are super-sized, and more powerful and much more economical than theirs.

2ND WOMAN: They do?

BROTHER: They suspect that we have discovered a secret weapon that can penetrate anything, and nothing they do can make the angel smile.

MAN: Us? They accuse us?

SISTER: They are sure we have discovered a way of mixing up sound so that nothing they say can be heard by their angel. But, worst of all, they are afraid we will attack them any minute.

BROTHER: They are so afraid they think perhaps they should attack us first!

CROWD (*Ad lib*): No! No! Not that! (*Etc.*)

SISTER: All their stonecutters and masons and potters and workmen and glassblowers and scientists and politicians and citizens have tried to make the angel smile. But no one has succeeded.

CROWD: Just like us.

CRIER: Ah, my friends, our enemies seem to be just as unfortunate as we are. And here we thought all along they were plotting against us. (*Sighs*) But still . . . how can we make the angel smile, before disaster strikes? This is our last chance, this Christmas Eve. We don't have much time.

BROTHER (*Looking toward wall*): There is a way. An easy way.

CROWD (*Excited; ad lib*): A way! What way? (*Etc.*)

SISTER: Tear down the wall.

MAN (*Amazed; frightened*): Tear down the wall? But what about our enemies?

SISTER: If we start tearing it down, they will help. They'll want it down, too. It's the only chance for all of us, on both sides. Walls make people afraid and suspicious and mean. Walls fence out all the best things,

310

like brotherhood and goodwill, and fence in all the worst things, like distrust and hate. We must tear down the wall! (BROTHER *and* SISTER *walk over to wall, begin to pry at stones.* SINGERS *begin to sing "Silent Night." A few members of crowd join in singing; some of them pry at stones. At the end of the first stanza,* 1ST WOMAN *turns to look at the statue.*)

1ST WOMAN (*Gasping; excited*): Look! Look! The angel is beginning to smile.

CROWD (*Turning; ad lib in amazement*): She's beginning to smile! Tear down the wall! (*Etc. All go to wall and begin pulling down stones.*)

CRIER: The angel's smiling! She's really smiling! (*Goes to* BROTHER *and* SISTER) You children have won the reward. One half the gold in the town. Ah, she's smiling. Wait until the Mayor hears about this!

BROTHER (*Hesitantly*): Sir, about the reward.

CRIER: Yes, what about it?

BROTHER: We'd like the Mayor to spend the money for a park between our two countries, where the wall was— a park, with trees and grass and flowers, where everyone can go, from both sides.

CROWD (*Cheering; ad lib*): Tear down the wall! Tear down the wall! A park, a park! (*Etc.*)

CRIER (*Ringing bell, holding up hand for silence*): Listen, my friends! Listen! (*Crowd becomes quiet. Then, from the other side of the wall, comes the sound of people singing the first stanza of "Silent Night." Crowd listens silently for a moment, then, facing the statue, begins to sing along. Slow curtain*)

THE END

Characters: 6 male; 6 female; 12 or more male or female for Singers, Town Crier, and Townspeople.
Playing Time: 15 minutes.
Costumes: Modern, winter clothing for all.
Properties: Roll of paper; bell; pen.
Setting: The town square. At the back is a conspicuous stone wall. A section of the wall may be made on painted cardboard boxes, so that it can be torn down. On either side of wall toward wings are low steps. At front, above audience, stands statue of an angel.
Lighting and Sound: No special effects.

Mr. Smithers Goes Shopping

Mrs. Smithers told her spouse:
"It's time to decorate the house,
so buy some mistletoe this year
and several holly wreaths, my dear.
You must admit it will be jolly
to hang up mistletoe and holly."

So Mr. Smithers made a stop
that evening at the florist's shop.
"Please wrap me up some greens," said he.
"A couple sprigs of mistletee,
I mean, some sprigs of tistlemoe,
and several wrolly heaths. No, no!
I mean . . ." he said between his teeth,
"I want to buy a mistle wreath,
and several pieces, four or so,
of Christmas-looking hollytoe . . ."

Then Mr. Smithers sighed, "The deuce!
Just wrap me up some pine and spruce!"

The Christmas Tablecloth

Characters

GRAM
MOTHER
KATHY
RICK
DAD

TIME: *Christmas Day, late in the afternoon.*

SETTING: *Living room of a comfortable old farmhouse, decorated for Christmas. There is a Christmas tree in one corner, and an unlighted red candle in front of the window. At center is table on which lies a big half-opened tablecloth full of names and dates embroidered in red.*

AT RISE: MOTHER *is knitting.* GRAM *sits near table.* KATHY *has spread large pieces of wrapping paper on floor and is drawing pictures in colored chalk.*

GRAM: It's been a nice Christmas, hasn't it? Except for the tablecloth . . .

MOTHER: I'm sorry about that tablecloth. It means so much to all of us. But this is just one of those days when plans didn't work out.

KATHY: It hasn't stopped snowing for twenty-four hours! (*Brightens*) But one of *my* plans worked out—getting this box of colored chalk for Christmas. (*Holds up picture*) Do you recognize this, Mom? See, Gram? It's the way our house looks in summer when the lilacs are in bloom. If I drew it the way it looks *now*, all I'd need would be white chalk.

MOTHER: Not bad, Kathy.

KATHY: I can do a better one. (*Goes back to drawing*)

MOTHER: I can't help wondering if Don and Phyllis started to come and got stuck. With the telephone out of order, there was no way to warn them about the snow drifts.

GRAM: Maybe the repair crew has been out by now, even if it is Christmas Day.

KATHY (*Jumping up*): I'll see. (*Picks up receiver, listens*) It's still dead. (*Puts receiver down*)

GRAM (*With a sigh, beginning to fold tablecloth*): Well, I might as well fold up the tablecloth.

KATHY: Don't, Gram. Christmas isn't over yet.

GRAM: But nobody can possibly come in such a storm, Kathy.

KATHY: You can't be *sure*. Dad and Rick are out shoveling.

MOTHER: Just to the barn. Even if they got as far as the road, the snowplow hasn't gone through.

KATHY: I'm for not giving in until the very, very last minute. (*Goes back to drawing;* GRAM *hesitates, then stops folding.*)

GRAM: It's the first time in forty years that somebody hasn't signed the tablecloth.

MOTHER: Is it really that long, Mother?

GRAM: Forty years today. I got the idea five years before you were born, Margaret. Your father fell right in with it . . . said it would make a wonderful heirloom for our grandchildren.

KATHY: That's Rick and me!

GRAM: I remember the Christmas I started the tablecloth we had Aunt El and Uncle Dave over for dinner. (*Finds place on cloth*) See, here are their signatures. I embroidered them over later in red floss. And here's the date underneath. 19— (*Fill in date, forty years before present year*) The next Christmas we had ten guests for dinner.

KATHY: It's good you didn't always have ten guests, or there wouldn't be any room for them to sign. (*Holds up picture*) How's this for a sprig of holly, Mom?

MOTHER: Very good, Kathy! Why don't you cut around it and pin it on the curtain?

KATHY (*Jumping up, starting for corner where Christmas tree stands*): Where's your work basket? The table's gone, to make room for the Christmas tree!

MOTHER: Oh, of course. Dad put the table in the bedroom when we put up the tree.

KATHY: I'll look in there. (*Exits*)

GRAM (*Still looking at tablecloth*): The year of the flu epidemic we nearly missed getting a signature. But old Dr. Herrington came in the afternoon and I remembered to have him sign. How I ever remembered with three of you sick in bed is a mystery.

MOTHER: The tablecloth has always meant so much to you, that's why. (KATHY *re-enters, carrying pin, scissors, and envelope.*)

KATHY (*Holding out envelope*): What's this, Mom? It was sticking out from under your work basket. It's addressed to Gram.

MOTHER: My goodness, I forgot all about that letter! (*To* GRAM) It's from your old friend Addie, Mother. Her daughter wrote me several weeks ago asking for my date bar recipe, and enclosed this Christmas letter for you. She asked me to hold it until nearer the holidays, and I forgot all about it when we moved the table. I'm sorry.

GRAM: I'm not, Margaret. Now I have it to read on Christmas Day. There couldn't be a better time to have a visit with Addie. (*Takes letter, opens it, adjusts glasses, reads.* KATHY *cuts around picture, pins it on*

315

curtain and stands back to admire it. Goes back to window and stands looking out. GRAM *looks up.*) Her son Arnold has another boy, born on Halloween. His name is Peter, but Addie calls him Punkins. Sounds just like Addie! (*Resumes reading letter*)

KATHY: The path to the barn is filling in already. Rick and Dad had better hurry with their chores, or they'll have to shovel their way back to the house again. (*Sighs*) Well, it does look as if nobody can get through to us today.

GRAM: Weren't you the one who wasn't willing to give up until the very, very last minute? (*Puts down letter*) Well, I must say reading Addie's letter was just like having a visit with her face to face. Just as if she'd been right here.

KATHY (*Suddenly inspired*): Gram, did she sign it?

GRAM: Of course, she did. Signed it "Your old friend, Addie."

KATHY: If it was just like having a visit with her, why couldn't you trace her signature on the tablecloth to embroider? Then you wouldn't break the record, Gram.

MOTHER: That's an idea!

GRAM (*Considering*): Trace it on the tablecloth? (*Shakes her head*) No, it wouldn't do. I'm afraid it wouldn't be fair. All the others have signed in person, crossed our threshold and been right here with us. No, it wouldn't be the same. I guess we'll just have to leave a blank space this year. (*Sound of door slamming shut is heard offstage.*)

KATHY: Dad and Rick must be finished with their chores.

MOTHER (*Calling out*): Shake your coats and caps on the porch. And take off your overshoes so you won't track up the floor.

316

KATHY: I'll bet they look like snowmen.

DAD (*Entering*): It's a good day to stay home, and a good night to go to bed early. There'll be a lot more shoveling to do in the morning. (RICK *enters.*)

KATHY: How deep is the snow, Rick?

RICK: Almost thirty inches, and still coming down.

DAD: It's slackening a little, though. Sky ought to be bright and clear by morning. But I doubt if the snow-plow will reach us today. (*Looks around, goes to turn on tree lights*) This is what I call a nice cozy family Christmas. It doesn't often happen we're alone on Christmas.

GRAM: Only once in forty years!

RICK: Poor Gram, there hasn't been any company to sign her tablecloth. And Christmas is almost over.

KATHY: It's dark enough now to light the candle in the window, isn't it, Mom?

RICK: Why light the candle? Nobody's going to see it.

KATHY: *We'll* see it. Let me take your matches, Dad. (*He hands her a box of matches, and she lights the candle.*)

RICK: What's for supper, Mom? I'm starved!

MOTHER: After all that turkey you ate for lunch, Rick?

KATHY (*Suddenly*): Listen! I hear something.

RICK: Just the nice quiet snow falling, that's all.

KATHY: No, I heard a funny sort of squeak. Listen! (*All are quiet for a moment. A faint squeaking noise is heard.*) There! On the window sill! (*Points*) Look, someone *did* see the Christmas candle!

DAD: Why, it's that little stray cat we saw out at the barn. I thought I told you to shut her in, Rick.

RICK: She must have slipped out with us when we finished the chores.

KATHY: I wonder whom she belongs to. She's cold and

hungry and lonesome, poor little thing. I'm going out to get her.

MOTHER: Just open the door and call, Kathy. She'll probably come. (KATHY *hurries out.*)

KATHY (*Calling from offstage*): Here, kitty, kitty, kitty. (*In a moment she re-enters, carrying cat.*) She's shivering and purring at the same time.

GRAM: Poor little mite.

MOTHER: Get her a saucer of warm milk, Kathy. And put the saucer on a paper so she won't drip on the floor. (KATHY *exits with kitten.*) Whose do you think it is?

DAD: Probably one of Sandersons'. They have about a dozen.

RICK: Well, Gram, we did get some company after all, didn't we? It's just too bad cats can't write on tablecloths.

MOTHER: Yes, it is. To think that after forty years—(KATHY *re-enters with saucer and cat.*)

KATHY: I'll put her down on one of my old pictures, so I can pet her while she drinks. Nice kitty. There! Enjoy your Christmas supper. (*Sets cat and saucer on papers on floor*)

DAD: It's a good feeling to have the cows under cover on a night like this.

RICK: And the chores done early.

KATHY (*Suddenly excited*): Gram!

GRAM: Goodness, Kathy, you made me jump. What's the matter?

KATHY: Gram, look. Come here, everyone. Look! (*They crowd around cat.*) The cat stepped on the lilac bush in my picture and look!

MOTHER: The colored chalk dust stuck to her paw, and she's made a purple footprint, like a little rose.

GRAM: What a pretty little print!

RICK: Only roses don't come in purple.

KATHY: The color doesn't matter, Rick. It's the *idea.*

RICK: What idea?

KATHY: Don't you see? It can be a signature . . . without having to be traced. A signature for Gram's tablecloth. We can hold the kitten up to put its footprint on the cloth, for Gram to embroider.

GRAM: Why, Kathy, you're right. The only visitor who crossed our threshold today! And the little print will be one of the nicest signatures of all.

KATHY: So the record will go on unbroken, won't it? And the print of a little red rose will mark a Christmas we'll never forget! (*Curtain*)

THE END

PRODUCTION NOTES
The Christmas Tablecloth

Characters: 2 male; 3 female.

Playing Time: 10 minutes.

Costumes: All the characters are dressed in warm, everyday clothes.

Properties: Christmas tree; red candle; large white tablecloth, half-opened, covered with names and dates embroidered in red; colored chalk, large pieces of wrapping paper; pin; scissors; envelope containing a letter; box of matches; kitten; saucer.

Setting: A comfortably furnished living room, decorated for Christmas. Window is up left.

Lighting: No special effects.

Sound: Faint squeaking noise off stage, as indicated in text.

The Night Before Christmas

Characters

MASTER OF CEREMONIES (M.C.)
CLEMENT CLARKE MOORE
CATHARINE, *his wife*
HARRIET, *a family friend*
PETER, *handyman*
FOUR CHILDREN

TIME: *Late afternoon of Christmas Eve, 1822.*
SETTING: *M.C.'s stand is at far left. At right is the living room of a fine house on the outskirts of New York City. Furnishings may be simple.*
AT RISE: M.C. *enters, stands at left, and addresses audience.*

M.C.: Some people spend a lifetime trying to attain fame and fortune, yet never do. Some achieve one or the other with great effort, and others with little work, but through a happy combination of circumstances. Still others have fame thrust upon them when least expected. The hero of this story belongs to the last group. And it is safe to say that his popularity surprised no one more than it surprised Clement Clarke Moore himself.

Moore was born the only child of a well-to-do family, and he enjoyed all the advantages of his time. At the age of 19, he was graduated from Columbia College, and (as he wrote in his journal) he hoped to dedicate his life "to the attainment of useful learning."

At the time this story opens, Clement Moore was 42 years old, married, and with a family of young children. He had achieved a certain amount of recognition as a scholar, college professor, and writer of learned papers, but was little known outside his own circle. For his amusement he wrote verses.

We see him now late in the afternoon of Christmas Eve, 1822, wrapping Christmas presents with his wife, Catharine, and Harriet, a close friend of the family. (*Spotlight comes up on living room side of stage, where* CLEMENT CLARKE MOORE, CATHARINE, *and* HARRIET *are wrapping Christmas packages.*)

CATHARINE: Always so much to do on Christmas Eve!

HARRIET: Yes, and isn't it exciting! You wouldn't have it any other way, Catharine.

CATHARINE: Indeed I wouldn't. Clement, there are still these packages to deliver, you know.

CLEMENT: Yes, I know. Peter will be bringing in the tree soon. I'll tell him to hitch Prancer to the sleigh . . . and off we'll go through the gathering dark, with a moon to light the way.

HARRIET: I envy you. The world will be dazzling after yesterday's new snow.

CLEMENT: You sound quite poetic, Harriet.

CATHARINE: Speaking of being poetic . . . have you remembered, my dear husband, that you promised to write a Christmas poem for the children?

CLEMENT: Why, so I did!

CATHARINE (*Surprised*): You haven't written it yet?

CLEMENT: Not yet. Christmas Eve has crept up on me somehow.

CATHARINE: There isn't much time, you know. After you get back from delivering the presents, the children will be coming in to hang their stockings and sing Christmas carols.

CLEMENT (*Calmly*): Perhaps I can think of something as we drive along. (*Sound of knocking*) That must be Peter now, with the tree. (*Goes to door*) Ah, Peter, you did well to find such a nice tree. (PETER *brings in tree, sets it down.*) And, Peter, please hitch Prancer to the sleigh. I'll need you to drive me around . . . I have these packages to deliver.

PETER: Yes, sir. (*Hurries out*)

HARRIET: Good old Peter. I always enjoy seeing him. He's so round and jolly. And how he loves wearing a red cap and muffler!

CATHARINE: Dear Peter. He's been with us for years. Now he has white hair, with whiskers to match.

CLEMENT: He served my father faithfully. We were indeed lucky to have him to help us.

HARRIET: Someone should put Peter into a story. Don't you think so, Clement?

CLEMENT: Indeed. (*Nods and exits*)

CATHARINE: When we finish here, Harriet, will you help me check on what's going on in the kitchen? There will be dozens of guests at the Christmas party tomorrow afternoon. . . . (*Spotlight goes out on living room, up on M.C.*)

M.C.: Dr. Moore and Peter made the rounds with the Christmas parcels. It was a clear, cold winter night. Jingle bells danced on Prancer's harness. The waxing moon gave "the luster of midday" to fields, streets, and houses. As they drove along, Dr. Moore talked to Peter about Christmas customs in the Netherlands, and in a flash it seemed to the professor that he was sitting beside jolly old St. Nicholas himself. A vague idea began to grow in his mind . . .

When they finished delivering the presents and Dr. Moore was back home, he went immediately to his study and closed the door. Meanwhile, Catharine and Harriet were decorating the room with spruce boughs

322

and holly, and the children were hanging up their stockings amid exclamations of excitement. (*Spotlight comes up on* CATHARINE, HARRIET, *and* CHILDREN *engaged in their activities.*) Soon, Clement Moore emerged from his study with a few sheets of paper in his hand. (*Spotlight up on* MOORE)

CLEMENT: Happy Christmas to all. (*Laughing*) Did I hear something about a poem for the occasion?

CATHARINE: Why, Clement, have you written one . . . so quickly?

CLEMENT: There is something magic about Christmas Eve, my dear. It ignores the element of time. (*Looking around at others*) Who wants to hear the Christmas poem?

CHILDREN (*Ad lib*): Oh, Father, I do! Please read it to us! (*Etc.*)

CLEMENT: Sit down, and I will read you what I've written. (CHILDREN *sit near tree,* CATHARINE *and* HARRIET *in chairs.*)

CATHARINE: Children, you must be very quiet. As quiet as mice.

CLEMENT (*Reading dramatically*): "'Twas the night before Christmas, when all through the house
Not a creature was stirring, not even a mouse;
The stockings were hung by the chimney with care
In hopes that St. Nicholas soon would be there.
(CLEMENT *continues reading through to the end of the poem. When he finishes, others clap and cheer.*)

CHILDREN (*Ad lib*): Read it again! Please, Father. That was wonderful. (*Etc.*)

HARRIET: Oh, I must have a copy for the children of our parish, and for the newspaper as well, Clement. All the children of New York must read your poem.

CATHARINE: I'm afraid it's a little late for this Christmas, Harriet. Maybe next year.

HARRIET: I *must* have a copy, Clement. I'm sure the editor of the *Troy Sentinel* will publish it. He's a friend of Father's.

CLEMENT: All right, Harriet, but on one condition: I would not want my name on it. How would it look for a staid old professor to be writing about St. Nicholas? If it is to be published, it must appear without the name of the author. (*Spotlight goes out on* MOORE, *up on* M.C.)

M.C.: And that is what happened. Harriet sent the poem to the *Troy Sentinel,* and it was published in December, 1823, without Dr. Moore's name on it as author. Children loved it. In a few years it was appearing in newspapers all over the country. But it took 15 years before Clement Moore admitted that he was its author. Since then the fame of "A Visit from St. Nicholas" has continued to spread. It has been published in many schoolbooks, magazines, and anthologies, and it's been translated into many languages. And Dr. Moore, who spent dedicated years as a scholar and professor, became famous for a merry Christmas poem that took him less than an hour to write.

THE END

PRODUCTION NOTES
THE NIGHT BEFORE CHRISTMAS

Characters: 2 male; 2 female; male or female for M.C.; four male and female for children.

Playing Time: 20 minutes.

Costumes: Early nineteenth century American dress.

Properties: Christmas packages; Christmas tree; spruce boughs; holly; Christmas stockings; few sheets of paper.

Setting: Divided stage. At left is lectern for M.C. At right is the living room of a fine home on the outskirts of New York City, suitably furnished.

Lighting: Spotlight, as indicated in text.

Sound: Knocking on door.

Santa, the Wise Old Owl

Characters

HORSE
PIG
OWL
GOAT
GOOSE
CAT
DOG

TIME: *Before Christmas.*
SETTING: *A barnyard. There is a bench on stage.*
AT RISE: HORSE *and* PIG *are talking together.* (*Children wear placards indicating animals they represent.*)
HORSE: Why so glum, friend Pig? Just a few days before Christmas, and you're grunting around more than usual. Cheer up!
PIG: Why should I? Christmas is such a pig in a poke. I never know what I'm going to get . . . if anything. Do you?
HORSE: Neigh, neigh! But, of course, I'm expected never to look a gift horse in the mouth . . . whatever I get. (GRANDMA OWL *enters briskly, arms full of parcels.*)
PIG: Good morning, Grandma Owl. You certainly seem to be in fine feather this morning.

OWL: Good morning. (*Sees bench*) Ah, here's a perch where I can rest a while. (*Sits*) I'm helping Santa this year, you know. He said he needed some wise old owl to help him with his Christmas problems, and he thought I looked like the right kind of bird. Now, what are you two acting so glum about? And only a few days before Christmas, too. . . .

HORSE: We're afraid we won't get much for Christmas.

PIG: What do *you* want, Grandma Owl?

OWL: Why, I haven't had time to give it much thought.

HORSE: You mean you don't give a hoot?

OWL: I've been busy. Besides, I discovered long ago that it isn't *getting* things that makes folks happy. It's . . . (*Looks offstage*) Well, I declare, Mrs. Goat and Miss Goose are coming down the lane. (*Calls out*) Whoo, whoo, ladies! (GOAT *and* GOOSE *enter, looking sad.*)

GOAT: Oh, Grandma Owl, what a lucky bird you are to be helping Santa Claus this year!

GOOSE: It certainly was a feather in your cap to be chosen. You're sure to get a handsome present.

GOAT: I can think of a dozen things *I'd* like to get, but when it comes to Christmas, I'm apt to be left out in the cold. It gets my goat.

PIG: Me, too.

OWL: Come, come. Don't you know it isn't what you get for Christmas that matters? It's what you . . . (*Looks offstage*) Why, here come Mrs. Cat and Mr. Dog, and they seem be quarreling like cats and dogs, as usual. So close to Christmas, too. (*Calls*) Whoo, whoo! (CAT *and* DOG *enter.*)

CAT (*Whining*): What's good about Christmas?

DOG (*Gruffly*): It's a sad time of year for me.

OWL: You two *do* look rather down in the mouth this morning.

DOG: It's a dog's life, not being sure you're going to get anything for Christmas.

CAT: For once I agree with Dog.

OWL (*Irritated*): Dear me, what's the matter with everyone? Spending your time moping around! If you put as much energy into thinking of what you could *give* instead of what you might *get*, you wouldn't have time to be grumpy.

OTHERS (*Ad lib*): Give? What could we give? *We* want presents. (*Etc.*)

OWL: That's just it . . . you have to take time to think about it.

GOOSE (*Cheerfully*): By some magic maybe I could lay a golden egg. Or, at least, a super white one.

GOAT: I could eat that scraggly old grass along the fence that Master hasn't been able to reach with the mower.

HORSE: I could give him an extra fine horseback ride.

DOG (*Animatedly*): I could show him some new trails in the woods.

CAT (*Grinning*): I could chase off that silly old mouse.

PIG: I could be nice about giving his son a piggy-back ride.

OWL: There! You see? You're all feeling better already. No doubt you'll come up with other things you can give, if you just put your minds to it. Christmas is a wonderful time of year, a merry time. You just have to look at it in the right way. Merry Christmas, everyone! (*Curtain*)

THE END

PRODUCTION NOTES
SANTA, THE WISE OLD OWL

Characters: 7 male and female.

Playing Time: 5 minutes.

Costumes: Children wear placards indicating animals they represent. (More elaborate costumes may be worn, if desired.)

Properties: Christmas parcels.

Setting: Barnyard. Bench is at one side.

Lighting and Sound: No special effects.

The Week Before Christmas

Characters

BOY
GIRL
NINE BOYS
NINE GIRLS

AT RISE: BOY *and* GIRL *are on stage.*
GIRL (*Gaily*): Christmas is coming,
   and laddies and lasses
   are wearing the rosiest
   rose-colored glasses.
BOY (*Glumly*): Christmas is coming . . .
   as slow as molasses!
GIRL (*Gaily*): Christmas is coming—
   it's very exciting,
   with presents for wrapping
   and greetings for writing.
BOY (*Glumly*): But waiting and waiting
   is not so inviting!
GIRL (*Gaily*): Christmas is coming—
   it's thrilling to tell it,
   to see it and hear it
   and sniff it and smell it.
BOY (*Glumly*): But oh, it is poky
   however you spell it! (*Nine pairs of* BOYS *and* GIRLS
   enter in turn, each pair with a letter to spell Christ-

mas. They may stand side by side or, if the stage is small, one behind the other. They pantomime their parts as much as possible.)

1ST BOY (*Carrying C, munching cookie*): C . . . for crunching cookie crumbs,

1ST GIRL (*Shaking head over calendar*): And counting days till Christmas comes!

2ND BOY (*Carrying H and holly sprig*): H . . . for hanging holly high,

2ND GIRL (*With clock*): And hoping time will hurry by!

3RD BOY (*Carrying R, and packages for mailing*): R . . . for rushing gifts galore,

3RD GIRL: Then reading, "Christmas—eight days more!"

4TH BOY (*Carrying I*): I . . . for idling near each gift,

4TH GIRL: And itching for the twenty-fifth!

5TH BOY (*Carrying S, and gaily wrapped presents*): S . . . for sealing secrets well,

5TH GIRL: And shush-ing sister not to tell!

6TH BOY (*Carrying T*): T . . . for trusting old St. Nick,

6TH GIRL: But thinking he's more slow than quick!

7TH BOY (*Carrying M*): M . . . for making plans complete.

7TH GIRL (*Marking time*): And marking time with restless feet.

8TH BOY (*Carrying A, and holding gilt halo over head*): A . . . for acting nice as pie,

8TH GIRL: And aching for the days to fly!

9TH BOY (*Carrying S*): S . . . for seeing snowflakes pelt,

9TH GIRL: And shouting for them not to melt!

ALL: That spells CHRISTMAS . . .
 Hold your thumbs,
 Hold your halo . . .
 Here it comes!

Now December's Here

ALL: Everything is secrets
            now December's here:
GIRL: Secrets wrapped in tissue,
            whispered in an ear,
BOY: Secrets big and bulky,
GIRL: Secrets small and slight,
BOY: In the strangest places,
            hidden out of sight.
GIRL: Packages that rattle,
BOY: Packages that squeak . . .
GIRL: Some say, "Do not open."
BOY: Some say, "Do not peek."
ALL: Secrets, secrets, secrets,
            now December's here . . .
            everything is secrets
            this Christmas time of year.

Christmas Shoppers

Oh, the wind is brisk and biting
and the cold is not inviting,
but there's music, merry music everywhere.
The streets are full of bustle
and our feet are full of hustle,
for there's Christmas, merry Christmas in the air.

Oh, the wind is cold and chilly
and it whistles at us shrilly,
but there's music, merry music everywhere.
The bells are full of ringing
and our hearts are full of singing,
for there's Christmas, merry Christmas in the air.

Shining Up the Halo

(A musical skit to the tune of "Jolly Old St. Nicholas")

1ST GIRL: Christmas Day is coming soon,
and I'm as good as gold:
I wear a halo 'round my head
and do the things I'm told.

1ST BOY: I never pout or answer back,
I'm gentle as a lamb.
I sometimes wonder at myself
to see how good I am.

2ND GIRL: Christmas Day will soon be here . . .
I'm helpful all day long,
and everybody seems to think
there must be something wrong.

2ND BOY: I ask for extra chores to do,
I'm cheerful as can be,
I'm so polite to everyone
I hardly seem like *me*.

GIRLS: Mother looks at us and smiles.

BOYS: Father does it, too:

ALL: Our halos are so shiny bright
they look entirely new!
Parents don't need calendars
to tell the time of year:
they merely look at us and know
what day will soon be here!

331

Standing Up for Christmas

Nine boys and girls stand in a line at back of stage.
Each holds a large letter to spell out Christmas. *Each*
steps forward in turn to show letter and recite lines.

C: I stand for carols
       and Christmas cheer.

H: I stand for holly
       that's hanging here. (*Points to sprig of holly hang-*
       ing from H)

R: I stand for reindeer
       I've never seen.

I: I stand for ivy
       of Christmas green.

S: I stand for Santa
       and skates and skis.

T: I stand for tinsel
       on Christmas trees.

M: I stand for message
       to you from me.

A: I stand for angel
       atop the tree.

S: I stand for secrets
       of every size,
       all wrapped and waiting
       for eager eyes.

ALL: We stand for letters
       that, one by one,
       spell out a season
       of joy and fun.

Christmas All Around

BOYS: You see it in the windows
   Of the houses and the stores
   Where holly wreaths and Christmas trees
   Look in and out of doors,
GIRLS: You smell it in the kitchen
   Where the tangy scent of spice
   Gets mixed with nuts and citron
   And everything that's nice,
BOYS: You hear it in the music
   That echoes down the street,
   And at the crowded counters,
   And in the busy feet,
GIRLS: You sense it in the whisper
   Of secrets in the air,
   And in the happy eagerness
   That twinkles everywhere . . .
ALL: Shiny lights on fir trees,
   Voices that resound,
   Goodies in the oven,
   Secrets that abound,
   You see it and you smell it
   And you hear it all around . . .
   CHRISTMAS!

Christmas Fun

(To the Tune of "Hickory, Dickory, Dock")

Hickory, dickory dock,
we sit and watch the clock:
the minutes creep
and we're sound asleep
when Santa fills our sock.

A Song for Christmas

(To the tune of "Sing the Song of Sixpence")

Sing a song of Christmas . . .
how patient can we be?
Four and twenty presents
piled beneath the tree!
When today is over
only ____ days more
Till we see the hidden gifts
That we've been waiting for.